Deleuze and Guattari and Terror

Deleuze Connections

'It is not the elements or the sets which define the multiplicity. What defines it is the AND, as something which has its place between the elements or between the sets. AND, AND, AND – stammering.'

Gilles Deleuze and Claire Parnet, *Dialogues*

General Editor
Ian Buchanan

Editorial Advisory Board

Keith Ansell-Pearson   Gregg Lambert
Rosi Braidotti   Adrian Parr
Claire Colebrook   Paul Patton
Tom Conley   Patricia Pisters

Visit the Deleuze Connections website at:
www.edinburghuniversitypress.com/series/delco

Deleuze and Guattari and Terror

Edited by Anindya Sekhar Purakayastha and Saswat Samay Das

EDINBURGH
University Press

Edinburgh University Press is one of the leading university presses in the UK. We publish academic books and journals in our selected subject areas across the humanities and social sciences, combining cutting-edge scholarship with high editorial and production values to produce academic works of lasting importance. For more information visit our website: edinburghuniversitypress.com

Edinburgh University Press Ltd
The Tun – Holyrood Road
12(2f) Jackson's Entry
Edinburgh EH8 8PJ

First published in hardback by Edinburgh University Press 2023

Typeset in 10.5/13 Adobe Sabon by
Cheshire Typesetting Ltd, Cuddington, Cheshire
printed and bound by CPI Group (UK) Ltd,
Croydon, CR0 4YY

A CIP record for this book is available from the British Library

ISBN 978 1 3995 0986 2 (hardback)
ISBN 978 1 3995 0987 9 (paperback)
ISBN 978 1 3995 0988 6 (webready PDF)
ISBN 978 1 3995 0989 3 (epub)

Contents

Acknowledgements

Perhaps this book was molecularised during our regular discussions since 2008 at various tea stalls at IIT Kharagpur on different debates in Continental philosophy and critical theory. Amid the surrounding cacophony and comforting greenery, we used to revisit the genealogies of the Frankfurt School, making Jurgen Habermas and his theory of public sphere communicative rationality the key point of our tea table talks for unending hours. Nostalgia has a soothing effect when reminiscing about those fascinating hours of pure discussion and vibrant glow. Those were indeed blissful moments of daring, emboldening us to intervene in these critical theoretical debates from our positions in the Global South. Needless to say, we were beginners at this job, but that did not diminish the thrill and excitement of walking with those great world-philosophical minds. Long walks on the sprawling campus of IIT Kharagpur, endless discussions and dreams along the empty corridors of the Humanities and Social Science Department, bouts of pure joy and humorous rides through different cobwebs of philosophy and Zizekean thunders sustained us, and we cruised along. Books were in short supply as very few were doing critical theory in that rigorous manner in India at that time, but thanks to Ravi Swamy and the Central Library of IIT Kharagpur, a generous flow of the latest books and journals in this field was supplied, a facility that whetted our appetite further, helping us to accentuate the momentum of critical theoretical practices. Giovanna Borradori's profound conversation with Derrida and Habermas in her *Philosophy in a Time of Terror* (2003) arrived, and as we pored over it, we realised the need to revisit the genealogies of the entire critical theoretical tradition. We decided to move beyond Kant, Habermas and Derrida, our first loves, and discovered the radical glories of Deleuze and Guattari, realising that we had chanced upon people who seemed to have analysed the problems afflicting the modern world in a better way. Our deeper investment in studying political, social as well as ontic violence drew us closer to Deleuzo-Guttarian schizoanalysis and the larger concepts of process philosophy.

Everyday news reports of political atrocities happening in different parts of the world at that time would intrude into our regular discussions, and we were deeply disturbed, confronting the same question time and again: how to offer some philosophical solace amid this descending gloom unfolding through neoliberal policies, systemic violence, heinous terror attacks and equally demonic counter-terror violence, militarism, the violence of 'homonationalism', right-wing political attacks, racial hatred, dogma-driven animosities, profiteering and ecocide – the list can go on. None of these, we felt, could be deciphered through normative critical theoretical frames, as they demand Deleuzean schizonanalysis. Our flirtation with Deleuze and Guattari was still quivering at the threshold of possibility until we invited Ian Buchanan to speak at IIT Kharagpur on Deleuzism. Ian's warmth and refreshing encouragement dispelled all hesitancy at our end, prompting us to think of working on a project related to Deleuze, Guattari and spirituality or Deleuze, Guattari and terror. A series of discussions followed at different locations in Kolkata, and Ian's valuable input during our sojourn at Kolkata's Park Street helped us to settle on the second option.

This was the beginning of an arduous journey, as we began to look for Deleuze scholars and potential contributors with proven track records in this field. Without Ian's constant support this would not have been possible. As often happens with edited volumes, the initial euphoria eclipsed as some contributors had to withdraw for health reasons or because of other personal difficulties, and so it took us longer to complete the project than we had thought initially in 2016. Finally, we gathered a brilliant constellation of wonderful contributors and we profusely thank all of them for being part of this project, and for agreeing to contribute in spite of their other academic preoccupations.

In between times, our love for Deleuze and Guattari brought us into close contact with other leading Deleuze scholars, and we take this opportunity to thank each of them for their support and profound input. We convey our gratitude to Ian Buchanan, Nathan Widder, Nicholas Tampio, Janae Sholtz, Ajay Gudavarthy, A. Raghuramaraju and Anup Dhar, who have been great interlocutors and guides in our Deleuzean journey. We benefited immensely through our conversations with them during their stays at IIT Kharagpur, where they spoke in detail as invited speakers on different aspects of Continental philosophy and Deleuze. The 2017 Deleuze conference at Tata Institute for Social Sciences, Mumbai, also proved to be immensely helpful as we learned from other leading Deleuze scholars such as Brian Massumi, Erin Manning, Kenneth Surin and many others. We remembered that academic gathering with fond memories as we worked through this manuscript. Special mention of our stay at Potsdam, Germany, during the 2014 ASNEL conference is in order here, as it saw us conversing with many scholars working on post-colonial interventions in critical theory. Our adventure around the Berlin Wall, Humboldt University and Hegel's grave in Berlin provided the impetus to continue our critical theoretical flirtations. We also remember people who helped us in different ways during the course of this book. Thomas Byers, former director of the Centre for Commonwealth Studies, University of Louisville, was a wonderful host and guide in picking up the latest books on philosophy and critical theory in Green Apple Books and City Lights at San Francisco when one of us went for a fellowship stay at the University of Louisville.

Both of us express our deep gratitude to our parents and family members who have been of constant support throughout. We also thank our friends and colleagues who provided moral and intellectual support. At Edinburgh University Press, we once again thank Ian Buchanan, the series editor, and Carol Macdonald and Sarah Foyle, the commissioning editors, who have been of wonderful support. We are grateful to the two anonymous readers for their remarkable comments which helped in improving the manuscript. We sincerely hope this volume will offer some fresh insights in the domain of Deleuze and Guattari studies.

Introduction: Chaosophy Notes: Terror, the Seventh War Machine

*Anindya Sekhar Purakayastha and
Saswat Samay Das*

a war-machine whose aim is neither a war of extermination nor a peace
of generalized terror, but revolutionary movement. (Deleuze and Guattari
1980: 590, as quoted in Patton 1984: 66)

Am I the enemy of the state . . . or am I a friend of the state (helping the
state in its surveillance practices of keeping constantly vigilant on the look-
out for potential terrorists as with the TIPS program)? . . . No longer is the
constitutive nature that of self and society, but rather self and nation. I am
part of the nation in-so-far-as I see (particular?) others as threats to the
nation. Through an internalization of the state logic of other as becoming
bomb, I accept my schizophrenia. I, in fact, am asked by the state to help
enact the logic of threat in my everyday life through a self-actualization of
surveillance and ever-readiness. (Packer 2006: 382–3)

As the 'war-machine' is not about war but about destratified plateaus, it
stands as a figuration of alternative nomad thoughts, and yet it runs the
risk of being both rhizomatic and at the same time arboreal. Otherwise,
how do we account for the desiring-production of terrorism as a war
machine combating the state apparatus of capture? Is terror a nomadic or
fascicular rejoinder to the 'military-Keynesianism' (Buchanan 2000: 113)
of the contemporary neoliberal social machine? Terror, being born of
and simultaneously militating against the capitalist mega-machine, might
invoke Deleuzo-Guattarian 'toolkits' or their hermeneutic apparatus to
reclaim its validity as a heuristic model of radical nomadism. That said,
and notwithstanding its global spread, does terror adumbrate planes of
over-codified desire that defeat the real schizophrenisation of desiring-
production? What are the 'dark precursors' or the 'flows and schizzes'
of terror? Does it destratify only for the dissolution of desire, arresting
its nomadism in its dogmatic figuration of desire? Destratification, the
process of liberating oneself from the yoke of strata, is, according to
Deleuze and Guattari, both easy and dangerous; it is a transformative

mechanism that abhors the death drive. Terror, on the other hand, thrives through an annulment of life-affirmation; perhaps it conjures up the

> schizo ... who took things too far, albeit by force of circumstance ... wildly destratifying is far worse than not destratifying at all, the first will almost certainly kill you while the second will merely stultify ... it is the life-affirming affects of destratifying techniques that are desired, not their deadly effects, so the great question of our age is whether one can be had without the other? (Buchanan 2000: 125–6)

This 'oscillation between breakthrough and breakdown' (Buchanan 2000: 162), between transformation and dissolution, is what determines the uncoded 'planomenon' of desire (Holland 2013: 56). To reiterate, terror is a mal-invested war machine, the latter, though, having little to do with actual war. The real object of Deleuze and Guattari's war machine, or the 'metamorphosis machine' (Patton 2000: 109), is not war but the actualisation of creative mutation. Given that, even though it maintains 'a necessary synthetic relation to war by virtue of its antipathy to the striated space of apparatuses of capture', it might be preferable to think of this type of assemblage not as a war machine but as a machine of metamorphosis (Patton 2000: 110). There are studies equating the Deleuzo-Guattarian war machine even with Gandhian *Ahimsa* or the non-violent experimentation of *satyagraha* (Rajeevan 2017), attesting a conceptual purity; an entity that refuses to be appropriated by the 'epistrata' of the state (Holland 2013: 59). Deleuze and Guattari call the 'postfascist' figure of the worldwide war machine, associated with state capitalism, 'a war-machine that takes peace as its object directly, as the peace of Terror or Survival' (Deleuze and Guattari 1987: 421). Their worry was that the 'war-machine is growing stronger and stronger' (1987: 422), and by that they mean the state or 'world war-machine'. There are new 'terror assemblages' as well, arguing for 'homonationalism' in 'queer times' (Puar 2007), an ideology that spawns patriotic racism and justifies the state-sponsored war on 'terror'. We argue that terror of both left, right and jihadi varieties as well as repressive counter-terror measures are inscribed within the logic of this global state machine. The nomad war machine, on the other hand, launches innocent war, war without war as its object, a war in the name of flow. Deleuze and Guattari promote this kind of nomad war, *A Thousand Plateaus* being a wonderful specimen of nomad propaganda (Miller 1993: 29–30).

Unlike terror, therefore, the Deleuzo-Guattarian war machine is not directed towards establishing an alternative form of authority; it simply destabilises or 'deterritorialises' authority (Rodgers and Jensen 2009), it is a 'minority' that denotes a 'line of flight', unstable, ambiguous and 'ever-moving' (Deleuze and Guattari 1987: 351–61). Recent critical studies on 'Deleuze, ISIS and Delirium' (Akil 2016), 'The Rhizome of Jihad' (Kuronen and Huhtinen 2017), 'Deleuze and the Event(s)' (Beck and Gleyzon 2016), 'Deleuze and the Grandeur of Palestine' (Gleyzon 2016), 'Gilles Deleuze: Writing in Terror' (Marks 2003), 'Addressing the Schizophrenia of Global Jihad' (Michelsen 2009), 'Revolutionaries, Barbarians or War Machines?' (Rodgers and Jensen 2009), and so on, while affirming the uniqueness of Deleuze and Guattari's political philosophy, run the risk of establishing a 'zone of indistinction' between Deleuze and Guattari's idea of the war machine and political theories of the postmodern radical left (multitude), the right-wing war machine (AltExploit Group Networks, Israeli war strategy) and rhizomatic networks of jihad, etc. This prompts us to critically intervene because, for Deleuze, any political move should organise itself in assemblages, or 'constellations of singularities', and the means of political transformation should be exercised cautiously and experimentally, warding off all arborescent roots, organisational or ideological epistrata (Tampio 2009: 384–5).

Terror, according to Hannah Arendt, is the defining feature of all totalitarian systems, and Arendt, engaging in what she called the 'interminable dialogue with the essence of totalitarianism', placed terror and the camps at the very centre of any analysis (Villa 1999: 13). Arendt's 1953 radio address entitled 'Mankind and Terror' provides a concise summary of the reasons why totalitarian terror is different from all other forms. Arendt begins, however, by discussing the terror of tyrannies and revolutionary terror, which (on the face of it) bear more than a little resemblance to totalitarian terror; both forms of terror are 'directed at an end and find an end' (Villa 1999: 17–18). Deleuze and Guattari articulated similar apprehensions in their cautious response to both radical left revolutionary terror as well as statist violence, offering us scope to speculate as to how they would have responded to terror as it is unfolding today.

In his 1990 interview with Antonio Negri, Deleuze refutes the Leninist assumptions embedded in the militant political imagination, demystifying the very concept of revolution. Historical revolutions, Deleuze observes, almost always have adverse consequences: the English Revolution led to Cromwell, the French Revolution gave us Napoleon, and the Bolshevik Revolution bolstered Stalin. Deleuze believes that revolutions are dangerous and they fail to change people's minds in a positive way (Tampio 2009: 390). 'Men's only hope', Deleuze explains, 'lies in a revolutionary becoming.' 'Becoming revolutionary' is a much more cautious form of political change than Lenin's 'experience of revolution'. 'As a rule, immanent to experimentation', Deleuze explains, we need to adopt 'injections of caution' so that it goes for a wild and destructive destratification (Deleuze and Guattari, as quoted in Tampio 2009: 390). Deleuze and Guattari's critique of left dogmatism can be applied to the contemporary politics of the 'tyranny of the majority' or the arborescence of identity-orientation.

Nomadic assemblages, on the contrary, are not committed to revolution; they rely more on the political principle of *A Thousand Plateaus* – 'gently tip the assemblage' – suggesting that revolution is a poor strategy for actualising the ideals of liberty and equality. Revolutionary extremism very often flirts with authoritarianism and violence, but the politics of 'schizophrenic utopianism' (Buchanan 2000: 143), on the other hand, prioritises liberty and respect for opposing views. Deleuze prefers 'local and specific struggles' to cataclysmic events and jurisprudence to revolution (Lefebvre 2005).

> The war machine is the joyful affirmative power (*puissance*), the desire or will to exist and express, state power, on the other hand, is a form of violence that captures everything into its striated spaces of constriction, confinement, and negativity ... the state form of power is not just an exterior machine of capture but also a negative striated form of power inherent with violence in advance for the future, whereas war machine is the life force that resists the monstrosity of this violence. Thus, war machine as the anti-violence machine becomes a positively non-violence machine. (Rajeevan 2017: n.p.)

This clearly distinguishes the war machine from the state war machine and organised revolutionary machines or terror machines. Terror, defined as evil by its detractors, is perceived differently by its apologists, and while few endorse its mindless perpetration of pernicious violence and destruction, terror also raises fundamental questions about the strata of brutal state power and the despotic tyranny of the capitalist axiomatic. This explains the growing appeal of terror and impels one to critically unpack the actual core of terror. In what follows we discuss how terror can be seen as a malformed or distorted version of the war machine, or what we call the seventh type of war machine.

The Seventh War Machine

Terror, at war with the neoliberal state and its military behemoth, also inflicts pain on innocent non-state actors. How can we then approach terror through 'Deleuzism' (Buchanan 2000)? Can terror be at all characterised as 'a vector of deterritorialization' or 'nomadism', which is

> a vital concern of every State that wants to vanquish nomadism . . . each time there is an operation against the State – subordination, rioting, guerilla warfare or revolution as act – it can be said that a war-machine has revived, that a new nomadic potential has appeared . . . (Deleuze and Guattari 1987: 50–60)

A Thousand Plateaus (1980) theorises six types of war machine, of which the first two do not have war as their definitional agenda. Nomadic bands legitimise the 'war' component of the term 'war-machine' in the concept's third variant, where war against the state is projected as their objective, with the aim of protecting or rescuing their smooth space from state striation (Holland 2013: 127). The state, on the other hand, assumes the role of the war machine itself in its fourth variant, in which war is adopted as a means to serve the state's essentially political ends: the aim of securing, striating, protecting and expanding its territory (Holland 2013: 127). This indeed throws up an interesting scenario in which the category of war machine attests polyvocality and multiplicities of line of flight, a condition in which the third and fourth variant of the Deleuzo-Guattarian war machine are locked in an endless battle with each other.

While these four different forms are essentially typological, the last two instances are historical, namely, Nazism and the subsequent emergence of the Cold War. The fifth example of the war machine, that is, historical fascism, strengthened the fourth variant to emerge as the sixth, because Nazism intensified limited war into eternal and comprehensive war, facilitating the state war machine to produce the war machine of global capitalism. In the current conjuncture the market war machine has completely engulfed the state machine, virtually replacing it as the final arbiter. Capital accumulation as the aim of the sixth war machine exceeds the control of the state and pervades society totally (Holland 2013: 128). The apprehension is that the war machine has

> taken charge of the aim, worldwide order, and the States are no longer anything more than objects or means adapted to that machine . . . the States reissue a war machine that takes charge of the aim, appropriates the States

and assumes increasingly wider political functions . . . setting its sights on a new type of enemy, no longer another State but . . . the 'unspecified enemy'. (Deleuze and Guattari 1987: 119–20)

This hunt for the 'unspecified enemy' induces the global-capitalist Terminator war machine to adopt new forms characterised by terms such as 'neoliberal securitisation'. Recognising global capitalism as a war machine helps us to understand how its axiomatic stratum has produced hydra-headed war machines such as terror, anti-terror (state-declared war on terror) and counter-terror (right-wing ultranationalist Islamophobia and anti-Muslim terror). This emboldens us to think aloud and speculate whether global terror is the seventh variant of the war machine, neither the fifth category of Nazism nor the stratum of *laissez-faire*, but a hydra-headed nomadic monster, a bastard child of the two that challenges and at the same time reinforces both the progenitors.

The Biometric State and the Other as Becoming Bomb

The global security *dispositif* born to suppress terror is a state-machine, generating stratified desires to internalise the state logic of seeing the 'other as becoming bomb' (Packer 2006: 382). It produces a vicious form of 'biometric state' (Muller 2008) and *societies of control*, something prefigured by Deleuze in his *Postscript on the Societies of Control* (1992). Popular narratives on worldwide risk management and corresponding security imperatives produce cultural forces and political rituals that sustain, prolong and determine our collective subjugation to the demands of this biopolitical security-society in which geopolitics and biopolitics are wedded together to define the micro-physics of state and everyday life, leading to militarisation, violence, counter-terror and fascistic control (Muller 2008).

How do we read Deleuze and Guattari within this climate of terror, 'war against terror', Islamophobia, hate speech and open endorsement of state repression? How does one characterise terror groups fighting against the hegemony of the global neo-imperial order? Do they evince signs of assemblages, of Deleuzian 'groupuscules'? Or should we brand groups such as Islamic State (ISIS) as a fascist arborescence relying on violent social organisation? Deleuzo-Guattarian 'toolkits', as they called them, are being appropriated by all camps nowadays – by pro-terror as well as anti-terror voices – deepening the need to rescue Deleuze and Guattari`s concepts from being misappropriated. A blog called AltExploit has a 2017 entry on 'Rhizomatic Extreme-Right'

(15 October 2017), hinting how contemporary right-wing forces are deploying Deleuze and Guattari's idea of the rhizome to establish their claims and functioning modes. WikiLeaks has been described as an exemplary 'rhizomatic, deterritorialized, itinerant war machine'. Even counter-insurgency theorist Shimon Naveh, who teaches at an Israeli military academy and speaks in 'fluent Deleuzo-Guattarese, narrates his effort to "smooth out" spaces that are "striated" in Palestinian towns' (Shatz 2010: 8). Does this signify a domestication and distortion of Deleuze and Guattari's revolutionary ideas? Is the language of desire and multiplicity being reduced to fashionable tricks and strategic ploys in the cyberspace of neoliberal capitalism? The philosophy of desire was always susceptible to this distortion, and both Deleuze and Guattari admit that

> Desire . . . is not always good: 'Hitler got the Fascists sexually aroused. Flags, nations, armies, banks get a lot of people aroused.' The appeal of reactionary politics lay in its ability to neutralise the 'deterritorializing' effects of capitalism with 'reterritorializing' narratives of God and country. All the more reason, then, for the 'revolutionary machine' to 'acquire at least as much force as these coercive machines have for producing breaks and mobilising flows'. But who would take part? The revolutionary machine in *Anti-Oedipus* is a band of outsiders, made up of avant-garde writers . . . non-Western tribes, outlaws, gays, minorities, freaks . . . The aim of 'schizo-analysis' . . . was to liberate the 'multiplicity' of the unconscious. ('We are all groupuscules.') (Shatz 2010: 4)

This affirms the non-totalitarian nature of the 'revolutionary machine', consisting of 'groupuscules' as distinct from 'coercive machines' of state power and state-like organisations or groups. *Anti-Oedipus* (1972) launches, as Foucault rightly observes, a practical critique or a political pragmatics of militant organisations and subjectivities. Foucault, as is quite well known, described *Anti-Oedipus* as 'a life style, a way of thinking and living, outlining how does one keep from being fascist, even (especially) when one believes oneself to be a revolutionary militant' (Foucault, in Deleuze and Guattari 1983: xii, as quoted in Thoburn 2008: 112). In a similar vein, Brad Evans and Julian Reid in their work on *Deleuze & Fascism* (2013) locate fascism in our heads, urging for a shift of focus from macro-historical perspectives to an understanding of micro-fascism as explained by Foucault in his brilliant introduction to *Anti-Oedipus*. Evans and Reid analyse 'terror' from this angle.

For us, the challenge lies in how to define terror or world terrorism as it stands today through a Deleuzo-Guattarian transversal lens. While analysing terror, we bring into focus Deleuze and Guattari`s larger concern for statist repression and machinic systems of securitised governance at large, resulting in violence, repression and counter-violence. We look into the fascistic, militant, radical and even the 'ethical' (Devji 2005) dimension of terror, and while doing that, the spectral and semiotic underpinnings of terror, state repression, as well as the rhizomicity or singularity formation of *jihad* are also brought into the discussion. We wonder whether this exercise of theoretical and philosophical understanding of terror involves, borrowing from Guattari, some form of 'chaosophy' (Guattari 2009a), or the axiomatic of dogma-ridden 'groupuscules'. This enunciation of violence and terror through a Deleuzo-Guattarian lens is also one way of doing 'philosophy at the edge of chaos' (Bell 2006).

Existing scholarly works have, over the years, engaged with 'Deleuze, Schizoanalysis and Fascism' (Holland 2008), with 'Homeland Security, Society of Control and Deleuze' (Packer 2006) or the 'Schizophrenia of Global Jihad' (Michelsen 2009), 'Deleuze and War' (Evans and Guillaume 2010) or 'Deleuze and Writing in Terror' (Marks 2003); and recently one comes across studies on 'Cinematic Terrorism: Deleuze, ISIS and Delirium' (Akil 2016), 'Organizing Conflict: The Rhizome of Jihad' (Kuronen and Huhtinen 2017) and 'Deleuze and Anarchy' (Heerden and Eloff 2019), demonstrating how newer studies on Deleuze, Guattari and terror have emerged consistently in recent years as the world continues to be rocked by terror and counter-terror measures.

As drone attacks, jihadi killings, state-sponsored war, market violence and right-wing terror continue to determine our living patterns, a volume on reading terror through a Deleuzo-Guattarian perspective is long overdue. Terror construes a blind ideological obedience to the doctrine of violence, justifying it as a legitimate force of social and political transformation. Most of the time, however, terror has been projected as a mode of revolutionary militancy. State terror, on the other hand, has capitalised on people's sense of insecurity, fear and national security, erecting a normative worldwide system of official repression, brute force, killings, torture and oppressive surveillance. Given this, how do we approach philosophy in the time of Guantanamo Bay, ISIS torture videos, right-wing ultra-nationalist lynchings, racial attacks, sporadic and indiscriminate firing at innocent victims in mosques, churches, shopping malls or railway stations? The long-drawn Syrian war, the unprecedented refugee exodus, cluster bombings, ISIS killings and counter-killings, macabre visuals of death and brutality – this apocalyptic chaos forces one to hunt for a schizoanalytical 'chaosophy' (Guattari 2009a) that helps us make sense of what is going on. If the

Holocaust motivated both Deleuze and Guattari to decode organised mass murder in the camps, resulting in their seminal studies on fascism and totalitarian tendencies, the contemporary resurgence of fascist and terror forces across the globe necessitates an innovative rereading of their works to understand the current conjuncture.

Despotism and Cancerous Bodies without Organs

As stated earlier, existing scholarly works have focused on Deleuzo-Guattarian interventions on war, fascism (Evans 2010; Evans and Reid 2013) and anarchism (Heerden and Eloff 2019), but what about Deleuze, Guattari and the reality of terror? If 'there is only desire and the social, and nothing else', as claimed by Deleuze and Guattari, then how do we explain terror as a desiring-machine? Does terror actualise monstrous forms of schizo-delirium? How do we explain the theologico-libidinal investment in terror acts? If every investment of desire is social, then is it imperative to inquire how the desiring-production of terror is socially inscribed? In other words, how do we go beyond, or get beneath, the molar aggregates of terror and investigate the 'molecular elements' forging multiple desiring-machines that constitute and motivate them? Both Deleuze and Guattari acknowledge that there are desiring-machines of a 'paranoid and perverted type too', and therefore the question remains as to whether we read terror as an insidious desiring-machine – a case that obscures the relation between desiring-production and desiring-machines.

> While careful and productive de-stratification is the ethical ideal, there is a danger of de-stratifying too rapidly or wildly—the danger of over-dosing, in both the literal sense (over-dosing on drugs) and the figurative sense (over-dosing on too much de-stratification). But there are also BwOs belonging to the strata themselves, BwOs that proliferate uncontrollably and end up being destructive, such as cancer, inflation, and fascism. The ethical challenge for desire, Deleuze & Guattari conclude, is 'distinguishing between that which pertains to stratic proliferation [cancerous BwOs], or else too-violent de-stratification [over-dosing], and that which pertains to the construction of the plane of consistency' ... where your BwO can intersect or merge productively with those of others, as you launch forth on the thread of a tune to improvise with the world. (Holland 2013: 100)

Can we therefore define terror as 'stratic proliferation' resembling 'cancerous BwOs', destratifying too violently, as opposed to real revolutionary nomadism, constructing the plane of consistency? Terror outfits are not segmentary or acephalous assemblages; they oppose the state machine and yet replicate most of the time the despotic or stratified repression of the state. The objective of schizoanalysis is said to be to analyse the specific nature of the libidinal investments in the economic and political spheres, and that entails how, for the agent/ agents who desire(s), desire can be made to desire its own repression – eliciting the role of the death drive in the circuit connecting desire to the social sphere (Buchanan 2000: 88). This role of the death drive is evident in the acts of terror outfits such as ISIS, who tried to establish a territorial caliphate based in the Middle East as a prefiguration of the contemporary territorial machine or a modern-day despotic machine, a form of social or religious machine that engulfs desiring-production. The despotic machine or the barbarian socius functions through new alliances and direct filiation, challenging the lateral alliances and the extended filiations of the old community. Despots, we have learned from Deleuze and Guattari, rally for a new alliance system and place themselves in the direct filiation with the deity which the people must follow (1983: 210). The despotism of terror is a form of social machine, causing great violence, even though this may not necessarily manifest itself always in direct military action.

> The despot, or his God, becomes the full body on which the socius inscribes itself, replacing the territorial machine's earth and this new despotic regime establishes the 'megamachine' of the state replacing the territorial machine, a new hierarchy is installed, placing the despot at the top. (Deleuze and Guattari 1983: 212, as quoted in Buchanan 2000: 104–5)

This mega-machine of the state is the new Body without Organs (BwO) and this fear of a despotic rise was flagged by Deleuze and Guattari in *A Thousand Plateaus*, warning us of the dangers inherent in the functioning of the BwO. This marks a departure from their previous enthusiasm for BwOs in *Anti-Oedipus*

> Staying stratified—organized, signified, subjected—is not the worst that can happen: the worst that can happen is if you throw the strata into demented or suicidal collapse, which brings them back down on us heavier than ever . . . And how necessary caution is, the art of dosages, since overdose is a danger. You don't do it with a sledgehammer, you use a very fine file. You invent self-destructions that have nothing to do with the death drive. Dismantling the [organism] has never meant killing yourself, but rather opening the body to connections that presuppose an entire assemblage, circuits, conjunctions, levels and thresholds, passages and distributions of intensity, and territories and de-territorializations measured with the craft of a surveyor. (Deleuze and Guattari 1983: 160, as quoted in Holland 2013: 99–100)

The politics of terror (whether state terror or terror combating the state, or counter-terror, one terror group confronting another terror machine) is basically monomaniac, and Deleuze and Guattari's plateau on politics in A Thousand Plateaus offered forebodings about terror or destructive lines of flight in politics. They mentioned four dangers that threaten the political lines: two, namely fear and power, encourage us to embrace rigidities, transforming 'metamorphosis-machines' into overcoded machines of rigid segmentation. Additionally, there is the danger of political lines degenerating into 'micro-Oedipuses' and 'microfascisms', even though they don't manifest in full-fledged macro-fascism:

> Instead of the great paranoid fear, we are trapped in a thousand little monomanias, self-evident truths, and clarities that gush from every black hole and no longer form a system, but are only rumble and buzz, blinding lights giving any and everybody the mission of self-appointed judge, dispenser of justice, policeman, neighborhood SS man. Finally, there is the fourth danger, that lines-of-flight themselves may go bad and turn into lines of abolition and pure destruction . . . the murder-suicide of German writer Heinrich von Kleist and Henriette Vogel, along with Hitler's declaration in 1945 that 'If the war is lost, may the nation perish' ('Telegram 71', as quoted in Holland 2013: 121)

Having discussed Deleuzo-Guattarian premonitions about the dangers lurking within the political line of flight, leading to 'fascist' consolidations, 'murderous suicides', 'paranoid fear' and 'monomanias', it becomes easier for us to analyse terror through Deleuzo-Guattarian optics. The hermeneutics of terror justifies itself as a liberating counter-current to the absolutist neo-imperial order or to multiple forms of ethnic hegemon. But contrary to what is claimed, is terror a liberation of desire or an incarceration of desire? Does it, in other words, schizophrenise the existing power structure or impose repressive social machines over desiring-production? Is terror a cancerous BwO as apprehended by Deleuze and Guattari? A line of flight towards death? Do we accept the terrorist as a delirious schizophrenic who has been touched off by a desiring flow that threatens the social order, invoking a demand for schizoanalysing complex power codes, repressive machines that determine the act of terror? It is in this sense, perhaps, that Deleuze and Guattari define the schizophrenic as the limit of the socius, the instance of a pure a-sociality which terrifies every social organisation. The schizophrenic is the living instance of the socially unassimilable being or organisation, the 'new barbarian' (the body incapable of obedience or submission) (Buchanan 2000: 44). But unlike the nomadology of the schizophrenic, does terror demonstrate desiring-production in its pure state or is it an interiorised pathological 'black hole' of death and destruction? Terror in all its variants partakes of doctrinal apparatuses of stratification that prevent the liberation of desire.

> It would be strange', Guattari remarked, 'to rely on a party, [doctrinal organisation] or state apparatus for the liberation of desire'.... Liberated desire means desire that escapes the impasse of private fantasy: it is not a question of adapting it, socialising it, disciplining it, but of plugging it in such a way that its process not be interrupted in the social body, and that its expression be collective. What counts is not the authoritarian unification, but rather a sort of infinite spreading. It is not a question of directing, of totalising, but of plugging into the same plan of oscillation. As long as one alternates between the impotent spontaneity of anarchy and the bureaucratic and hieratic coding of a party organisation, there is no liberation of desire. (Buchanan 2000: 8–9)

Desire is revolutionary in itself, but terror binds desire in its doctrinal stratum. For Deleuze and Guattari, desire runs the risk of being shackled to, or converted into, interest, and as interest it is susceptible to capture, domestication and pacification (Buchanan 2000: 89).

Terror, Micro-fascism, Global Schizo-delirium

Eugene Holland's study (2008) of Hitler's Germany and George Bush's America in terms of micro-fascism or micro-oedipalisation tried to scrutinise the idea of Palingenesis and the absolutist force of obeying with a mythic promise of rebirth of the community or the nation, a force that galvanised people to obey the despot or the state war machine to deliver the nation out of this abjection. This is where, according to Holland, the rot of fundamentalism lies, and therefore, along with oedipalisation, one situates one's understanding of terror or terrorism within the theoretical frame of the war machine and schizoanalysis. Recent studies on cinematic terrorism (Akil 2016) use Deleuze's concept of the *time-image* discussed in *Cinema 1* and *Cinema 2* as a heuristic tool to analyse the brutal internet films of ISIS, arguing that these may be experienced as actualisations of a 'global schizophrenic delirium'. Akil claims that ISIS films of killing and torture demonstrate what Deleuze describes as the 'powers of the false', showing a reality that it is unbearable to witness. As the Marquis de Sade exhibited in his works images of violence and perversion, reflective of the brutal realities of the reign of terror during the French Revolution,

ISIS itself, and not only its film productions, becomes the foci of a symptomatic and cinematic realization of the failures of our globalized society in the post-Cold War/Arab Spring era. We experience the unbearable violence in the form of schizophrenic delirium, as if this violence is being performed somewhere else, by someone else, to someone else. (Akil 2016: 366)

According to Akil, we learn from the ISIS videos about

a horrifying flaw, or error, not only in the psychotic minds of ISIS as a fascist organization, but more generally in our own contemporary status as a civilization. Only through the realization that at the core of all our experiences in humanity lies a pervasive state of delirium that one begins to relate to some fundamental understanding. . . . '[w]e're not threatened by error. It's much worse: we're swimming in delirium'. (Deleuze 2004b: 165, as quoted in Akil 2016: 367)

This emphasis on delirium, connecting it with terror acts, is crucial as it has larger global ramifications. Akil's reference to the concept of 'delirium' is explained through Deleuze and Guattari, theorising it as 'the general matrix by which the intensities and becomings of the body without organs directly invest the socio-political field' (Deleuze 2004b: 165). Delirious formations 'are neither familial nor personal but world historical' (Smith 2012: 210–12). The reason we expound at length on delirium in this study on terror and Deleuze can be ascribed to Deleuze's idea of the delirious inscription of the social field. Akil rightly argues that delirium is not about what we witness and how we react to it, but about what constitutes the state of delirium in the first place.

According to Deleuze, 'the unconscious is a factory, and not a theatre.' In fact, in their criticism of psychoanalysis, Deleuze and Guattari specifically argue that 'psychoanalysis does not understand what delirium is, because it does not see how delirium invests the social field in its widest extension.' To understand delirium, we need to understand the specific interaction between the psychological and the social, the 'molecular micro-machines' and the 'large molar social machines': 'how they interact and work in one another' . . . Delirium is completely invested in the social, the historical, the cultural, the economic. As stressed by Deleuze, delirium 'is by its nature a libidinal investment of an entire historical milieu, of an entire social environment. What makes one delirious are classes, peoples, races, masses, mobs.' (Deleuze 2004b: 275, as quoted in Akil 2016: 367)

The upshot of this argument can be summarised as a reading of terror both as fascistic delirium as well as radical insurrection. In both ways, the deeper social and economic inscription of terror becomes evident as a way for us to understand the underlying implications of the market-driven globalisation that has embroiled us in the larger libidinal investment of the current historical milieu. The delirious dance of terror, warmongering and other pervasive forms of regular systemic violence – the larger molar social machine – determines a corresponding molecular micro-machine of individual or group acts of terror or violent delirium.

> What the ISIS videos reveal is not only the barbarity of our human race, but specifically, the glitch in a global system that hides that barbarity. According to Deleuze and Guattari: Well, we say that we've never seen a schizophrenic delirium that is not first and foremost racial, racist, and political, that is not running off in every direction of history, that does not invest cultures, that does not talk about continents, kingdoms, etc. . . . The real problem of delirium is the extraordinary transitions between two poles: the one is a reactionary pole, so to speak, a fascist pole of the type: 'I am a superior race,' which shows up in every paranoid delirium; and the other is a revolutionary pole: like Rimbaud, when he says: 'I am an inferior race, always and forever.' (Deleuze 2004b: 235, as quoted in Akil 2016: 367)

If terror brutalities and the visual projection of that delirium reflect the larger libidinal structure of the social and the cultural, then conventional psychoanalytical and official modes of security studies are inadequate to understand the inherently systemic and psychic root of terror. For that we need schizoanalytical frames as theorised by Deleuze and Guattari.

Landscapes of Jihad and Schizoanalysis

Terror groups are generally supposed to function through ideologies of radicalisation or principles of militancy, valorised as modes of revolutionary agency. Jihadi radicalisation is connected to the schizophrenia of its narrative-drivers, but the popular concept of identity-oriented construction of jihadi groups needs re-evaluation, especially in the light of Faisal Devji's study of global jihad in his seminal *Landscapes of the Jihad: Militancy, Morality and Modernity* (2005). Going beyond stereotyped readings of a monocultural Islamic identity, Devji argues for an 'enormous variance in Jihadi identity' (Michelsen 2009: 454), and that allows it to be seen through Deleuzo-Guattarian concepts of rhizome and the war machine. Generally speaking, when we speak of terror, the popular tendency as governed by media narratives and state propaganda mostly speaks of Islamic terror or jihad, and this strategic singling out of one particular type of terror act hides the overall molar machinic arrangement of social and systemic terror.

Mark Sedgwick (2009), in his reading of Devji's thesis on global jihad, highlights fresh insights offered by Devji on Islamic terror. Contrary to conventional perception, jihadism is not a twentieth-century phenomenon; rather, Devji locates its historical precedents in the eighteenth and nineteenth centuries, when jihads were generally described as 'anti-colonial' resistance mobilisations practised on the Islamic periphery – in Libya, Somalia, parts of India and Afghanistan. According to Devji, today's jihad too emerges from the periphery, even though certain Arabic names are projected in the media as leading identity-oriented blocks. Historically, anti-colonial jihads were generally messianic, mystical and apocalyptic movements led by charismatic figures. The concept of jihad as practised in the eighteenth and nineteenth centuries was, therefore understood in these terms, and not in standard political terms, as it is perceived today.

Contrary to popular images of a pernicious assemblage of terror outfits, Devji went to the extent of underlining the democratic nature of contemporary jihad, which is marked by the absence of messianic figures – an absence that might be explained in terms of the 'democratisation' of the messiah into 'a collective figure' (Devji 2005: 48). Sedgwick locates another aspect of this democratisation by describing jihadism as a 'broad church' as there is no requirement for ideological conformity, or even conformity to Islamic norms in terms of religious practice. Jihadism then, in this analysis, is not seen as politically 'instrumental', as the jihadists themselves are not sure about what exactly they are trying to achieve in political terms. Devji rightly points out that honour, respect and revenge are more prominent as motives than anything political, in the classic sense of that word. The vast disproportion between the terror acts of al-Qaeda (such as 9/11) and enormous anti-terror acts (such as the invasion and occupation of Afghanistan and Iraq) made the local causes of al-Qaeda's jihad vanish into the immensity of their own global effects (Sedgwick 2009: 353).

So the question is, if jihad is not to be understood in instrumental or political terms, how is it to be perceived? Sedgwick quotes Devji who suggests that

> it might be understood in 'ethical' terms, as consisting of actions that are 'complete in themselves.' 'Martyrdom,' argues Devji, borrowing from Kierkegaard, 'neither represents an idea nor is it in any way instrumental, but constitutes rather the moment of absolute humanity, responsibility and freedom as a self-contained act shorn of all teleology' ... Less controversially, the jihad may also be understood in terms of globalization, of the new world order, and of the new media ... Even when one may not

agree with Devji's interpretation of his evidence or with the conclusions he draws from it, the questions raised are important ones that are too often ignored. And sometimes one will agree with Devji ... the effects of the jihad matter more than the jihad itself, that it is a phenomenon of the Islamic periphery more than of the Arab world, that it is little interested in states or citizenship, and that non-instrumental or 'ethical' motivation matters a lot. (Sedgwick 2009: 353)

This is a significant shift from the way we investigate global jihad, enabling us to identify the ethical aspect involved in it as well as other issues such as globalisation and media narratives around the idea of Islamophobia. Having looked into these unexplored dimensions, we realise that the issue of terror demands further scrutiny, and in a world engulfed in continuous battles about questions of economic fundamentalism, market-terror and ethnic assertion, a renewed approach to understanding the deeper molecular aspects of jihad or global terror is very much in order.

All jihadi groups or any other militant group affiliated to ideologies that are involved in various resistance mobilisations are said to draw their sustenance from a certain amount of radicalisation. In popular parlance, radicalism too has been understood in narrow identitarian ways, but when seen through the schizoanalytical lens, one can conceptualise the schizophrenia of global jihad which transcends all identitarian closures. Michelsen addressed the schizophrenia of global jihad, arguing that

If radicalisation is a schizo-effect rather than a product of fundamental identity, then a successful address of radicalisation ... requires a molecular rather than molar approach; abandoning myths of identitarian path-dependence into radicalism for a more pragmatic openness to the complexity of reasons for waging Jihad. Only a 'molecular politics' or schizo-engagement offers avenues for productively engaging the complex dynamics of embodied desire that drive mobilisation for Jihadi violence. (Michelsen 2009: 455)

The schizophrenia of global jihad denies a central narrative-identity of jihad, as that would closely resemble the tendency to oedipalise identity found in Freudian psychoanalysis. Michelsen argues that it seems plausible to hypothesise that the pervasive tendency in public diplomacy literature to formulate jihad as driven by purely identitarian forces may simply reflect the habitual return to the identitarian axioms of the contemporary world (Michelson 2009).

Guattari and Jihad

Throughout his life Félix Guattari organised support networks for the release of militant leaders connected with the Italian Red Army; he and some of his friends created the CINEL (Collective of Initiatives for New Spaces of Liberty), whose primary objective was to ensure support for militants persecuted by the justice system. Guattari's *Soft Subversions: Texts and Interviews 1977–1985* includes a chapter on 'Minority and Terrorism' which forms a part of a long 'dialogue' between Guattari and Maria-Antonietta Macchiocchi on minoritarian struggle *vis-à-vis* Italian 'terrorism'. Evidence of Guattari's ongoing collaboration with Deleuze also emerges in this book, bearing testimony to how they thought of attempting in *A Thousand Plateaus* to retheorise the minor in a broad socio-semiotic way. Details about this are available in 'Minority and Terrorism: Dialogue between Maria Antonietta Macciocchi and Felix Guattari' held at the Namur Colloquium in May 1978 (translated by Emily Wittman [Paris: Payot, 1979]). In another section of this book, Guattari focuses on the film *Germany in Autumn* as a way to reflect again on the so-called 'terrorist phenomenon' and to contrast German repression with its Italian counterpart (Guattari 2009b: 12). In a long 1982 interview with Sylvère Lotringer on a possible 'New Alliance', Guattari speaks of the 'rhizome' of political and conceptual tools and instruments available to continue to struggle in a new political era, that of molecular revolution. All these testify how, while supporting militant causes, both Deleuze and Guattari were aware of the tendency of militant ideologies to run the risk of verging towards fascistic structures.

Nicholas Thoburn in his essay 'What is a Militant' included in *Deleuze and Politics* (Buchanan and Thoburn 2008), while drawing a genealogy of modern militancy, introduces a critique of the militant, notwithstanding its revolutionary roles. This again helps us in surmising how Deleuze and Guattari would have responded to terror today. The militant terror-machine, while lauded for its revolutionary role, is also exposed to unconceal its cold, brutal act as a monomaniacal machine. Thoburn seeks to

> understand the ways militancy effectuates processes of political passion and a certain unworking or deterritorialisation of the self in relation to political organisations and the wider social environment within which militants would enact change. To this end the paper traces a diagram or abstract machine of militancy, a diagram comprised of Guattari's cartography of Leninism and the model of struggle set out by the Russian nihilist Sergei Nechaev ... this militant machine [Terror?], Guattari argues, is

characterised by: the production of a field of inertia that restricts openness and encourages uncritical acceptance of slogans and doctrine; the hardening of situated statements into universal dogma; the attribution of a messianic vocation to the party; and a domineering and contemptuous attitude – 'that hateful "love" of the militant' – to those known as 'the masses'. (Guattari 1984: 130, as quoted in Thoburn 2008: 98)

The militant machine as articulated in Guattari's cartography denotes a passional struggle and its relation to a deterritorialisation of the self. Thoburn characterises this in Deleuze and Guattari's terms as the constitutive 'line of flight' of militancy, of the formations of the 'passional' and the 'subjective' regime of sign that subsequently takes a singular and dangerous route. Genealogically speaking, Thoburn refers to Sergei Nechaev's 1869 *Catechism of the Revolutionist* to locate the birth of modern militancy:

In the forty-seven principles that comprise the Catechism, Nechaev outlines an image of revolutionary action, operating through the closed cell of the political organisation, as a singular, all-encompassing passion. It is a cold, calculated passion that . . . requires a dismantling of all relations to self and society that could be conceived of in any manner other than its own furtherance, even at the cost of death . . . it has had a persistent presence in radical cultures: Lenin expressed admiration for the tenets of the Catechism . . . [it] was popular among, and published and distributed by, the Black Panther Party, having some presence in the Panthers' formulation of 'revolutionary suicide'. . . Militancy thus posed not only a moral standard against which revolutionary commitment would be assessed, but a kind of 'quasi-spiritual test' . . . premised on the purification of subjectivity that could only be found through an ever-renewed and ever-intensified struggle whose limit was constituted ultimately by a preparedness for death . . . Such was the force of . . . revolutionary passion . . . exemplifying Deleuze and Guattari's understanding of the characteristic delusion of the passional regime – as a monomania . . . 'I'm monomaniacal like Captain Ahab in Moby Dick . . . We should be like Captain Ahab and possess one thought – destruction of the mother country.' (Thoburn 2008: 101–2)

Thoburn inquires as to how we deterritorialise this militant diagram and think of a political practice beyond militancy. Thoburn explores the a-militant diagram, by problematising the relation between the political group and that which lies outside it, what might be known by militant assemblages as 'the masses' – as Guattari implies, it is on this axis that the question of an 'other machine' beyond that of the militant should be posed (Guattari 1984: 190, as quoted in Thoburn 2008: 108).

Guattari envisions the 'subject group' as a mode of political composition oriented towards innovative collective composition and enunciation, and open to its outside and the possibility of its own death – in contrast to the 'subjugated group', cut off from the world and fixated on its own self-preservation. As Deleuze and Guattari's project unfolds, the model of the subject group thus loses prominence in favour of an opening of perception to, and critical engagement with, the multiplicity of groups – or, in Deleuze and Guattari's terms, assemblages or arrangements – which compose any situation, following their notion that 'we are all groupuscules'. Guattari mentions in a 1980 interview that once he came up with the idea of the 'subject-group', he contrasted that with 'subjected groups' in an attempt to define modes of intervention which

> I described as micro-political. I've changed my mind: there are no subject groups, but arrangements of enunciation, of subjectivization, pragmatic arrangements which do not coincide with circumscribed groups. These arrangements can involve individuals but also ways of seeing the world, emotional systems, conceptual machines, memory devices, economic, social components, elements of all kinds. (Guattari 2009b: 227–8, as quoted in Thoburn 2008: 113)

So there is a politics to be extracted from Deleuze and Guattari's works that provides a plank to resist terror, rooted in issues of perception. Deleuze, it is argued, 'refuses to write "in terror", preferring to write "before" terror', a distinction which can be elucidated through references to Deleuze's engagement with Primo Levi's treatment of the issue of shame as it emerged through his encounter with the Holocaust (Marks 2003: 115). Giorgio Agamben too has mentioned this traumatised abjection of Levi in his *Remnants of Auschwitz*. Levi developed his sense of shame at the concentration camps, and felt repulsed post-Holocaust for belonging to humankind. The feeling of shame that Levi explores emanates out of his recognition that we all as humans are capable of perpetrating terror.

Terror functions similarly in Deleuze's work, in that he explores terror as an ensemble of affects and percepts which might enable us to start thinking. Deleuze is seldom prescriptive, opting instead to focus on the need to transform our perceptions of the world. Deleuze's work is,

> in the terms employed by Jean Cayrol, 'Lazarean'... Lazarean precisely because he returns from death, from the land of the dead; he has passed through death and is born from death, whose sensory-motor disturbances he retains. Even if he was not personally in Auschwitz, even if he was not personally in Hiroshima ... He passed through a clinical death, he was

born from an apparent death, he returns from the dead, Auschwitz or Hiroshima, Guernica or the Algerian war . . . In this way, Deleuze, although he acknowledges that terror has undermined the Greek philosophical ideal of 'friendship', refuses to write in terror. Instead, he finds in some art and thought, and particularly in cinema, the possibility of writing before terror. (Marks 2003: 123)

Interwar Italy and Germany, according to Deleuze and Guattari, witnessed the masses desiring fascism, and any discussion on terror must identify this collective love for the fascist machine, reminding us of Foucault's prefatory remarks in *Anti-Oedipus* about fascism being in our head. Schizoanalysis argues that the masses were not coerced or tricked into supporting fascism, they actively desired it. Deleuze and Guattari are more interested in this central question – why did the masses desire fascism? Their explanation of this phenomenon of wilful endorsement of fascistic terror focused on the relation between desire and the social field. Deleuze and Guattari were concerned with how desire invests the social field as well as with what desire actually invests, what its object is

Mid-century European masses weren't ideologically tricked into fascism: they actively desired it because it augmented their feelings of power. There is little or nothing psychological about this, except perhaps in one of its results (and then only to the extent that affects of power could be attributed to individuals, as 'subjective feelings'): the historical circumstances under which and the social institutions by means of which that augmentation of power occurred are of primary importance, as we shall see. (Holland 2013: 76)

According to Eugene Holland, if *Anti-Oedipus* perceives fascism (along with paranoia) as a fixation opposed to the fluidity of desire, *A Thousand Plateaus* projects fascism as a peculiar kind of acceleration of desire. Fascism is presented there as a matter of speed: desire moves too fast rather than too slow. The idea of fascism as 'excess speed' relates to two crucial differences between the first and second volumes of *Capitalism and Schizophrenia*. The second volume argues about a 'cancerous' Body without Organs and of a 'suicidal' line of flight.

The general tendency to locate terror or ideologies of terror within the theological practices of Islam has led to Islamophobia and the subsequent resurgence of the securitised state, the 'hightech-military/information-economy/fossil-fuel complex', or what Deleuze and Guattari would call the society of control. This simplistic demonisation of Islamism as inherently embedded in violence, approving the doctrine of terror, detracts from any close analysis of terror or terrorism as a political or philosophical category. Such targeted and strategic categorisation of a particular community as terror-prone is itself an act of terror. All the different chapters in this book expose the fallacies of such generalisations; they focus instead on closer analysis of the question of terror through Deleuzo-Guattarian tools.

Chapter Outline

Claire Colebrook in 'The War on Terror versus the War Machine' shows how the English translation of Giorgio Agamben's *Homo Sacer* in 1998 allowed for a theorisation of the post-9/11 war on terror. Agamben's claim was that Western power, down to its very conception of the subject and language, was premised upon a sovereignty that constituted itself by marking out a political mode of life that would set itself off from bare life. Agamben was indebted to Carl Schmitt and Walter Benjamin, both of whom – in different ways – regarded the emergence of sovereignty and law as necessarily violent events that could always (in moments of crisis or emergency) require the violent suspension of law for the sake of preserving the law. Colebrook inquires about better ways to think about the war on terror that mostly rely on suspension of law for the sake of sovereign expediency. She suggests that there is indeed a better way, and that another conception of power, law, war, terror and the state was offered by Deleuze and Guattari in *Anti-Oedipus* and *A Thousand Plateaus*.

Janell Watson's chapter 'Guattari and Terror: Radicalisation as Singularisation' narrates how terrorist attacks, defined as an intentional act of violence by a non-state actor, increased between 1970 and the early 1990s, then declined until around 2000, and have increased rapidly over the past decade. These include mass-causality attacks, which kill more than a hundred people in a single country on a single day. She argues that many mass attacks occur in conditions of war, civil unrest or extreme economic instability, but those against prosperous targets garner a disproportionate share of empathy and attention from the international mainstream media, such as high-profile cases in New York (2001), Moscow (2002), Madrid (2004), Mumbai (2008), Nairobi (2013) and Paris (2015). Given the terrorist organisations' appeal to religion, as well as the fear-based response of right-wing Europe and America, Watson is struck by the pertinence of Guattari's observation that the 'global diffusion of the mass media' has enabled 'subjective factors' to play a more dominant role in history than in the past. She examines the mass-mediated appeals to religion and fear as manifestations of 'rising demands for subjective singularity' around the world. These demands can be understood as a refusal by the masses to accept the standardised models of subjectivity offered by global capitalism, which serves the wealthy elite to the detriment of the vast majority of the world's population. Schizoanalysis, she argues, offers tools for understanding this demand, as well as for seeking responses less lethal and less fascist than those promoted by current extremist groups.

Janae Sholtz's chapter 'Creative Resistance: An Aesthetics of Creative Affect in a Time of Global Terror' thinks of art or the affect in the time of global terror. Images of violence and injustice, generated through media and photography, have opened, Sholtz argues, a visual window and increased our participation, on an affective level, with the atrocities that are occurring all over the world (for example, war photography, the drowned Syrian refugee). The optimistic claim is that these images bring the suffering of others before us and demand a response, that they generate empathy and awareness. But equally one might point to the use of image and spectacle to propagate terror itself, through the mass release of videos of beheadings, hangings and brutal executions. In one case, the affects that are ideally being evoked are empathy, disgust and indignation, while in the other, what is desired are affects of fear, despair and terror. One of the issues that Sholtz addresses, then, is how and if artworks differ from the utilisation of images for purposes of creating and spreading terror. Is there an ameliorative possibility in the artistic image, the photographic image in particular, meant to document and crystallise the intensity of injustice, suffering, etc. that makes it rise above the fray of this perpetual stream of affects to which we contemporaries are subject? In many respects, for Sholtz, Rancière's formulation of the distribution of the sensible draws upon a similar mode of analysis as Deleuze's methodology of schizoanalysis and intersects with Deleuze's understanding of artworks as particular blocs of sensation, which capture forces. The creative affect is an opening up of the sensible to new potential assemblages and relations. If power, state power, is the domestication of force (Massumi), then creative affect is its liberation, or at least one form.

Don Johnston's essay on 'The Inhospitality of the Global North: Deleuze, Neo-colonialism and Conflict-caused Migration' argues that although Deleuze himself identified *Anti-Oedipus* (and arguably much of the work he produced with Félix Guattari) as 'from beginning to end [. . .] political philosophy' (Deleuze 1995: 170), Deleuze and Guattari's work is not commonly used to examine contemporary world politics. However, their philosophical concepts are useful tools for the evaluation of the character of current political events. Johnston contends that Deleuze and Guattari's concept of 'becoming-democratic' provides a means to consider the Kurdish region of Iraq's response to the considerable displacement of Iraqis by ISIS forces into and within their territory in 2014. It also enables a comparison with and evaluation of the differing Greek and European responses to the massive influx of refugees into and through the Hellenic republic in 2015 and 2016. Yet a consideration of the humanitarian aid sustaining those who have fled the world's many conflagrations suggests that we may be experiencing a becoming that runs counter to the violence and bellicosity prevalent in the world today. Such a becoming – imperfect and imperilled as the humanitarian endeavour is – indicates that this 'becoming-humanitarian' might be considered an ethical response on the part of civil society to the life-negating violence of global terror.

S. Romi Mukherjee's chapter 'Suicided by *A Life*: Deleuze, Terror and the Search for the "Middle Way"' begins by arguing that the oeuvre of Deleuze and Guattari is characterised by their radical politics of affirmation and refusal of all forms of negativity, lack and violence. While Deleuzo-Guattarian tropes can be deployed to rethink the question of terror and terrorism in the contemporary world, there remains the question of how to reconcile Deleuzo-Guattarianism's protracted line of flight from the negative with a Deleuzo-Guattarian reading of terror. In other words, these thinkers, who never ceased to side with 'A Life' against the cult of death, seem strangely ill-equipped to conceptually engage with the 'excess' that is terrorism, whose victims' deaths cannot be rhetorically explained in terms of Spinozan vitalism or the return of organic matter to substance. Through an examination of their biographies and their theoretical interventions, Mukherjee explores how and why Deleuze and Guattari registered and repudiated the negative, thus complicating a Deleuzo-Guattarian reading of really existing trauma. With Deleuze's suicide as an allegorical image of this breakdown of the plane of immanence, Mukherjee goes on to explore how the politics of affirmation can and should be tempered to engage with violence – how a 'middle way' between 'Immanence: A Life' and the realities of finitude can be forged.

Anup Dhar's argument on the psychoanalysis of terror and the terror of psychoanalysis contends that a spectre is haunting the West; the spectre of the 'suicide bomber'. The (deeply troubling) figure of the suicide bomber operating at what Freud calls the 'border of the knowable', the uncanny and inexplicable 'ethico-politics' of such a figure – an ethico-politics that goes beyond the paradigmatic 'acting out' of legitimate violence: *war* – is putting into crisis the pure logic of reason, as also the simple division between an ordered social and the unanticipated irruption/break/event: terrorism. The 'hauntology' of such a figure, problematising, on the one hand, the logic of the self-directed violence of suicide and, on the other, the other-directed violence of fascism, forms the context of the question this chapter asks: what is 'terror' (*what is terror*, and not the psycho-diagnostic question: *who* is the terrorist, or the question the security-state asks: *where* is the terrorist). In other words, it also asks: what is *not* terror, where is the limit point of terror, and who is not perpetuating terror. Dhar argues that oedipalisation *is* terror. The displacement of the simple (sexual) might of the father by the 'Law of the Father', the displacement of the 'overt might of the sovereign' by the (legal) might of the community is also terror. In that sense, *being* anti-oedipal is the Other of terror. Foucault sees *Anti-Oedipus* as a book *of* (and not 'on') ethics; a book of ethical action and living; a book that is not on ethics (which is usual in philosophy) but a book of ethics, a book that itself, in itself, exudes ethics. The question of *Anti-Oedipus* or the 'anti-oedipal question' is how does one keep from being fascist, even (especially) when one believes oneself to be a revolutionary militant? Dhar's chapter marks a sharp distinction between *Anti-Oedipus* the book, and 'anti-Oedipus' the subject/schizo-position; between *Anti-Oedipus* the written text, and 'anti-Oedipus' the being (being anti-Oedipus), the process of becoming, the praxis, the art – not art as an object, but art as artisanal, art as the *art of*, art of doing-living-being anti-oedipal or being anti-terror. *Anti-Oedipus* thus renders the anti-oedipal question *asketic*. Deleuzian schizoanalysis doesn't just offer a theorisation of terror; he also offers a road map for the *praxis of anti-terror*, which oedipalised psychoanalysis cannot.

Clayton Crockett's discussion of 'Terror and the Time-Image: How Not to Believe in the World' analyses terror in terms of Deleuze's philosophy of cinema. He also analyses sections of *A Thousand Plateaus* and *Cinema 2* to show how Deleuze's philosophy resists terror as a false solution to the need to believe in this world. *Cinema 2*, he posits, is not simply a philosophy of cinema; it is a profoundly political text, and it offers resources to think about global terror. Terror is a reaction to state violence, power and control that takes the form of a mediatised spectacle. The state is based on territory, and Crockett shows how Deleuze and Guattari adopt Paul Virilio's terms of territorialisation, deterritorialisation and reterritorialisation to think about global politics in *A Thousand Plateaus*. They affirm absolute deterritorialisation in their work, but rather than being a genuine deterritorialisation, modern terror constitutes a false time-image in the form of a sublime spectacle. A terrorist spectacle might appear to resemble a Deleuzian time-image, but this is not the case because the image of terror collapses the interstices of the time-image that contribute to creativity and thought. The spectacle of terror as seen in explosive and violent images, Crockett argues, ultimately serves to reinforce rather than resist the mechanisms of capitalist control, which serve to reterritorialise the field that has been evacuated by terror and catastrophe, shock and awe. For Crockett, Deleuze offers resources to combat capitalism and state-supported violence in his and Guattari's invocation of the nomadic war machine in *A Thousand Plateaus*, and in his concept of the time-image in *Cinema 2*, but none of these can be viewed in any way as a sympathy for terrorism.

Julian Reid, in his exposition 'The Image of Terror: Art, ISIS, Iconoclasm and the Question of the People to Come', raises a provocative question regarding whether we could consider ISIS as an example of experimentation in the creation of Deleuzian 'people to come'. Reid argues that ISIS's appeal to those who followed and joined with the struggle for the creation of an Islamic state rested partly on its denunciation of present social relations and desire for the creation of a differently constituted world. The leaders of ISIS offered their very own apocalyptic narrative and prophecies, and denunciations of present world conditions, by way of recruiting followers (Fromson and Simon 2015). At the same time Reid qualifies this proposition by inquiring whether it would be an affront to Deleuze, given what Jon Protevi has described as his 'gleeful anti-clericalism' (Protevi 2013). ISIS, Reid demonstrates, was also a very explicit and deliberate attempt at the creation of a territorial state, something that many have argued is anathema to a Deleuzian political sensibility and his 'nomad science' (Lenco 2012: 100–5). For Reid, the question Deleuze posed was how, on the peripheries of global order, 'communities embark on another kind of adventure, display another kind of unity, a nomadic unity, and engage in a nomadic war-machine' (Deleuze 2004a: 259). In this context it would seem repressive not at least to entertain the idea of ISIS as a somewhat ironic attempt at the fullfilment of a Deleuzian 'people to come'.

Yasmin Ibrahim's take on 'Deleuze, the Simulacrum and the Screening of Terror Online' shows how Deleuze encounters the phenomenon of the simulacrum not as a copy of the original, but as the enunciation of difference in intrinsic form and reality. For Deleuze, Ibrahim argues, we enter a world in which 'Simulacra are those systems in which the different relates to the different by means of difference itself. What is essential is that we find in these systems no prior identity and internal resemblance:

it is all a matter of difference' (Deleuze 1990: 299). The transcendence of violent images online and their movement as affective screen images remakes the spectatorship of terror, where consuming terror through the simulacra of immateriality online (re-)produces new modes of birthing the terror-bound subject and terror as subsumed through post-indexicality. Here terror imagery reterritorialises the virtual sphere, producing new subjecthood with and through the semiotic capitalism of the internet. Terror imagery and its movement online reveals the simulacrum as a spectre in which circuits of consumption and assemblages re-enact it as a commodity for the masses, revitalising digital terror through capitalism and its hidden algorithms. In the process, it unleashes violence and the imaginary of terror as part of the 'sharing' economy, celebrating simulacrum as both the recombination of (im)material forms and its abstraction by capital online.

Arthur Kroker's chapter 'Islands of Sorrow, Ships of Despair: Nativism Resurgent and Spectacles of Terror' offers four meditations in honour of the thought of Gilles Deleuze. His is a description from afar of the intellectual and political rupture in the order of everything that was the sure and certain mark of Deleuze's lasting contribution, but he argues for something else, a form of writing that is at once faithful to thinking power in terms of the language of descent promulgated by Deleuze and, at the same time, reflecting on the question of contemporary terror as the limit experience in this time after Deleuze. Here, the bodies of abuse that are the subject of Islands of Sorrow, Ships of Despair; the bodies tortured with all the signs of vengeful cruelty that inhabit the dreams of Caliphate; the bodies of broken dreams struggling on the streets of all the Maidans of the contemporary world; and the psychically possessed bodies of Trump's American 'Id Slipping its Chain' – all these are applications, in fact as well as in theory, of Deleuze's primary political insight, namely that the spirit of the fascist within has now broken out of the cage of individual solitude, becoming the emblematic geist of the twenty-first century.

Finally, Samir Gandesha's essay on the spectacle of terror argues that terrorism's effect – which, of course, principally lies, he argues, in its *affect* – is transmitted and felt not via the event-like eruption violence of itself, but via the *threat* of its purely arbitrary, contingent, random manifestation. Terrorists don't trade in fear as such, insofar as fear takes a specific, finite object, but rather in an infinite atmospheric anxiety. While *fear* results from a direct confrontation with the object that presents itself before us, *anxiety* is produced by a sense that the potential violence that surrounds us could be dynamised from what

Deleuze calls the 'virtual' into the actual with lightning speed at the flip of a switch or, more likely, the click of a mouse, the swipe of a smartphone or tablet. The seemingly sheer randomness of terrorism is, furthermore, compounded by the very nature of a society that keeps the truth about itself from itself: a society that both knows yet at the same time doesn't know the truth about terrorism; a society that is unable to face the way in which its own deterritorialisations constitute terroristic forms of reterritorialisation.

References

Akil, H. N. (2016), 'Cinematic Terrorism: Deleuze, ISIS and Delirium', *Journal for Cultural Research*, 20 (4): 366–79, <https://doi.org.10.1080/14797585.2016.11 68973>.

Arendt, H. (1994), 'Mankind and Terror', in *Essays in Understanding, 1930–1954*, ed. Jerome Kohn, New York: Harcourt Brace.

Beck, C., and F.-X. Gleyzon (2016), 'Deleuze and the Event(s)', *Journal for Cultural Research*, 20 (4): 329–33, <https://doi.org.10.1080/14797585.2016.1264770>.

Bell, J. A. (2006), *Philosophy at the Edge of Chaos: Gilles Deleuze and the Philosophy of Difference*, Toronto: University of Toronto Press.

Buchanan, I. (2000), *Deleuzism: A Metacommentary*, Durham, NC: Duke University Press.

Buchanan, I. (2013), *Deleuze and Guattari's Anti Oedipus: A Reader's Guide*, London: Bloomsbury.

Buchanan, I., and A. Parr (2006), *Deleuze and the Contemporary World*, Edinburgh: Edinburgh University Press.

Buchanan, I., and N. Thoburn (eds) (2008), *Deleuze and Politics*, Edinburgh: Edinburgh University Press.

Casaca, P., and S. O. Wolf (2017), *Terrorism Revisited: Islamism, Political Violence and State-Sponsorship*, Switzerland: Springer.

Deleuze, G. (1990), *Logic of Sense*, trans. M. Lester and C. Stivale, New York: Columbia University Press.

Deleuze, G. (1992), 'Postscript on the Societies of Control', *October*, 59: 3–7.

Deleuze, G. (1995), *Negotiations: 1972–1990*, trans. M. Joughin, New York: Columbia University Press.

Deleuze, G. (2004a), 'Nomadic Thought', in *Desert Islands and Other Texts 1953–1974*, ed. D. Lapoujade, trans. M. Taormina, New York: Semiotext(e), pp. 252–61.

Deleuze, G. (2004b), *Desert Islands and Other Texts 1953–1974*, ed. D. Lapoujade, trans. M. Taormina, New York: Semiotext(e).

Deleuze, G., and F. Guattari (1980), *Mille Plateaux: Capitalisme et Schizophrenie, II*, Paris: Minuit.

Deleuze, G., and F. Guattari (1983), *Anti Oedipus: Capitalism and Schizophrenia*, trans. R. Hurley, M. Seem and H. R. Lane, Minneapolis: University of Minnesota Press.

Deleuze, G., and F. Guattari (1987), *A Thousand Plateaus: Capitalism and Schizophrenia*, trans. B. Massumi, Minneapolis: University of Minnesota Press.

Devji, F. (2005), *Landscapes of the Jihad: Militancy, Morality, Modernity*, London, Hurst.

Evans, B. (2010), 'Terror in all Eventuality', *Theory & Event*, 13 (3), <https://doi.org.10.1353/tae.2010.0009>.

Evans, B., and L. Guillaume (2010), 'Deleuze and War: Introduction', *Theory & Event*, 13 (3), <https://muse.jhu.edu/article/396498> (last accessed 19 June 2022).

Evans, B., and J. Reid (eds) (2013), *Deleuze & Fascism: Security, War, Aesthetics*, Abingdon: Routledge.

Fromson, J., and S. Simon (2015), 'ISIS: The Dubious Paradise of Apocalypse Now', *Survival: Global Politics & Strategy*, 57 (3): 7–56.

Gleyzon, F.-X. (2016), 'Deleuze and the Grandeur of Palestine: Song of Earth and Resistance', *Journal for Cultural Research*, 20 (4): 398–416.

Guattari, F. (1984), *Molecular Revolution: Psychiatry and Politics*, trans. R. Sheed, Harmondsworth: Penguin.

Guattari, F. (2009a), *Chaosophy: Texts and Interviews, 1972–77*, Los Angeles: Semiotext(e).

Guattari, F. (2009b), *Soft Subversions: Texts and Interviews, 1977–85*, trans. C. Wiener and E. Wittman, Los Angeles: Semiotext(e).

Heerden, C. G. van, and A. Eloff (2019), *Deleuze and Anarchism*, Edinburgh: Edinburgh University Press.

Holland, E. W. (2008), 'Schizoanalysis, Nomadology, Fascism', in I. Buchanan and N. Thoburn (eds), *Deleuze and Politics*, Edinburgh: Edinburgh University Press, pp. 74–97.

Holland, E. W. (2013), *Deleuze and Guattari's A Thousand Plateaus: A Reader's Guide*, London: Bloomsbury.

Kuronen, T., and A.-M. Huhtinen (2017), 'Organizing Conflict: The Rhizome of Jihad', *Journal of Management Inquiry*, 26 (1): 47–61.

Lawlor, L. (2016), *From Violence to Speaking Out: Apocalypse and Expression in Foucault, Derrida and Deleuze*, Edinburgh: Edinburgh University Press.

Lefebvre, A. (2005), 'A New Image of Law: Deleuze and Jurisprudence', *Telos*, 130: 103–26.

Lenco, P. (2012), *Deleuze and World Politics: Alter-Globalizations and Nomad Science*, Abingdon: Routledge.

Marks, J. (2003), 'Gilles Deleuze: Writing in Terror', *Parallax*, 9 (1): 114–24.

Michelsen, N. (2009), 'Addressing the Schizophrenia of Global Jihad', *Critical Studies on Terrorism*, 2 (3): 453–47.

Miller, C. L. (1993), 'The Postidentitarian Predicament in the Footnotes of *A Thousand Plateaus*: Nomadology, Anthropology, and Authority', *Diacritics*, 23 (3): 6–35.

Muller, B. J. (2008), 'Securing the Political Imagination: Popular Culture, the Security "Dispositif" and the Biometric State', *Security Dialogue*, 39 (2/3): 199–220.

Packer, J. (2006), 'Becoming Bombs: Mobilizing Mobility in the War on Terror', *Cultural Studies*, 20 (4–5): 371–99.

Patton, P. (1984), 'Conceptual Politics and the War-Machine in "Mille Plateaux"', *SubStance*, 13 (3/4), Issue 44–45: 61–80.

Patton, P. (2000), *Deleuze and the Political*, London: Routledge.

Peters, M. A. (2000), '"The fascism in our heads": Reich, Fromm, Foucault, Deleuze and Guattari – The Social Pathology of Fascism in the 21st Century', *Educational Philosophy and Theory*, <https://doi.org/10.1080/00131857.2020.1727403>.

Protevi, J. (2013), *Life, War, Earth: Deleuze and the Sciences*, Minneapolis: University of Minnesota Press.

Puar, J. (2007), *Terrorist Assemblages: Homonationalism in Queer Times*, Durham, NC: Duke University Press.

Rajeevan, B. (2017), 'Can Thinking of Gandhi's Ahimsa as "War Machine" Revive the Non-Western Revolution?', *Economic and Political Weekly*, 52 (48), <https://

www.epw.in/engage/article/ahimsa-war-machine-revival-gandhian-non-western
-revolution> (last accessed 19 June 2022).

Rodgers, D., and S. Jensen (2009), 'Revolutionaries, Barbarians or War Machines?
Gangs in Nicaragua and South Africa', *Socialist Register*, 45: 220–38.

Sedgwick, M. (2009), 'A Review of Faisal Devji, *Landscapes of the Jihad: Militancy,
Morality, Modernity*', *Terrorism and Political Violence*, 21 (2): 352–4.

Shatz, A. (2010), 'Desire Was Everywhere', *London Review of Books*, 32 (24),
<https://www.lrb.co.uk/the-paper/v32/n24/adam-shatz/desire-was-everywhere>
(last accessed 19 June 2022).

Smith, D. W. (2012), *Essays on Deleuze*, Edinburgh: Edinburgh University Press.

Tampio, N. (2009), 'Assemblages and the Multitude: Deleuze, Hardt, Negri, and the
Postmodern Left', *European Journal of Political Theory*, 8 (3): 383–400.

Thoburn, N. (2008), 'What is a Militant?', in I. Buchanan and N. Thoburn (eds),
Deleuze and Politics, Edinburgh: Edinburgh University Press, pp. 98–120.

Villa, D. R. (1999), *Politics, Philosophy, Terror: Essays on the Thought of Hannah
Arendt*, Princeton: Princeton University Press.

Chapter 1

The War on Terror versus the War Machine

Claire Colebrook

> Georges Dumezil, in his definitive analyses of Indo-European mythology, has shown that political sovereignty, or domination, has two heads: the magician-king and the jurist-priest. Rex and flamen, raj and Brahman, Romulus and Numa, Varuna and Mitra, the despot and the legislator, the binder and the organizer. Undoubtedly, these two poles stand in opposition term by term, as the obscure and the clear, the violent and the calm, the quick and the weighty, the fearsome and the regulated, the 'bond' and the 'pact,' etc. But their opposition is only relative; they function as a pair, in alternation, as though they expressed a division of the One or constituted in themselves a sovereign unity. . . They are the principal elements of a State apparatus that proceeds by a One-Two, distributes binary distinctions, and forms a milieu of interiority. It is a double articulation that makes the State apparatus into a *stratum*.
>
> It will be noted that war is not contained within this apparatus. (Deleuze and Guattari 1987: 351–2)

Common sense would seem to suggest that the war on terror is an event within history, that it requires two competing conceptions of the state (states generated by the free consent of individuals versus states that are imposed by fiat), and that war can only be just when states of democracy are threatened by totalitarian or other existential threats. If one accepts such an account then various suspensions of democratic procedure – such as extraordinary renditions, enhanced interrogation, internment camps, drone warfare, travel bans and increased surveillance – would all be necessary to allow democracy to be preserved. War would be external to the state to the extent that war would only be required to maintain the state. One dominant conception of sovereignty would make sense of today's war on terror by scrutinising the logic whereby democracies suspend their own modes of operation. If sovereignty is achieved by establishing a domain of law, recognising citizens whose life is human insofar as it takes part in civility, self-determination and mutual recognition of right, then its exterior is one of bare life, no longer protected by the law, but the very matter excluded in order for law to generate its political legitimacy. It was felicitous that the English translation of Giorgio Agamben's *Homo Sacer* in 1998 allowed for a theorisation of the post-9/11 war on terror. Agamben's claim was that Western power, down to its very conception of the subject and language, was premised upon a sovereignty that constituted itself by marking out a political mode of life that would set itself off from bare life. Agamben was indebted to Carl Schmitt and Walter Benjamin, both of whom – in different ways – regarded the emergence of sovereignty and law as necessarily violent events that could always (in moments of crisis or emergency) require the violent suspension of law for the sake of preserving the law. What better way to think of the war on terror than as just this suspension of law for the sake of sovereign expediency?

I will suggest that there is indeed a better way, and that another conception of power, law, war, terror and the state was offered by Deleuze and Guattari in *Anti-Oedipus* and *A Thousand Plateaus*. One of the reasons why Agamben's work has become so significant for the theorisation of the state and power today is because it follows Benjamin in always seeing the suspension of law for the sake of the law as necessary for state sovereignty. It would follow that the twenty-first-century war on terror would exemplify one tendency of the state: rather than the constituted form of order that may have required violence at its origin, we increasingly find power operating as self-constituting and violent – as a police state – at every turn. The war on terror sees everyday life take on the form of a state of war. The potentiality of terror becomes a means for the state to treat every body as though it were not fully human, always a potential threat to the state, to 'humanity'.

Carl Schmitt's definition of sovereignty ('Sovereign is he who decides on the state of exception') became a commonplace even before there was any understanding that what was at issue in it was nothing less than the limit concept of the doctrine of law and the State, in which sovereignty borders (since every limit concept is always the limit between two concepts) on the sphere of life and becomes indistinguishable from it. As long as the form of the State constituted the fundamental horizon of all communal life and the political, religious, juridical, and economic doctrines that sustained this form will still strong, this 'most extreme sphere' could not truly come to light ... Today, now that the great State structures have entered into a process of dissolution and emergency has, as Walter Benjamin foresaw, become the rule, the time is ripe to place the problem of the originary structure and limits of the form of the State in a new perspective. (Agamben 1998: 11–12)

For Agamben, then, it is necessary to think outside the form of the state to the state's threshold, and that threshold's dependence on a conception of life that it at once requires and excludes. For Agamben, beyond the state there is an extreme passivity that is not one of modernity's produced fragile bodies or refugees, stateless persons and the dispossessed ('bare life'), but an even more radical life that is not yet divided between political man and mere existence. On this model the state's relation to terror is constitutive of sovereignty: the possibility of statelessness allows those beyond the borders of the state to be so much disposable life, but it creates a permanent terror within the state. In the United States, to take just one example, there are not only border detention centres to contain supposed threats from without, but ongoing police violence against Black Americans, such that the flagrant display of being disposable produces an ongoing force of law (Sexton and Martinot 2003).

This is not what Deleuze and Guattari mean when they argue that war is 'not contained' within the state apparatus. It is important to note this contrast between theories of sovereignty (where war is internal to the state and where states secure their supposed non-violent domain of order through a violence that might always re-emerge in moments of existential threat) and Deleuze and Guattari's positive conception of the war machine. Sovereignty, in the tradition that runs from Carl Schmitt and Walter Benjamin through to Giorgio Agamben, begins with an event of constitutive violence that establishes a border between the order of the state and then a capacity for terrorising violence that keeps state power in place. One could, then, consider events such as Guantanamo Bay or the war on terror in general as exposures of what the supposedly peaceful state has been all along: what appear to be exceptions – or moments when polities revert to police states – are really business as usual. The state is always a war on terror, always a use of violence that will draw a border between law and violence. John Lechte, providing a critical overview of this tradition, argues that life outside the state and outside forms of politically meaningful freedom is assumed to be void of sense and form (Lechte 2020). Lechte seeks to challenge the notion that statelessness amounts to a condition void of meaning, and does so by suggesting that there is no such thing as bare life void of sense. Life 'itself' is always a form of life. David Graeber and David

Wengrow have also criticised the fetishised attachment to the state and the assumption that statelessness is neither desirable nor sustainable (Graeber and Wengrow 2021). These criticisms of the state form insist on meaningful existence beyond the political structures of capitalism and modernity.

Deleuze and Guattari are also critical of the supposed inevitability of the state, but instead of positing the form and meaning of pre-state existence, they argue for an originary or transcendental war. (If, in the beginning, there is war, then there is strictly speaking no beginning, but rather relations among forces from which narrations and senses of origin might be forged.). Before there is a border between state forms of sovereign violence and some putatively senseless outside or 'war of all against all', there is what Deleuze and Guattari refer to as the 'war machine'. Rather than a state of natural harmony there are forces from which relations (and therefore composed stabilities) are formed. This is *not* a theory of emergence, where order emerges from chaos; instead, by positing something like the 'war machine' Deleuze and Guattari grant more complexity and difference to forces that will be reduced and homogenised in the form of the state. One might think of them as belonging to a counter-tradition, running from Hegel and Nietzsche to the present, in which cruelty and violence are constitutive of relations and bodies, *and* in which terror occurs as a specifically modern modality. Terror would occur not when states of war become general, but when what Deleuze and Guattari refer to as the war machine – constitutive relations of force – are repressed to the point that there can *only* be an ongoing, and yet impossible, war on terror. Terror is at once the repression of the war machine, the seizing of the means of violence by single states, *and* the phantasm deployed by those same states to prevent the unleashing of stateless forces.

One mode of political theory would begin with sovereign violence, a constitutive act that creates a space of law, an inside of the polity versus an outside of bare life; such sovereign powers would be engaged in a constant war on terror, always shoring up the polity by means of expelling, abandoning and destroying modes of life not marked out by the political order. Another mode, offered by Deleuze and Guattari, would situate war outside the state: in the beginning are relations of force without law, and it is from those forces that bodies are formed. Such bodies would be nothing more than their ongoing relations of encounter, or what Nietzsche referred to as 'festive cruelty' – the pure force of suffering. Such cruelty is suppressed with the transition to monotheism, where there is now a perpetual, distant, always-deferred threat:

You will already have guessed *what* has really gone on with all this and *behind* all this: that will to torment oneself, that suppressed cruelty of animal man who has been frightened back into himself and given an inner life, incarcerated in the 'state' to be tamed, and has discovered bad conscience so that he can hurt himself, after the *more natural* outlet of this wish to hurt had been blocked, – this man of bad conscience has seized on religious presupposition in order to provide his self-torture with its most horrific hardness and sharpness. Debt towards *God*: this thought becomes an instrument of torture. (Nietzsche 1994: 63)

Here, we might want to mark out a different modality of the primacy of affect: affect, if taken seriously, is not always or necessarily the joyous affirmation of a body's own life, but a capacity to be affected, to feel force, to suffer. Life is (despite all the claims made otherwise for a Deleuze and Guattari of joyous becoming) better thought of as transcendental cruelty: not selves who fear this or that harm, but forces of life always on the brink of loss, extinction and catastrophe. Writing through Kleist, Deleuze and Guattari tie affect to the war machine. Affects are not emotions; they are forces that destroy subjective unity. This is why it is possible to see their philosophy of desire and the war machine as one of proto-terror, where forces have the power to operate beyond subjects and interests, with one path generating a general dispersal and another tending towards capture and organisation:

> Similarly, feelings become uprooted from the interiority of a 'subject,' to be projected violently outward into a milieu of pure exteriority that lends them an incredible velocity, a catapulting force: love or hate, they are no longer feelings but affects. And these affects are so many instances of the becoming-woman, the becoming-animal of the warrior (the bear, she-dogs). Affects transpierce the body like arrows, they are weapons of war. (Deleuze and Guattari 1987: 356)

This is why, in *Anti-Oedipus*, Deleuze and Guattari reject the notion of states as beginning with anxiety (1983: 117); anxiety is an effect of the state, not its ground. Rather than thinking of a war of all against all, which would prompt individuals to submit to states for the sake of stability, it is better to think of the stability of the state as that which produces formed individuals *and* their subsequent anxieties about deformation. From forces that have no centre and operate across a space that is constantly marked and unmarked, or organised and freed, states emerge by harnessing the war machine into military forces. There can only be anxiety, or a self that fears the disruption of its integrity and interiority, once states have harnessed violence and terror as their means for maintaining a centred and organised power:

It is the social machine that has profoundly changed: in place of the territorial machine, there is the 'megamachine' of the State, a functional pyramid that has the despot at its apex, an immobile motor, with the bureaucratic apparatus as its lateral surface and its transmission gear, and the villagers at its base, serving as its working parts. The stocks form the object of an accumulation, the blocks of debt become an infinite relation in the form of the tribute. (Deleuze and Guattari 1983: 194)

There is no contradiction at all in situating desire *and* the war machine prior to the constitution of the state: desire, like the war machine, is pre-personal, and it is relations among forces that produce points of relative stability. Such stabilised fields create the conditions from which bodies and persons are generated. Desire and war would always be directly revolutionary, combative of the state, destructive of all the forms of capture that turn force against what it can do. Terror, as Deleuze and Guattari detail in their history of the state and capitalism, marks the first stage of organisation; the emergence of centralised power and the state occur with deterritorialisation. Rather than bodies being marked, scarred or tattooed, the system of power takes the form of signs and an external archive. The body no longer responds immediately to the cruelty of warring forces, but to an ongoing threat of terror. When an elevated body inflicts force and cruelty on another but does so as a form of punishment, the warring relations among bodies become inscribed into forces of memory. The despot's capacity to view and mark bodies from on high shifts towards one of deterritorialised terror, the anticipation of threat and dissolution:

One might think that the system of imperial representation was, in spite of everything, milder than that of territorial representation. The signs are no longer inscribed in the flesh itself but on stones, parchments, pieces of currency, and lists. According to Wittfogel's law of 'diminishing administrative returns,' wide sectors are left semiautonomous insofar as they do not compromise the power of the State. The eye no longer extracts a surplus value from the spectacle of suffering, it has ceased to evaluate; it has begun rather to 'forewarn' and keep watch, to see that no surplus value escapes the overcoding of the despotic machine. For all the organs and their functions experience a detachment and elevation that relates them to, and makes them converge on, the full body of the despot. In point of fact the regime is not milder; the system of terror has replaced the system of cruelty. (Deleuze and Guattari 1983: 230)

In response to the 13 November 2015 terrorist attacks in Paris, at least two of the US Republican party presidential candidate hopefuls suggested establishing a database to track Muslims, with such monitoring being aligned with the reasoned care one would take to protect one's children.[1] In response, then president Barack Obama declared such suggestions to be 'not American'; whatever terrors others might deploy one will have lost the 'war on terror' if one falls into undemocratic ways of operating. Let us leave aside for now the question of how exceptional Ben Carson's and Donald Trump's suggestions for containment, religious testing, water-boarding and database monitoring would be; let us not raise the question of the post-9/11 security measures and detainment camps that Barack Obama had allowed to stay in place, nor consider President Trump's later 'travel ban' that would ward off potential terrorists from zones deemed to be hotbeds for breeding radicalism and contagion. Let's accept, however difficult such a thought experiment might be, that there is a radical difference in kind between a war on terror and terrorism itself. Theories of sovereignty would allow for such a distinction: terrorism would be the rogue, dispersed, state-destroying power that state procedures (however terrifying and terrorising) would be targeting in their ongoing efforts to shore up legitimated power. How does a war *on terror* operate? What is war such that it can set itself apart from terror?

One possible answer that was suggested – but not explored – by a 2015 opinion piece on ISIS in the *London Review of Books* was that war is bound up with nation-states, sovereignty and an authentic contestation of territory, whereas terrorism is ad hoc, stateless and (in ways not fully clarified) not a legitimate opponent of war. One can undertake a war *on terror*, but not a war *with terror*:

> With a single night's co-ordinated attacks, IS – a cultish militia perhaps 35,000 strong, ruling a self-declared 'caliphate' that no one recognises as a state – achieved something France denied the Algerian FLN until 1999, nearly four decades after independence: acknowledgment that it had been fighting a war, rather than a campaign against 'outlaws'. In the unlikely event that France sends ground troops to Syria, it will have handed IS an opportunity it longs for: face to face combat with 'crusader' soldiers on its own soil. (Shatz 2015: 11)

If the Paris attacks by IS achieved 'recognition', and that recognition was signalled by a declaration of war, and if such recognition was, indeed, sought by ISIS, then it seems that (for all the talk about clashing civilisations) IS, France and the USA share a rhetorical and conceptual field that ties national recognition with war. The logic would seem to go something like this: in order to be at war one must already possess an identity that is intrinsically intertwined with the possibility of combat.

I would not be 'American' (say) if there were not definitive norms and procedures that would constitute what I would and would not do. To undertake any tactic at all, to be outside nations and the rules of sovereignty, would be to possess no identity through time.

One might think of this internal relation between war and nations in at least three ways. The first would be legal and minimal; there can only be war among declared nations, where nations themselves are bound by constitutions and *politics* (or relations among its members). The second would be rhetorical; as the quotation from Shatz suggests, one simply does not recognise those one does not deem 'worthy' of war. Neither of these ways of dividing war from terror would make sense without thinking of the genealogy of the modern state, and liberal theory's fantasies of the logic of recognition.

The third way of thinking about war and terror would be classically Hegelian and would be in accord (however counter-intuitively) with the liberal tradition of norms and personhood. Identity and personhood are defined, not by simply living, but by a certain finitude and death. If I were to live for eternity, then I would pass through all possibilities, eventually becoming anything and everything. But my being is *not* extended infinitely in time; I must decide to be who I am, and in relation to what I am not. Without struggle and difference I would not be who I am. (This combative account of the self, defined through negation, was crucial to Schmitt's account of nationhood and borders defined through relations of friend and enemy.) True recognition occurs when I would fight to the death; if two bodies engaged in combat would desist from struggle if their lives were to be threatened, then such relations would be bound and limited by mere life (nothing more than mere and punctual animality). If, however, I would rather die than submit to defeat, I am motivated by an idea or ideal beyond mere life. Further, if I am viewed as one who would die or would sacrifice my life for something other than life, then I achieve a greater degree of mastery and pure prestige. The capacity to imagine and then project beyond one's death does two things; any combatant who values life above all else is in the position of the enslaved (attached to life, bound to its needs). Nothing is more powerful, more *masterful* than elevating oneself above life. Second, the struggle between one who can imagine recognition beyond their own life and one who is still bound to life is no longer a battle between forces that differ in degree, but becomes a difference *in kind*. The opponent who battles for life is in a game of more or less, of survive or die, of preservation. The opponent who is fighting for an idea beyond life (fighting for what they believe) has shifted relations into a condition of dissymmetry (enslavers and the enslaved, those fighting for what makes life worth living, versus those fighting merely to live).

One can see how Hegelian conceptions of recognition are definitive for the liberal state. A state of terror would be a war of all against all; there would be no rationale, no limit and *no recognition* if nothing were more important than life. This would be Hobbes's state of nature and the war of all against all; no one has sacrificed or invested anything in a social whole, and for that reason everyone is exposed contingently and randomly to the force of everyone else. By contrast, in a world of those prepared to die for something more than life, and those prepared to fight to the death for recognition, there would be some masters and some slaves. Perhaps this master/slave political dialectic has, for the most part, been the world of colonisation, imperialism and war; those countries capable of generating a belief in the flag, or the meaning of the nation, could recruit armies, send bodies abroad, have them risk their lives for the world they have left, and then conquer those hapless others who were too attached to life. (Jared Diamond has claimed that those who can store sufficient energy to enable a caste of priests would then have the advantage of producing a populace prepared to die for their territory [Diamond 1997: 277].) John Protevi (2015), providing a genealogy of warfare and its difference from tribal conflict, poses the question of just what establishes *a state*: how is it that a history of conquering, capture and enslavement emerges from what was once a milieu of tribal contestation? Perhaps it is monumental architecture; perhaps it is the capacity to store grain. Perhaps, though, this is the story the state tells itself; from the position of the polity, stateless existence seems null and void and must be warded off at all costs. Avoid terror and save the state! Suspend the law of the state for the sake of vanquishing terror that would dissolve the state form! In this state-based narrative, one would mark a difference or threshold between the nasty, brutish and short attachments to existence that characterise the state of nature, or the war of all against all, and the establishment of social wholes where individual security is generated by the collective attachment to the polity, and – ultimately – by each individual being defined through the collective. If I were asked to act in a manner that was contrary to the very definition of personhood that characterised my nation, I would rather not live. When Barack Obama responded to certain measures advocated by Donald Trump and Ben Carson by arguing that databases and water-boarding were 'not American', he retained (however inauthentically) the idea that a war on terror could not take any means whatsoever, but could only be a war *on terror* if there were some limits beyond which one would not go if one were to remain *who one is*. I would suggest, then, that according to this logic only nations can be at war, because only nations are defined by recognition. Not only does the nation relate to other nations and values, against whom it might then wage war, it can be itself only by retaining that difference from its others.

One does not have to be enslaved to Hegelian theories of recognition to think this way; even the most staid Kantians argue that attachment to norms *makes me who I am*, and acting contrary to those norms would be self-destructive, suicidal even (Korsgaard 1992: 83). If I am prepared to die for my country, then this is because my country *means something*. In this light one can see why Deleuze and Guattari refer to the 'despotism of the signifier', and see the state as a way of *repressing* the war machine. It is by establishing a value beyond life, or by means of inscription, that one forms nation-states, militaries, and those whose lives are deemed to be stateless, inhuman and beyond political recognition. It is only by establishing themselves as transcendent to life, by way of deterritorialisation and terror, that states can set themselves apart from terrorism – rogue and anarchic forms of violence that destroy transcendence.

Now, one might at first be alarmed by the intrinsic relation between the modern state and death. Surely, we want to respond, it is the stateless terrorist who dies and destroys for what he believes; surely it is the dispossessed and wretched of the earth who would commit suicide, and take many random and 'innocent' others along with them? Well, such a claim would be at odds not only with the Hegelian tradition of recognition, but most theories of political personhood. It is the person – the master – who values more than mere life; it is the stateless who are poor in world. Further, one might want to look a little more closely at the supposed stateless and dispossessed terrorist before concluding that perhaps we can understand and mitigate this desperation if we look to the history of imperialism, and explain terrorism as undertaken by those who have been denied personhood, citizenship and proper belonging. The problem with *that* response is threefold: as I have already suggested, the self-conception of the modern state is bound up with an identity that is defined through death, recognition, mastery and personhood. Theorists as far apart from each other as Charles Taylor (1994), Jacques Derrida (2005) and Carl Schmitt, however critically, have defined the modern possibility of politics by way of an agonistics of recognition. Without the otherness or irritant (and possible enmity) of nation-states that are *not one's own* one would not have an identity or social whole worthy of one's life. For Derrida this defines the state as structurally tied to a logic of auto-immunity, which – in turn – generates a curious hospitality. I could not be a self without relation to an other, and that other could only *really* be other if their possible inclusion would threaten the very polity into which I grant refuge. Those who responded to the Paris attacks by suggesting that Syrian refugees be refused entry have, it seems, forgotten the logic of modern nation-states. One is a nation *only* by way of a sense of 'who we are'; but that persona, far from precluding antagonistic and threatening relations to others, *requires alterity* in order to be itself. Barack Obama's response that certain measures were 'not American' was at least minimally aware of the logic of states, if conveniently unaware of the way that logic has been violated at least since the emergency measures following 9/11.

The *ideal* of the liberal state, at least in its political theoretical manifestation, is one of a world of masters and (hence) an end of ideology. If one were to live in a world where there were no slaves, where everyone lived for the social whole or ideal that gave them their unique personhood, we would have arrived at liberal democracy and the end of history. If *everyone* is a master, always already deferred beyond their *mere life* to some grander idea, then 'we' transcend the narcissism of small differences and arrive at liberal democracy. The modern state is defined *not* by holding on to a static and transcendent identity, but through an awareness that it is nothing more than an ongoing collective formation of its own making. This is how Francis Fukuyama (1992) conceives the end of history, as the end of ideology: if one recognises values and personhood as the outcome of social organisation, then one would, in turn, recognise other social formations as self-created and semi-autonomous wholes. Without the otherness or irritant (and possible enmity) of nation-states that are *not one's own* one would not have an identity or social whole worthy of one's life. For Derrida this defines the state as structurally tied to a logic of auto-immunity, which – in turn – generates a curious hospitality. The other whom I welcome, if it is genuine hospitality, must be genuinely other, and therefore a possible antagonist.

So where does this leave the war *on terror*, and the possibility that 'we' have shifted to being 'at war' – no longer a warring nation defined *against terror* but a new modality of terror war, where everybody is subject to surveillance, emergency measures and day-to-day policing because terror's potentiality is everywhere? It is worth noting that the ongoing war on terror is enabled by the use of the word 'state', however contested: if one can localise an Islamic State then the war on terror has a target. And if one follows this logic it would make sense to think that what is *other* than the war on terror would be an ongoing programme of recognition, not allowing individuals to feel stateless, abandoned or without citizenship. By contrast, Deleuze and Guattari's political theory suggests an opposite path; the problem is not those who have been abandoned or cast outside the polity, but the polity itself. Theirs is a utopian theory of statelessness: not post-apocalyptic, where the end of the state sees us wandering the earth abandoned to various police states, but profoundly apocalyptic, where we can live without terror or the state, without the war on terror, and without the terrorisms it brings in train. (As to what this might really amount to, one might think of Nigel Clark's 'Aboriginal Cosmopolitanism' in which he notes that climate change ought to prompt us to think beyond the high-consumption modes of humanity that we equate with being human [Clark 2008].) If we follow Deleuze and Guattari's notion of the war machine as that which has always haunted, but been repressed by, the state we can begin to see that the terror that seems to threaten the state from without is endemic to the state form.

There is yet more to consider; even on its own terms the state that would set itself off from terror by way of a monopoly on violence that would be used only to maintain the state's law and order is barely in existence. We are already stateless insofar as sanctioned violence is all-pervasive. Everything that supposedly defines the nation – possessing a higher rational moral wholeness that transcends *mere life* – has disappeared. When emergency security measures such as the Patriot Act, the intrusions of the NSA, drone attacks, detention centres and extraordinary renditions become the means for the war on terror, the logic of war *is over*. There is not a nation defined by who it is that is attacked by a chaotic opponent who is hungry for nothing more than life and survival at all costs. On the contrary, everything is suspended – including the constitution – for the sake of vanquishing terror. If one's only way of opposing terror is by saving one's life, then one is back in the Hobbesian state of all against all.

Further, one should not, then, romanticise and yearn for the good old days of nationhood, when empires were all masters and fought wars for the sake of recognition. On the contrary, what the war on terror has exposed is that what passed itself off as war was *always a war on terror*. That is to say, the supposed state of nature that is mere terror – where no one would die for their country, their flag, their god, mired as they are in mere existence – is a world of meaningless force, of antagonism, and of life that is always close to its own death. The masterful nation-state where individuals secure identity and security by investing in the social whole – where one would die rather than be not American, and where *war* for the sake of who one truly is displaces terror – always generated terror for someone else. The possibility of war – the bounded nation-state – relies on displacing and imposing terror elsewhere. Put quite simply, the empires that managed to generate self-defining nation-states built on security, personhood, liberty and fraternity emerged from a war on terror, from appropriating, destroying, extorting and *not recognising* others who were not playing the game of recognition. It is not the case that there were once the good old days of warring nations that have now fallen prey to those whose only goal is destruction, thus pitting terror against the civility of war. War – noble, agonistic combat among recognising adversaries – was only possible because of a mass appropriation and extortion by way of terror (or the desire to live at all costs).

More importantly, this should preclude us from granting bodies such as ISIS the badge of honour and authenticity because it is *they* who are now dying for what they believe, happy to wreak destruction even on their own kind, while we look with shame upon an over-consuming and increasingly myopic West. It is not that 'we' have lost the nobility of war, thereby allowing ourselves to be threatened by terrorists who have no respect for life. Rather, the mania for mastery, for living with a sense of dying for *who one is*, is not only no longer the privilege of 'we' Western liberals. It has been definitively and irreversibly stolen from 'us'. The moment at which antagonism is no longer bound to ideals of civility, nationhood and who 'we' are is the moment at which life is no longer subjected to some ideal of what makes life worth living, what one would die for. The 'war of all against all' – the supposed rapacity and terror from which the state would save 'us' – is actually better thought of as a possibility of statelessness in which war would no longer take on a transcendent or life-ordering power:

> It is necessary to reach the point of conceiving the war machine as itself a pure form of exteriority, whereas the State apparatus constitutes the form of interiority we habitually take as a model, or according to which we are in the habit of thinking. What complicates everything is that this extrinsic power of the war machine tends, under certain circumstances, to become confused with one of the two heads of the State apparatus. Sometimes it is confused with the magic violence of the State, at other times with the State's military institution. For instance, the war machine invents speed and secrecy; but there is all the same a certain speed and a certain secrecy that pertain to the State, relatively, secondarily. So there is a great danger of identifying the structural relation between the two poles of political

sovereignty, and the dynamic interrelation of these two poles, with the power of war. (Deleuze and Guattari 1987: 354)

Deleuze and Guattari's 'great danger' is captured by the phrase 'war on terror', as though there were a state with war as a means that might set itself against rogue states that were intrinsically (rather than opportunistically or occasionally) tied to war. Rather, beyond nation-states versus rogue states, beyond nations of fundamentalism versus nations of post-ideological neoliberalism, there would be something like nomadism: a capacity to live without recognition, where war would *mean nothing.*

Note

1. <http://www.theguardian.com/us-news/2015/nov/20/muslim-databases-and-ra bid-dogs-gop-in-ugly-scramble-to-vilify-syrian-refugees> (last accessed 5 May 2022).

References

Agamben, G. (1998), *Homo Sacer*, trans. D. Heller-Roazen, Stanford, Stanford University Press.

Clark, N. (2008), 'Aboriginal Cosmopolitanism', *International Journal of Urban and Regional Research*, 32 (3): 737–44.

Deleuze, G., and F. Guattari (1983), *Anti-Oedipus*, trans. R. Hurley, M. Seem and H. R. Lane, Minneapolis: University of Minnesota Press.

Deleuze, G., and F. Guattari (1987), *A Thousand Plateaus*, trans. B. Massumi, Minneapolis: University of Minnesota Press.

Derrida, J. (2005), *Rogues: Two Essays on Reason*, trans. P.-A. Brault and M. Naas, Stanford: Stanford University Press.

Diamond, J. (1997), *Guns, Germs and Steel*, New York: W. W. Norton.

Fukuyama, F. (1992), *The End of History and the Last Man*, New York: Free Press.

Graeber, D., and D. Wengrow (2021), *The Dawn of Everything: A New History of Humanity*, New York: Farrar, Straus and Giroux.

Korsgaard, C. (1992), *The Sources of Normativity: The Tanner Lectures on Human Values*, Cambridge, MA: Harvard University Press.

Lechte, J. (2020), *The Human: Bare Life and Ways of Life*, London: Bloomsbury.

Nietzsche, F. (1994 [1887]), *On the Genealogy of Morality*, ed. K. Ansell-Pearson, trans. C. Diethe, Cambridge: Cambridge University Press.

Protevi, J. (2015), 'Economies of Violence', <http://www.protevi.com/john/ECONO MIES-28-March-2015.pdf> (last accessed 3 May 2022).

Schmitt, C. (1974 [1950]), *Der Nomos der Erde*, Berlin: Duncker and Humblot.

Sexton, J., and S. Martinot (2003), 'The Avant-Garde of White Supremacy', *Social Identities*, 9 (2): 169–81.

Shatz, A. (2015), 'Magical Thinking about Isis', *London Review of Books*, 37 (23): 11–14.

Taylor, C. (1994), 'The Politics of Recognition', in A. Gutman (ed.), *Multiculturalism: Examining the Politics of Recognition*, Princeton: Princeton University Press, pp. 25–73.

Chapter 2

Guattari and Terror: Radicalisation as Singularisation

Janell Watson

Radicalisation has burgeoned into a multidisciplinary subfield of terrorism studies. Many recent publications describe it as a 'process', as in this typical definition: 'radicalization can be loosely defined as a process where a previously passive individual changes to become more revolutionary, militant or extremist, and has been closely tied with those involved in terrorism' (McGilloway, Ghosh and Bhui 2015: 39; see also Aistrope 2016: 182; Crone 2016; Demetriou and Bosi 2016; Hafez and Mullins 2015: 959; Leistedt 2016; Maskaliūnaitė 2015: 9; Neumann 2013: 874; Powers 2014: 2; Pruyt and Kwakkel 2014; Tsintsadze-Maass and Maass 2014). Radicalisation is a process of subjectivation, given that it indicates a transformation in thoughts, beliefs, opinions, behaviours or belongings. This subjective mutation consists in departing from a status quo to follow a path along a political continuum, with 'moderate' at one pole and 'extremist' at the other (Richards 2015). However, what counts as moderate or extreme 'varies depending on what is seen as "mainstream" in any given society, section of society or period of time' (Neumann 2013: 876–7). Otherwise stated, radicalisation is historically and contextually specific, and it 'occurs in all societies and cultures, and arises in many types of movements, including ethno-nationalist, ideological, and non-Muslim religious ones' (Hafez and Mullins 2015: 968).

As of the writing of this chapter in 2018, Islamic extremism had received the most attention in recent global mainstream media reports, because 'right-wing extremist attacks are seen mostly as isolated events when compared with other attacks, such as those by Islamist extremist terrorists', even though 'statistics clearly show the significant risk posed by violent right-wing extremists in Western countries' (Koehler 2016: 84, 86). While Euro-American far-right militancy and Islamic fundamentalist extremisms dominate headlines today, in the 1970s far-left radicalism stood out. Whether it refers to the far right, the far left or religious fundamentalism, the very idea of radicalisation defines extremes in relation to a sociopolitical centre. For the purposes of this chapter, I redefine radicalisation as a movement away from a centre, in any direction.

Radicalisation scholarship, by default, situates itself at the prevailing centre, the zero point from which extremes are perceived, defined and represented. A great deal of English-language scholarship on radicalisation addresses terrorism that occurs in the centres of global capitalism, even though the vast majority of terrorist attacks occur far from this centre, in conditions of war, civil unrest or severe economic instability (Miller 2015; 2017). Studies show that those living in prosperous, relatively secure capitalist centres perceive the actual risk of terrorism (political violence perpetrated by a non-state entity) as much greater than it really is (Githens-Mazer 2012). High-profile terrorist attacks aimed at centres of prosperity have occurred regularly during the early twenty-first century, including those in New York (2001), Moscow (2002), Madrid (2004), Mumbai (2008), Norway (2011), Nairobi (2013), Paris (2015), Nice (2016) and Orlando (2016). Although they are not geographically located in the West, Mumbai and Nairobi have become centres of global wealth, as emblematised by the specific sites of the attacks – a luxury hotel and an upscale shopping mall, respectively.

In the context of these politically motivated attacks carried out in global centres, radicalisation names a distancing from what Tariq Ali calls 'the extreme centre', the political position claimed by the triumphant neoliberalism born from the collapse of actually existing socialism and communism. Ali argues that Western European social democracy fell with the Berlin Wall, 'the founding moment of the extreme centre', a regime which 'places capital above the needs of citizens' because it is ruled by 'corporate power rubber-stamped by elected parliaments' (2015: 2–3). Given the global scope of financial capitalism today, the extreme centre cannot be geographically localised in the so-called West, but includes wealthy enclaves on every continent. Global capitalism maintains the growth that sustains it by constituting itself as an extreme centre, a vortex, a black hole that absorbs all matter and energy within its reach. As Guattari puts it, global capitalism, which he aptly calls Integrated World Capitalism, 'generate[s] a global super-machinism integrating every "originary" human activity' (2010: 226). Integrated World Capitalism expands through integration, incorporating ever more of the world's resources and wealth by subsuming its labourers, consumers, markets, cultures and high-value products. Capitalism today integrates not only the means of material production, but also the means of production of subjectivity (Guattari 1995; 2013). To highlight the importance of subjectivity to Integrated World Capitalism is not to discount the continued supremacy of economic, juridical, administrative and military power, but rather to recognise the subjective factors which play an essential role in maintaining any mode of power, especially in the current age of mass media, big data and global communication networks. Capitalism has managed to integrate all of these apparatuses of power, enabling them to resonate together, forming a gigantic machine of subjectivation.

Not content to control its existing integrated urban centres, world capitalism expands its integrating mission by exporting its subjectivities to populations that it has not yet fully assimilated. For example, Guattari characterises the 1991 Persian Gulf War as 'an attempt to bring the Arab populations to heel' by demonstrating 'that the Yankee way of subjectivation could be imposed by the combined power of the media and arms' (1995: 3). Late capitalism synchronises the soft power of the media with the hard power of the state war machine, and yet this simultaneously ideological and physically violent imposition of American-style subjectivity meets resistance. 'Beyond material and political demands' made by those who resist, in the Arab world and beyond, Guattari writes, 'what emerges is an aspiration for individual and collective reappropriation of the production of subjectivity' (1995: 133). Individuals and collectives wish to reclaim subjectivity production from the extreme centre. Like Guattari, the radicalisation literature also emphasises material, political and subjective demands, as Rahimi and Graumans demonstrate in their list of causal factors frequently identified with conversion to extremism: 'poverty, social marginalization, weak or threatened identities, lack of connection to native culture' (2015: 28). Scholarship thus suggests that material and political conditions (poverty, marginalisation) must be studied alongside subjective conditions (identity, cultural belonging) when analysing radicalisation.

Many discussions of terrorist attacks carried out in prosperous global centres implicitly ask the question explicitly posed by Hafez and Mullins: 'Why and how do individuals residing in relatively peaceful and affluent Western societies come to embrace extremist ideologies that emanate from distant places?' (2015: 959). The 'relatively peaceful and affluent' centre marvels that anyone might choose ideas and values from afar. This is made clear by the widely touted cultural integration model of radicalisation, which presumes that everyone would enjoy capitalism's centrist way of life, if only they were afforded the opportunity. 'Academic

WAR MACHINE: CRIMINAL VIOLENCE
ORGANIZED CRIME
mafias, cartels, transnational gangs,
human traffickers

WAR MACHINE: TERROR
CULTURAL CONSERVATISM
Islamic extremism
ISIS, Al Qaeda, Uighur militants
Christian Far Right
neo-Nazis, neo-fascists,
white supremacists

WAR MACHINES: TERROR, REVOLUTION
FAR LEFT
antifa, anarchists, FARC,
Zapatistas

WAR MACHINE: STATE VIOLENCE
(POLICE, MILITARY, INTELLIGENCE)
AUTHORITARIAN CAPITALISM
Chinese Communist Party,
United Russia Party, Saudi monarchy

WAR MACHINE: STATE VIOLENCE
(POLICE, MILITARY, INTELLIGENCE)
EXTREME CENTER
Republicans, Democrats, New Labour, Tories, French
Socialists, French centrists, Christian Democrats,
Bharatiya Janata Party, United Nations, European Union

Figure 2.1 Political assemblages and their war machines.

literature as well as governmental strategies have shown a consistent interest in the basic formula that a lack of cultural integration equals an increased threat of radicalization' (Rahimi and Graumans 2015: 28). This integration–radicalisation binary underpins counter-terrorist strategies that promote social integration in the hope of preventing radicalisation (Galam and Javarone 2016). However, Rahimi and Graumans find little or no empirical support for the cultural integration model. Research suggests that most radicalised extremists living in liberal capitalism's global centres are in fact well integrated and 'normal' (McGilloway, Ghosh and Bhui 2015: 39; see also Tsintsadze-Maass and Maass 2014: 736). These studies debunk the claim that so-called homegrown terrorists tend to be social outcasts who feel excluded.

Perhaps the capitalist centre is not the neutral space of existential comfort that radicalisation studies presume it to be. Perhaps those who radicalise find no comfort in the modern, secular, consumerist lifestyles on offer in the global centre. Rather than suffering from exclusion, perhaps these well-integrated radicals instead reject inclusion. I suggest that radicalisation should not be understood as failed integration, but rather as an attempt at subjective singularisation, as defined by Guattari. To singularise in the age of late capitalism is to reject the stultifying standardisation imposed by mass production, mass consumption, mass marketing and mass media. To radicalise in the age of Integrated World Capitalism is to resist subjective integration by seeking singularisation. In what follows, I propose a Guattarian cartography of the political assemblages of the 2010s, with their adjacent war machines, as illustrated in Figure 2.1. My map overlays these assemblages on to a swirling vortex centred on Integrated World Capitalism which, I argue, acts as a material, energetic and subjective black hole, against whose forceful pull radical extremists struggle.

'Rising demands for subjective singularity'

Chaosmosis, first published in 1992, opens with a discussion of the growing role of subjectivity in history, citing post-Soviet social movements revolving around ethnic identity, national belonging, ideologies or religious beliefs. Guattari characterises these populist movements as an 'irruption of subjective factors at the forefront of current events', proclaiming that 'History is increasingly dominated by rising demands for subjective singularity—quarrels over language, autonomist demands, issues of nationalism and of the nation' (1995: 1–3). Rejecting global capitalism's attempts at integration, sociopolitical movements making subjective demands seek singularisation. His examples include the 1989 Chinese student demonstrations in Tiananmen Square; the national independence rallies that followed the 1989 collapse of the communist Eastern bloc; the 1979 Iranian revolution; and the more general rise of Islamic fundamentalism across the Middle East. These examples occupy very different positions along the political spectrum. Guattari labels the 1989 Chinese student demonstrations and post-Soviet Eastern bloc uprisings as liberation movements, thus placing them to the left; he refers to the Iranian revolution and the rise of Islamic fundamentalism as resurrections of 'archaic' conservative values, thus placing them on the right; and he describes the new post-independence states emerging in the former communist sphere as 'moderately conservative' (1995: 2–3, 21). This map of global politics features an emancipatory left and a reactionary right, with a moderate conservatism in between. Unfortunately, Guattari laments, 'large movements of subjectivation don't necessarily develop in the direction of emancipation' (1995: 2).

Whether liberatory, conservative or fundamentalist, all of these populist uprisings exemplify collective reactions to the social and psychic devastation wrought by the cultural uniformity imposed by Soviet or capitalist subjectivation, according to Guattari. To the shock of many in the capitalist West, the overthrow of Soviet communism did not result in a wholesale embrace of capitalist modernity. Ethnic traditions re-emerged. The prominence of these subjective demands (for traditional modes of identity, belonging, religions, lifestyles and so forth) surprises anyone who associates personal freedom with modernist, secular, multicultural democracy. What Guattari wrote in the early 1990s still rings true in 2018. I read our current era of global terror as a continuation of these collective attempts to reappropriate the means of subjectivity production. I am not saying that violent responses from radical movements are justified by the centre's greed, military operations or political interventions abroad. My argument is that the centre is just as historically contingent, ideologically dogmatic, materially destructive and socially stifling as its periphery. Political formations as diverse as al-Qaeda, Islamic State, neo-Nazism and neo-fascism appeal to their followers by making material and political demands of the extreme centre, in search of alternatives to its homogenised subjectivities.

How can collective movements reclaiming seemingly archaic traditions possibly manifest a desire for subjective singularity? It is important not to mistake singularity for individualism. Schizoanalysis never studies individuals outside of their social, political and environmental contexts, because it conceptualises subjectivity as 'the product of individuals, groups and institutions' (Guattari 1995: 1). This approach responds well to Rahimi and Graumans's call for radicalisation studies to move 'from traditional ego-based models to new theories of subjectivity which promise culturally and historically embedded models of subjective experience and political affect'. They hope that these newer 'models . . . can unpack sociocultural, political and historical ingredients of human psychological experience and political affect much more effectively' (Rahimi and Graumans 2015: 49). The subjective factors which Guattari sees as irrupting at the forefront of contemporary history do not originate within individualised egos, but from collective assemblages of enunciation – a subjectivity produced by individuals, groups and institutions. These assemblages, which never exactly correspond to an individual subject, include an existential territory ('the body proper, the self, the maternal body, lived space, refrains of the mother tongue, familiar faces, family lore, ethnicity') coupled with a virtual universe of reference or value (religion, belief, values, ideology, nation, ethnicity, legend, myth, abstract ideas, imagery, aesthetic constellations; the 'Cultural Unconscious') (Guattari 1995: 95, 67). Radicalised individuals are driven to reconstitute their existential territories because capitalist subjectivity of the late twentieth and twenty-first centuries destroys 'social territories, collective identities and traditional systems of value' (Guattari 2013: 37). Guattari replaced the notion of collective identity with that of existential territories and universes of reference 'because we cannot live outside our bodies, our friends, some sort of human cluster, and at the same time, we are bursting out of this situation' (Guattari 1996: 216).

Compare Guattari's notion of an existential territory incarnating a universe of value to a typical individual ego-based model, that of an alienated individual joining a radical group. Following this (overly) simple membership model, Stern finds that 'individuals are mobilized to join terrorist organizations as they would any other organization' (2016: 104). The idea of joining or becoming a member posits an ego motivated by factors such as a shared mission, influence from people close to them, perceived membership benefits or seduction by a charismatic recruiter or online propaganda (Stern 2016; Greenberg 2016; Jones 2017). A recent article identifies three phases of radicalisation: '(1) Sensitivity; (2) Group membership; and (3) Action' (Doosje et al. 2016: 79). 'Sensitivity' to radicalisation may take the form of a vulnerable individual with a fragile ego who undertakes a 'quest for significance', according to an egocentric model of radicalisation which posits that 'when people experience loss of personal significance (e.g., due to social rejection, achievement failures, or abuse) the motivation to restore significance may push them toward the use of extreme means' (Jasko, LaFree and Kruglanski 2017: 815; see also Kruglanski et al. 2014). Horgan appears to deviate from ego-centred models of radicalisation when he describes the group as an external force that subsumes the individual. He argues that 'individual personality factors in themselves are neither useful nor predictive', and so it is instead necessary to 'identify the significance of the group and organisational context that maintains involvement and sustains behaviour and eventually contributes to the commission of acts of terrorism' (Horgan 2008: 81). Horgan's statement does not actually eliminate individual egos, but instead hides them behind the passive voice: it is the individual whose 'involvement' and 'behaviour' are maintained and sustained by the group. All of these models map a relationship between a pre-existing group and an individuated ego.

In contrast, schizoanalysis always situates subjectivity in the context of assemblages composed of a heterogeneous array of components arranged in a machinic agglomeration. Each heterogeneous array is singular, resisting any attempt to impose a general model. Analysing assemblages therefore requires metamodelling, or metamodellisation, which borrows from multiple existing models, inventing new ones as necessary. Also known as schizoanalytic cartography, this technique draws new maps for each assemblage, respecting its singularity. Schizoanalysis thus avoids 'reductionist modelisations which simplify the complex', instead favouring 'complexification', in order to accommodate the 'ontological heterogeneity' of subjectivities and assemblages (Guattari 1995: 61). Metamodelling accepts that there can be no single model that accounts for all instantiations of phenomena as complex as subjectivities or social movements.

Recent terrorism scholarship itself attests to the impossibility of finding an overarching explanatory model. Numerous researchers note that empirical studies have yet to identify a common profile or a consistent pattern of behaviour among known terrorists (see, for example, Greenberg 2016; Klausen et al. 2016; Leistedt 2016; Stern 2016). Even though 'the combination of cognitive and behavioural radicalization usually precedes violence', those who have undergone 'cognitive radicalization' are far more numerous than 'the statistically infinitesimal number of behaviorally radicalized individuals with which security agencies are mainly concerned' (Hafez and Mullins 2015: 961). This is bad news for counter-terrorism scholars charged with developing a model capable of assessing an individual or group's likelihood of committing terrorist acts (Blackwood, Hopkins and Reicher 2016), given that each radicalised subject follows different 'pathways' and 'routes' towards political violence (Horgan 2008). Of the many available models of radicalisation, none applies universally enough to predict who will radicalise to the point of committing a terrorist act (Hafez and Mullins 2015: 959; Neuman 2013). Rahimi and Graumans observe that 'Researchers and governmental organizations alike have come to admit that, when it comes to radicalization and the social factors influencing its processes, it is extremely unlikely that any single model or theory would adequately integrate the range of known possible drivers, influences, or pathways' (2015: 45). Rather than claiming to build a model of how individuals come to join radical groups, Hafez and Mullins compare radicalisation to a 'puzzle' whose 'pieces . . . consist of grievances, networks, ideologies, and enabling environments and support structures'. In order to put the puzzle together, they pursue 'a theoretical synthesis' of its pieces (2015: 959, 961). However, synthesis implies the possibility of overcoming disorderly, unpredictable complexity, an impossible task. Recognising the impossibility of tidy synthesis, schizoanalytic cartography reveals an amorphous array of chaosmic mutation, of assemblages coming into existence or dissolving into entropy, showing where the puzzle pieces came from in the first place.

Assembling Components

Assemblages, without which subjectivities cannot survive, require component parts, both virtual and actual, but these building blocks of subjectivity do not materialise out of thin air. Available components of subjectivity can be culled from assemblages of all types and scales, from families to cultures to empires. Arguing that subjectivity mutates in direct relation to larger social mutations, Guattari proclaims that 'fundamental subjective mutations' coincide with 'the birth of the great collective religious and cultural' assemblages and 'the invention' of new materials, energies, machines, biotechnologies and aesthetic techniques (2013: 5–6). The grandest social mutation of the past millennium has been the emergence of Integrated World Capitalism, an enormously powerful cultural apparatus that has 'radically devalued old ideologies, social practices and traditional politics' (Guattari 1995: 120). This 'prodigious mutation' brought about 'the destruction of social territories, collective identities and traditional systems of value'. As a result of this radical devaluation and destruction, 'collective subjectivity' has given in to 'the absurd wave of conservatism that we are currently experiencing', writes Guattari in *Schizoanalytic Cartographies* (2013: 37), in which he first laid out a schema of 'fundamental capitalistic components'. I combine this schema with a variation on it that appears in *Chaosmosis* (2013: 5–15; 1995: 101–8; see also O'Sullivan 2012: 91–6).

1. Territorialized Assemblages

These take the form of land-based political regimes, such as principalities, kingdoms, ancient empires, fiefdoms, tribes, clans, peasants, or nomads. They correspond to archaic existential territories which take the form of homeland, self-belonging and ancestral attachments. The corresponding universes of value, aggregated and territorialized, are supported by initiation rites, myths, chants, dances, stories, local deities and sacred sites.

2. Deterritorialized Assemblages

European Christianity. This assemblage is composed of 'relatively autonomous territorial entities' plus a new subjectivity centred on the transcendent body of Christ.

Capitalism. The capitalist assemblage emerges in full during the eighteenth century. Capitalist values overcode all other systems of value by imposing sectorization, bipolarization, neutralization, standardization. This results in the destruction of previous universes of value, which devastates the existential territories which fed on them. Technologies of transportation, communication and securitization eventually enable the formation of Integrated World Capitalism.

3. Processual Assemblages

The aesthetic paradigm plays a key role in the composition of these relatively more autopoietic assemblages, made possible by 'planetary computerization'. Heterogeneous, diverse, multiplied, and particularized Existential Territories connect up with Universes of value crystallized in singularized, dynamic constellations, producing subjectivities 'capable of connecting with the singularities and mutations of our era'. (Guattari 1995: 106)

Despite the historical references in his descriptions of these three assemblage types, Guattari insists that this schema does not represent a chronology or evolutionary progression. He observes that 'capitalistic drives are found at the heart of the Egyptian. Mesopotamian and Chinese empires, then throughout the whole of classical Antiquity' (1995: 105), and that remnants of archaic territorialised assemblages continue to exist today. Any particular assemblage may emerge and come to the forefront at a specific historical moment. Assemblages may also overlap and mingle in rhizomatic fashion, remixing cultural fragments borrowed from other 'great collective religious and cultural Apparatuses'. These remixings follow a regressive path when they pursue 'a politics of return to archaic territorialities'. In contrast, they can forge a progressive path by 'crossing ... an additional degree of deterritorialization' (Guattari 2010: 227). Guattari had hoped that newly emerging interactive media would bring about a 'postmedia era' in which individual creativity could flourish. He did not live to see the internet and social media overrun by the world's largest corporations, while darker corners of the web traffic in pornography, hacking, scamming, conspiracy theories and extremist politics. The world is no closer to a post-media era of processual enrichment today than it was when Guattari died in 1992.

Radical political assemblages of the 2010s (Figure 2.1) continue to engage in 'conservative reterritorializations of subjectivity' (Guattari 1995: 3), borrowing from religious and authoritarian assemblages of the territorialising type (described in the schema above). For example, a US-based white supremacist assemblage may construct its existential territory by incorporating a Nazi universe of reference, with its nostalgic reinvention of an idyllic fatherland claiming direct descent from classical Greek culture; it may at the same time borrow components from the Ku Klux Klan universe, with its burning crosses and medieval-inspired robes. This reassembled assemblage consolidates, promotes and reproduces itself with the help of the internet and, fuelled by libidinal resentment, creates an explosive 'mixture of archaic attachments to cultural traditions that nonetheless aspire to the technological and scientific modernity characterizing the contemporary subjective cocktail' (Guattari 1995: 3–4). Many scholars have studied the prominence of social media and digital communication in the radicalisation process, as well as in the carrying out of attacks (see, for example, Greenberg 2016; Majeed 2016; Palasinski and Bowman-Grieve 2017). Guattari had already begun to observe that machinic components have come to prominence in the deterritorialised assemblages of late capitalism: 'Archaic forms of enunciation rested in the main on speech and direct communication, whereas the new Assemblages have more and more recourse to mediatic informational Flows, carried by machinic channels . . . which everywhere exceed the old individual and collective subjective territories' (2013: 20).

Although wary of conservative revivals of archaic attachments (such as the Iranian revolution), Guattari did not categorically reject cultural traditions. 'Any ideology or cult, even the most archaic, can do the job' of producing new subjectivities, he says, as long these archaic elements are only used 'as existential materials' (2013: 3–4). He distinguishes between reactionary nationalism and the emancipatory 'nationalitarianism' of marginalised or persecuted minorities such as the Palestinians, Basques, Irish, Corsicans, Uighurs, Roma or various Indigenous peoples. He describes these new nationalitarian movements as revolts against the 'beastly caging of subjectivity' of liberal modernity (1986: 76). He observes that 'current geopolitical developments continuously reactivate oppressed nationalities, as well as issues of ethnicity, clans, even tribes'. These reactivations can either sink into conservative reactionary nationalism or, more optimistically, they can set off 'processes of singularization', opening up 'spaces of freedom, desire, and creation' (1986: 73–4). He predicts that these nationalitarian spaces will play an increasingly important role in international relations, bringing 'a decisive renewal of cultural values, social practices, and models of society', saving humanity from 'major plagues' such as 'capitalist and state standardization' (1986: 72). In Guattari's view, these nationalitarian movements share the project of 'recomposing a social fabric mutilated by capitalism and state apparatuses' (1986: 77). Unfortunately, many of these revivals have further mutilated the social fabric by devolving into oppressive authoritarianism and, too often, political violence.

War Machines of the 2010s

Few individuals who radicalise or join radical groups actually engage in terrorist acts. Many radicals oppose violent means and pursue only legal avenues. Guattari himself was a political and social radical who advocated collective action, but he abhorred both state and non-state violence, even if it came from the far left opposition to the neoliberal centre. He denounced the 'stupid and repugnant' terrorism carried out in the 1960s and 1970s by European leftist groups such as Germany's Red Army Faction or the Italian Red Brigades. He equally abhorred European states' use of non-state terrorism as a pretext for increased repression (Guattari 1986: 78). Radical politics does not always involve acts of political violence. Guattari admired radical movements like the Velvet Revolution. Why do some radicals choose violence while others remain peaceful or passive? In A Thousand Plateaus, Deleuze and Guattari explain that the 'man of war' taps into an 'adjacent' non-state 'war machine' (1987: 403).

A war machine is a special type of assemblage in which the machinic phylum comes to prominence, enabling material-energetic flows to become tools and weapons. Because existential territories include the body, they require flows of body fluids, libido and energetic force. Radical assemblages rely on material and energetic flows of capital, desire, blood, violence, biopower and waves of bandwidth, while the machinic phylum offers technologies, strategies, tactics and systems. The war machine also requires subjective components in order to function, although this may take the form of a proto-subjective 'founding instance of intentionality' (Guattari 1995: 22) that enables the machinic assemblage to react to inputs from other assemblages and the surrounding environment. This proto-subjective intentionality resides within an existential territory coupled with a universe of value.

A pattern of behaviour can be understood as a set of assemblages. There are at least three types of behavioural assemblage among baboons, delineated according to their having to do with hierarchical relations, collective territorial defence or individual flight (Guattari 2010: 123–4). Similarly, protest movements and counter-cultures 'draw on' various collective assemblages – 'large repertoires of collective action, which may range from entirely peaceful and legal to high-risk, coercive, illegal and occasionally violent tactics' (Neumann 2013: 884). The man of war draws on the violent tactics within these behavioural repertoires of group action.

Today's jihadi or neo-Nazi militant stands ready as a modern man of war, whether claiming the banner of Che Guevara, the Nazis, jihad or medieval Islam. The figure of the terrorist appears as a defender of archaic traditions against modernity's tolerant cosmopolitanism, defended by the state's military man. Deleuze and Guattari describe the difference between the rebellious man of war and the military man loyal to the state:

Undoubtedly, nothing is more outmoded than the man of war: he has long since been transformed into an entirely different character, the military man ... And yet men of war reappear, with many ambiguities: they are all those who know the uselessness of violence but who are adjacent to a war machine to be recreated, one of active, revolutionary counterattacks ... They do not resuscitate old myths or archaic figures; they are the new figures of a transhistorical assemblage (neither historical nor eternal, but untimely). (1987: 403)

Even after the modern age has produced military men (and women) tamed by the state, the untimely man of war (or, more rarely, woman) always revives old war machines in order to enter into new transhistorical assemblages. War machines stand ready whenever the man of war re-emerges, as verified by Crone, whose research suggests that

many of these young men were acquainted with violence and violent milieus *before* embracing an extremist ideology: they had, for instance, been involved in drug dealing, gang violence and weapon use. Similarly, through their involvement in criminal environments many have experienced legitimate state violence: some have been in contact with police or intelligence services; some have been put in prison. (Crone 2016: 592)

This suggests that drug assemblages, gang assemblages, criminal assemblages and even police assemblages contribute war machines to radical political assemblages.

The body, at the beating heart of the existential territory, acquires 'an *embodied* know-how' which 'the perpetration of a terrorist attack presupposes', argues Crone. 'Processes of radicalization also imply a transformation of physical capacities and acquisition of the skills of violence' (Crone 2016: 588, 600–1). In Guattarian terms, this 'embodied know-how' resides in an existential territory fed by material flows shaped by the machinic phylum's martial branches. The man of war transforms himself 'into a weapon of jihad' (Jenkins, cited in Neumann 2013: 875–6). In the case of suicide attacks, the human is literally weaponised, but only if hooked up with a war machine. Just as the horse rider and lance formed a new war machine thanks to the invention of the stirrup (Deleuze and Guattari 1987: 89–90, 399), so an embodied human subjectivity transforms an aeroplane or rented truck into a weapon. The assemblage combines a human with a weaponised vehicle, forming a terrorist war machine.

The state in turn wields its own war machines, supported by national and international counter-terrorism agencies (Deleuze and Guattari

1987: 403). States controlled by late capitalism's extreme centre unleash a great deal of legally sanctioned political violence, as they defend the fruits of Integrated World Capitalism, which they disproportionately enjoy. The threat of non-state terror sets off states' securitisation machines at home and war machines abroad, all in the name of domestic security. In *On Suicide Bombing*, Asad argues that terrorism is 'an integral part of liberal subjectivities' of the centrists, who exhibit the 'urge to defeat political terror, the fear of social vulnerability, the horror and fascination with death and destruction' (2007: 2–3). Capital itself enables the state apparatuses controlled by the extreme centre to amass powerful security agencies, police forces, military troops and sophisticated weapons necessary for extreme securitisation at home and proxy wars abroad.

Processual Hope

Hope for liberating humanity from the grip of global capitalism's black hole lies in the 'general plasticity of Assemblages' (Guattari 2013: 19), their capacity to mutate exponentially starting from a minute point of singularity. Existential singularisation emerges from such points, creating the processual assemblages of the third type (as listed above). 'A singularity, a rupture of sense, a cut, a fragmentation, the detachment of a semiotic content—in a dadaist or surrealist manner—can originate mutant nuclei of subjectivation', writes Guattari (1995: 18). After all, black holes not only absorb matter and energy, but can also emit particles (Guattari 2010: 291). Those who oppose both extreme neoliberal centrism and conservative returns to archaic authoritarianism must seek out these rogue particles, encouraging the formation of new universes from which existential territories can embrace additional degrees of freedom with which to escape the grip of Integrated World Capitalism's extreme centre.

References

Aistrope, T. (2016), 'The Muslim Paranoia Narrative in Counter-Radicalisation Policy', *Critical Studies on Terrorism*, 9 (2): 182–204, <https://doi.org/10.1080/17539153.2016.1175272> (last accessed 15 September 2017).

Ali, T. (2015), *The Extreme Centre: A Warning*, London: Verso.

Asad, T. (2007), *On Suicide Bombing*, New York: Columbia University Press.

Blackwood, L., N. Hopkins and S. Reicher (2016), 'From Theorizing Radicalization to Surveillance Practices: Muslims in the Cross Hairs of Scrutiny', *Political Psychology*, 37 (5): 597–612, <https://doi.org/10.1111/pops.12284> (last accessed 6 October 2017).

Crone, M. (2016), 'Radicalization Revisited: Violence, Politics and the Skills of the Body', *International Affairs*, 92: 587–604, <http://onlinelibrary.wiley.com/doi/10.1111/1468-2346.12604/abstract> (last accessed 15 September 2017).

Deleuze, G., and F. Guattari (1987), *A Thousand Plateaus: Capitalism and Schizophrenia*, trans. B. Massumi, Minneapolis: University of Minnesota Press.

Demetriou, C., and L. Bosi (eds) (2016), *Dynamics of Political Violence: A Process-Oriented Perspective on Radicalization and the Escalation of Political Conflict*, Abingdon: Routledge.

Doosje, B., F. M. Moghaddam, A. W. Kruglanski, A. de Wolf, L. Mann and A. R. Feddes (2016), 'Terrorism, Radicalization and De-Radicalization', *Current Opinion in Psychology*, 11 (Supplement C): 79–84, <https://doi.org/10.1016/j.copsyc.2016.06.008> (last accessed 6 October 2017).

Galam, S., and M. A. Javarone (2016), 'Modeling Radicalization Phenomena in Heterogeneous Populations', *PLOS ONE*, 11 (5), e0155407, <https://doi.org/10.1371/journal.pone.0155407> (last accessed 6 October 2017).

Githens-Mazer, J. (2012), 'The Rhetoric and Reality: Radicalization and Political Discourse', *International Political Science Review / Revue Internationale de Science Politique*, 33 (5): 556–67, <http://www.jstor.org/stable/23353159> (last accessed 15 September 2017).

Greenberg, K. J. (2016), 'Counter-Radicalization via the Internet', *The ANNALS of the American Academy of Political and Social Science*, 668 (1): 165–79, <https://doi.org/10.1177/0002716216672355> (last accessed 15 September 2017).

Guattari, F. (1986), *Les années d'hiver, 1980–1985*, Paris: Barrault.

Guattari, F. (1995), *Chaosmosis: An Ethico-Aesthetic Paradigm*, Bloomington: Indiana University Press.

Guattari, F. (1996), *The Guattari Reader*, ed. G. Genosko, Oxford: Wiley-Blackwell.

Guattari, F. (2010), *The Machinic Unconscious: Essays in Schizoanalysis*, trans. T. Adkins, Los Angeles: Semiotext(e).

Guattari, F. (2013), *Schizoanalytic Cartographies*, London: Bloomsbury Academic.

Hafez, M., and C. Mullins (2015), 'The Radicalization Puzzle: A Theoretical Synthesis of Empirical Approaches to Homegrown Extremism', *Studies in Conflict & Terrorism*, 38 (11): 958–75, <https://doi.org/10.1080/1057610X.2015.1051375> (last accessed 6 October 2017).

Horgan, J. (2008), 'From Profiles to Pathways and Roots to Routes: Perspectives from Psychology on Radicalization into Terrorism', *The Annals of the American Academy of Political and Social Science*, 618: 80–94, <http://www.jstor.org/stable/40375777> (last accessed 15 September 2017).

Jasko, K., G. LaFree and A. Kruglanski (2017), 'Quest for Significance and Violent Extremism: The Case of Domestic Radicalization', *Political Psychology*, 38 (5): 815–31, <https://doi.org/10.1111/pops.12376> (last accessed 6 October 2017).

Jones, E. (2017), 'The Reception of Broadcast Terrorism: Recruitment and Radicalisation', *International Review of Psychiatry*, 29 (4): 320–6, <https://doi.org/10.1080/09540261.2017.1343529> (last accessed 14 September 2017).

Klausen, J., S. Campion, N. Needle, G. Nguyen and R. Libretti (2016), 'Toward a Behavioral Model of "Homegrown" Radicalization Trajectories', *Studies in Conflict & Terrorism*, 3 (1): 67–83, <https://doi.org/10.1080/1057610X.2015.1099995> (last accessed 15 September 2017).

Koehler, D. (2016), 'Right-Wing Extremism and Terrorism in Europe: Current Developments and Issues for the Future', *Prism: A Journal of the Center for Complex Operations; Washington*, 6 (2): 84–104.

Kruglanski, A. W., M. J. Gelfand, J. J. Bélanger, A. Sheveland, M. Hetiarachchi and R. Gunaratna (2014), 'The Psychology of Radicalization and Deradicalization:

How Significance Quest Impacts Violent Extremism', *Political Psychology*, 35: 69–93, <https://doi.org/10.1111/pops.12163> (last accessed 14 September 2017).

Leistedt, S. J. (2016), 'On the Radicalization Process', *Journal of Forensic Sciences*, 61 (6): 1588–91, <https://doi.org/10.1111/1556-4029.13170> (last accessed 14 September 2017).

Majeed, K. (2016), *Combating Violent Extremism and Radicalization in the Digital Era*, Hershey, PA: IGI Global.

Maskaliūnaitė, A. (2015), 'Exploring the Theories of Radicalization', *International Studies: Interdisciplinary Political and Cultural Journal*, 17: 9–26, <10.1515/ipcj-2015-0002> (last accessed 15 September 2017).

McGilloway, A., P. Ghosh and K. Bhui (2015), 'A Systematic Review of Pathways to and Processes Associated with Radicalization and Extremism amongst Muslims in Western Societies', *International Review of Psychiatry*, 27 (1): 39–50, <https://doi.org/10.3109/09540261.2014.992008> (last accessed 6 October 2017).

Miller, E. (2015), 'Overview: Terrorism in 2014', START, College Park, MD, <http://www.start.umd.edu/publication/overview-terrorism-2014> (last accessed 5 November 2017).

Miller, E. (2017), 'Overview: Terrorism in 2016', START, College Park, MD, <http://www.start.umd.edu/publication/overview-terrorism-2016> (last accessed 5 November 2017).

Neumann, P. R. (2013), 'The Trouble with Radicalization', *International Affairs*, 89 (4): 873–93, <https://doi.org/10.1111/1468-2346.12049> (last accessed 15 September 2017).

O'Sullivan, S. (2012), *On the Production of Subjectivity: Five Diagrams of the Finite-Infinite Relation*, Basingstoke: Palgrave Macmillan.

Palasinski, M., and L. Bowman-Grieve. (2017), 'Tackling Cyber-terrorism: Balancing Surveillance with Counter-communication', *Security Journal*, 30 (2): 556–68, <https://doi.org/10.1057/sj.2014.19> (last accessed 14 September 2017).

Powers, S. M. (2014), 'Conceptualizing Radicalization in a Market for Loyalties', *Media, War & Conflict*, 7 (2): 233–49, <https://doi.org/10.1177/1750635214538620> (last accessed 6 October 2017).

Pruyt, E., and J. H. Kwakkel (2014), 'Radicalization under Deep Uncertainty: A Multi-model Exploration of Activism, Extremism, and Terrorism', *System Dynamics Review*, 30 (1–2): 1–28, <https://doi.org/10.1002/sdr.1510> (last accessed 6 October 2017).

Rahimi, S., and R. Graumans (2015), 'Reconsidering the Relationship between Integration and Radicalization', *Journal for Deradicalization*, 5: 28–62, <https://journals.sfu.ca/jd/index.php/jd/article/view/34> (last accessed 18 November 2021).

Richards, A. (2015), 'From Terrorism to "Radicalization" to "Extremism": Counterterrorism Imperative or Loss of Focus?', *International Affairs*, 91: 371–80.

Stern, J. (2016), 'Radicalization to Extremism and Mobilization to Violence: What Have We Learned and What Can We Do about It?', *The ANNALS of the American Academy of Political and Social Science*, 668: 102–17.

Tsintsadze-Maass, E., and R. W. Maass (2014), 'Groupthink and Terrorist Radicalization', *Terrorism and Political Violence*, 26 (5): 735–58, <https://doi.org/10.1080/09546553.2013.805094> (last accessed 6 October 2017).

Chapter 3

Creative Resistance:
An Aesthetics of Creative Affect in a Time of Global Terror

Janae Sholtz

> The invisible forces, the powers of the future, are they not already upon us, and much more insurmountable than the worst spectacle and even the worst pain? . . . It is within this visibility that the body actively struggles . . . [I]t is as if combat had now become possible. (Deleuze 2003: 52)

> Not knowing how to share our own passion to see with another gaze, not knowing how to produce a culture of the gaze: this is where the real violence begins against those who are helplessly abandoned to the voracity of visibilities. It is thus the responsibility of those who make images to build a place for those who see, and it is the responsibility of those who present images to understand their modes of construction. (Mondzain 2009: 33)

The demands of revolutionary politics and recourse to aesthetic creativity do not always sit well together. My thinking attempts to straddle these unsettled boundaries, resisting the notions that, given the extent of the violence and injustice that floods the modern world, positing transformation on the basis of art is not radical or political enough. In part this is because the brutalities and political manipulations to which we are witness are often themselves affectively driven, requiring greater sensitivity and attunement to the aesthetically infused, affective components of our shared existence; and, in part, because I have found resources in Deleuze's aesthetics to sustain my belief in the potency and necessity of creative resistance through art. The transformations that I believe are necessary begin from a change in the very nature of our thinking and desires, and according to Deleuze, art acts as the catalyst for changing both.

The Uses and Abuses of Image and Affect

The question that I want to address bears upon the intersection between art and the political in light of contemporary intensifications of violence and abuses of power. What is the role of art in a time of global terror? A straightforward response might be to interrogate the ways that images manifest themselves within this contemporary framework. Images of violence, brutality and injustice, generated through media and photography, have opened a visual window on to, and increased our participation in, the atrocities that are occurring all over the world (photographs of drowned refugees, the aftermath of bombings, videos of police brutality). Another would be to analyse the modes of affect that are generated from these images. Optimistically, photographs or paintings can bring images of the suffering of others before us, demanding our response and thereby generating affects of empathy and concern. Equally, one might point to the use of spectacular images of violence to propagate terror itself.[1] In one case, the affects that are ideally being evoked are empathy, disgust and indignation, while in the other, what is desired are affects of fear, despair and terror.

Even more insidious, spectacles of violence are also part of our habituation to the overarching framework of the social order itself.[2] Not only have we become desensitised to violent spectacles through consumerist appropriation and media sensationalism, we have been taught to desire them through a variety of strategies which all serve to maintain a hegemonic social and economic order.[3] Evans and Giroux's scathing critique of neoliberalism in *Disposable Futures* (2015) suggests that fear, uncertainty and terror generated through the production of systematic violence is one of the fundamental features utilised to depoliticise and strip agency from the populace (and justify massive inequality in wealth and power).[4] In other words, our modern world of global terror (broadly construed) is saturated with spectacles of violence, some of which reflect a sinister radicalisation of Marcuse's (1964) 'manufactured distraction'[5] and some of which operates primarily as a means of feeding our collective consumerist desires. Terror and state-sponsored counter-terror both operate through the affective ritualisation of periodic violence,[6] and the social capacity for consuming atrocity has reached a voracious pitch: 'the power of death, the power of life, [has become] utterly mundane' (Massumi 1998: 48).

As theorists such as Adorno, Marcuse and Benjamin have argued,[7] the invocation and manipulation of images and media has saturated (and moulded) American culture for decades, and recent interest in the field of affect studies has led to even more precise identification of the problem as a constricting and paradoxical feedback loop whereby the desire for perpetually intensified experiences contributes to mass desensitisation, which then demands more intensive affective experiences, rendering the populace even more susceptible to control through the capture of their desires (see Jameson 1984; Colebrook 2011). Not only does 'mass media directly instill and effectively circulate politically and morally operative affect' (Massumi 1998: 46), but our institutions regularly trade in colonising collective desire through discourses of insecurity, catastrophe and inescapable danger (Evans and Giroux 2015: 51). However, it is precisely because modern operators of power and control manoeuvre themselves through affect and image that these must be our starting point for addressing this time of global terror.

Leading back to the initial question: what is the role of art in this time of global terror? Is there an ameliorative possibility in the photographic image, for instance, when its intent is to document and crystallise the intensity of injustice and suffering, which makes it rise above the fray of this perpetual stream of affects to which we contemporaries are subjected? Undoubtedly, art is frequently invoked as an agent of change or a catalyst that inspires human beings to see the world differently; the idea is that by framing certain content, art interrupts, or even transfigures, the commonplace (Danto 1983). Moreover, do the normalisation of systemic violence and the capitalist appropriation of affect, as catalysts to a kind of cultural desensitisation, render affect impotent and altogether frustrate our attempts to articulate or locate any transformative potential in art itself?

These questions will be contextualised through thinkers such as Siegfried Kracauer, Vilém Flusser, Roland Barthes, Susan Sontag and Georges Bataille, who have devoted substantial work to thinking through the significance of the image, particularly in relation to photography as an ambiguous psychological and sociocultural phenomenon. In several instances, their attempts to ascertain the true significance of the image, what we could call its artistic potential, provide some guidance for our inquiry, but also lead us to recognise that the attempt to find a truer or deeper significance to the image operates according to a model of representation that may be inadequate to our purposes. Because of Deleuze's emphasis on the non-representational nature of the image and the non-signifying, affective aspects of the artwork in general, his aesthetics provides an amended framework for analysing the current forms of collective desire and obsession with spectacles of violence. By conjoining his aesthetic vision to his understanding of machinic desire, as underlying our perceptual field and social institutions, we can posit a new, liberatory potential of what I call 'creative affect'. Finally, I address the ethical question that I believe is implicit in Deleuzian aesthetics – what *kinds* of affects do we need in the time of global terror?

Representation of the Image

Returning to the question of the ameliorative potential of the image, we might point to journalistic photography as an attempt to bring global attention to horrific events and thus 'make a difference' by appealing to our common humanity. When applied to the current cultural and political landscape, we may say that these images can potentially change our attitudes towards violence and open us to the suffering of others. Yet this view, that the photographic image depicting the violence and atrocity of war, terror, etc. can or should be used to produce empathy, is problematic.[8] In her analyses of visual representations of violence in *Regarding the Pain of Others*, Sontag presents several arguments against the assumption that images (photographs) of gross violence necessarily produce empathetic responses, arguing that all images are subject to manipulation of their message and, further, that images of violence and brutality are never transcendent to their context; we do not experience images as neutral observers but as members of groups, nations and peoples (Sontag 2003: 29, 30–1). Thus, a photograph of the ravages of war could inspire a repudiation of violence as easily as it could foster greater militancy (Sontag 2003: 8–12). Sontag's analysis in *On Photography* (1977) construes the relation between photography and violence even more pointedly, in that she argues that the photographic image is a method of exerting control over the world and, as such, manifests a kind of aggressive self-assertion which is itself a kind of metaphysical violence: 'To photograph is to appropriate the thing photographed. It means putting oneself into a certain relation to the world that feels like knowledge – and, therefore, like power' (Sontag 2001: 4). Sontag insinuates that this use of photography can no longer be considered artistic, but is rather psychological, 'a defense against anxiety and a tool of power' (Sontag 2001: 8). If anything, the proliferation of photography has led to the anaesthetisation of violence, rather than critical consciousness.

We need also consider what the representational utilisation of an image endorses on epistemological and ontological registers. Specifically, there is a certain relation of viewer to knowledge based on transparency, which, itself, implies the present as *true*, and, more troubling, *inevitable* – which is to say, tacitly endorsing the reproduction of the world, rather than calling for its transformation. In *Towards a Philosophy of Photography* (1984), Vilém Flusser identifies this assumption of transparency on the part of the spectator as resulting from photography itself. Flusser claims that the emergence of photography marks the transition from textual to visual culture, and analyses how this shift leads to different social forms (Flusser 1984: 17–18). In particular, whereas the rise of text ushered in the development of a universal consciousness of history, the rise of the photograph suggested an immediate access to the representation ascertainable for all society, which resulted in a cult of transparency. The danger with the belief that the representation, and therefore reality, was immediately transparent to the spectator is twofold: 1) we lose our critical consciousness, and 2) reality becomes something manipulable. Flusser interprets the photograph in terms of a sort of complicity with post-industrial negativity, as complicit with the passage of pure information, the devaluation of materiality and the rise of programming as power (Flusser 1984: 53). Photographic proliferation through cinema, media and television ushers in mass culture, habitualised through the redundant repetition of images (Flusser 1984: 20). Society slips into image illiteracy: 'the vector of significance has been reversed; reality has slipped into being a symbol, has entered the magic universe of the symbolism of images' (Flusser 1984: 62). This and the fetish for the proliferation of images explains the ease with we become consumed by what he calls (capitalist) photographic programming.

Of course, Flusser is not the only one to advance a critical stance concerning photography, especially in relation to the potential for massification that technology allows. As early as 1927, Siegfried Kracauer worried about the rise of what he called the 'extraordinary validity' of photography and its promulgation through methods of mass media. According to him, the ease of consumption (of the image) both chides us about what is supposed to be understood – *the legitimacy and authority of the original* – and how we are supposed to understand – *the present as a temporal and spatial continuum* (Kracauer 1993: 425, 431–2). For Kracauer, the massification of the image, its superficial manipulation by mass media, destroys its potential for anything ameliorative or transformative and excludes deeper knowledge and understanding of its contextual and historical framework (Kracauer 1993: 432).

The critiques of Flusser and Kracauer suggest that the problem with the image is its easy assimilation into the metaphysics of presence, promulgated by our tendency to assume the transparency of the image and its message. Moreover, our own complicity with, or desire for, the infinite production of affects, corresponding as it does to the practical and material conditions of capitalist consumption and exchangeability of objects, leads to what Sontag refers to as the aestheticisation of violence. The problem of representation seems to collude with the massification of the image. Images of this kind are insufficient to engender social transformation or shift the concentrations of desire and pathos that motivate us.

Yet these factors are not inherent to the image itself, which means, theoretically, that these tendencies could be overcome. Possible solutions would either be to carve out an alternative usage of the image beyond or above its massification, to challenge the primacy of its representational function and, perhaps simultaneously, to address its mode of reception. This final objective would demand careful consideration of how to overcome the contemporary condition of cultural hyper-saturation and desensitisation.

Indeed, the ambivalence concerning the potential of the image shows up in several attempts to unearth the true nature of the photograph as opposed to its vulgar use, but also to grapple with the new modes of perception that are made possible through it. Benjamin's (1935) elucidation of the loss of aura caused by photography evinces this sense of ambiguity, in that he identifies this phenomenon in art as both revolutionary and potentially totalitarian. Indeed, Kracauer's larger point in critiquing the derivative use of the image is to offer a different possibility for the photographic image. He asserts that the conditions of photography imply a disarticulation of consciousness and nature that actually confounds the assumption of a natural representation and transparency between the two.[9] Therefore, the photographic image can reveal a fragmentation between consciousness and the world, which in turn provokes greater intelligibility of our material and practical conditions: 'a revolutionary understanding of the economic base of a disenchanted nature in the wake of capitalism' (Bly 2016: n.p.). This is the more profound possibility inherent in the image and what separates its mundane use from its creative aspect.

The need to define what elevates the image to art is in fact exacerbated by the onset of the technological reproducibility of the image. In some cases, this has translated into the question of what gives the image its (artistic) integrity. In *Camera Lucida*, Barthes' rumination on the essence of photography reveals that the true potential of the photograph is that, in the recognition of its own paradoxical relation to its subject, it restores the infinite to thought (1980: 107–9). The photographic image is transformed into an illuminative beyond through the incongruity of two planes, the studium, or manifest subject and context, and the punctum, a flash that disrupts and crosses the studium. The punctum 'takes the spectator outside its frame, and it is there that I animate this photograph and that it animates me. The punctum, then, is a kind of subtle beyond – as if the image launched desire beyond what it permits us to see'

(Barthes 1980: 59). The idea is that the designation of the image *as* art requires the interruption of casual perception or the significant break in the fluidity of the image.

Likewise, Rancière (2005) thinks that for the image to be transformative, to produce a critical or *political* art, it must include a clash of heterogeneous elements. The tension within the image reveals alternative political realities normally covered over in the dominant regime. The presence of heterogeneous worlds exposes a certain 'distribution of the visible' that constructs certain individuals as legitimate and refuses even to acknowledge the visibility of others.[10] The ameliorative power of the image – that which induces critical awareness – is a function of the conscientious juxtaposition of content within the image. For Rancière, this is the artistic intervention that opens the image to its deeper significance and forestalls the ability of the viewer to easily consume or merely enjoy it.

Kracauer suggests that photography will usher in a new form of consciousness; Barthes identifies the punctum as something that we will be immanently moved by; Rancière implies that tension induces a kind of motivational or critical circuit. Yet here we are, more susceptible to the vicissitudes of media and more enamoured with the circulation and indiscriminate consumption of affect than ever before. So, how do we become aware of a positive or transformative potential of the photographic image (or the artwork) and how do we become engaged in the image to the extent that it might have these effects on us in the first place? What appears to be needed, beyond merely viewing or experiencing the image, is a willingness to engage and the cultivation of an awareness or sensitivity of engagement.

As a preliminary response, consider one of the most profound philosophical examples of intensive engagement with the photograph: Georges Bataille's fascination with a photograph of an individual undergoing the punishment of *Lingchi*, a form of execution in which the victim is kept alive while being methodically sliced into pieces.[11] Bataille's meditative engagement with this tortuous image illuminates the ethical imperative to establish a particular attunement from which to engage with images or certain affects. Bataille suggests that methodical viewing and contemplation of such images quite literally shatters the boundaries of the viewer, who enters into an affective contagion with the pure violence of the image itself.

Philosophically, this correlates with Bataille's larger 'goal' to induce extreme experiences that expose one to the raw existence that conditions and provides a limit to ipseity. There are certain experiences that offer a glimpse of the liminal paradoxical tension at the core of our subjectivity: laughter, ecstasy, torture or anguish. Yet Bataille expresses frustration that these liminal moments are ephemeral: 'I [can] never remain there' (2014: 48), and it is this practice of meditation on the image that intensifies and sustains these moments of suffering/ecstasy. In other words, the intensification and meditation on the image is a method of maintaining or elongating the opening of our being, creating a profound, lasting laceration – one that does not immediately reclose.[12]

Tarrying with this image of torture, its senseless cruelty and excess, forces a confrontation with the anguished, intolerable pain of the other which demands a response, yet to which it is impossible to respond; this impossibility is the possibility of an ethical disposition, shattering spectatorship in favour of affective communion: 'What counts is the alteration of the habitual order, in the end, the impossibility of indifference' (Bataille 2011: 28). Bataille initiates a new way of looking that challenges the spectator to remain vigilantly engaged with the impossible liminal spaces between self and world, sense and senselessness, life and death, power and impotence. What I find valuable about this is the recognition of the need for a particular attunement to extend the longevity of our affective involvement and to increase the motivational power of the image, as well as the sustained deliberation on how to achieve it. Bataille prompts us to think of a particular temporality of the image, a temporality of slowness and delay.

These considerations provide the context for my own philosophical intervention. Bataille's work illustrates clearly that the mode of reception of the image is extremely important for positing its transformative potential, which I take as an imperative for cultivating engagement both in terms of thoughtful attunement to the immanent conditions of the image and a renegotiation of spatio-temporal dynamics of engagement – temporal delay and spatial opening. Further, what these attempts to identify an artistic or elevated potential of the image have in common is the identification of characteristics that elevate its representational value, either through fragmentation, interruption, tension or intensification. Yet they are still interrogating the image from how its representation is modulated. If we want to effect change in the affective engagement with images, we cannot rely on art that solely represents or exposes violence, terror and injustice, however complicated these representations are. Addressing the effects (representations) of terror does not help us understand the underlying desires that lead to these gross displays. By merely replicating the proliferation and saturation of images to which we are already accustomed, it does nothing to disrupt that paradigm.

Thus, we need to reconsider the image and outline an alternate use or potential. In the next section I will begin with this imperative by invoking Deleuze's theory of the image, and then return to the former, considering the artwork as a means of renegotiating spatio-temporal dynamics.

Deleuzian Image, Art and Affect

Rather than interrogating the image as a representation of reality, Deleuze contemplates the *reality* of the image. In fact, for Deleuze, the image concerns the nature of the real itself. In *The Logic of Sensation*, Deleuze notes how non-representational aspects of the image become the focus of modernist painters as a response to the invention of photography. His analysis of abstraction in painting allows him to come up with an entirely different understanding of the power and function of the image beyond symbolism, narration or representation, one that he develops into a full-fledged ontology in *Cinema I* and *II*. Deleuze's point is not to privilege painting over photography, but to recognise a more fundamental potential or power inherent in the image, that is, to express the violence of sensation itself, which he understands as a fundamental encounter with hitherto imperceptible material forces.

In *Cinema I*, Deleuze's elevation of the ontological status of the image is indebted to Bergson, for whom the image is constitutive of matter itself: 'Matter, in our view, is an aggregate of "images". And by "images" we mean a certain experience which is more than that which the intellect calls a representation, but less than that which the realist calls a thing' (Bergson 1988: 9). Bergson's definition suggests that the image is fundamentally non-representational in at least two respects: 1) the image is not a representation in the mind of a beholder – it has its own materiality and independence; and 2) the image does not *re*-present anything – it has its own unique existence. Deleuze interprets this to mean that images are the fundamental features of the real: 'The infinite set of all images constitutes a kind of plane (plan) of immanence. The image exists in itself, on this plane' (Deleuze 1997: 58–9). We gain a better understanding of what the being of the image is by appealing to Deleuze's understanding of reality as a univocal plane of becoming, populated by forces, intensities and movements (also indebted to Bergson's monist understanding of duration as a continuous field of differentiation). With respect to this ontological framework, the image has priority over the object. Every 'thing' is a conglomeration of forces in states of more or less stability or instability (assemblages). As Bergson/

Deleuze explain, 'at this level of universal variation, where there is only movement, these movements are called images in order to distinguish them from everything that they have not yet become' (Deleuze 1997: 58–60). Thus, these movement-images 'are not yet bodies or rigid lines, but only lines or figures of flight', which are 'blocs of space-time' (1997: 58–60). In continuous variation and relation, these images move at infinite speed, and it is only with the introduction of a gap or interval, what Deleuze likens to a 'cooling down', that images become matter. Rather than reacting according to all facets, these images react according to specialised facets, the beginnings of the sensorial and perceptive (living) level of existence. Therefore, there is always a double system of reference of images: 1) a system in which each image varies for itself and all images act and react; and 2) a system in which all vary for a single one, receiving actions of the other images (Deleuze 1997: 62).

According to Bergson, the tendency of natural (human) perception to assume a fixed, instantaneous view obscures the dual nature of the image, hypostasising the state of things in constant change, and obscuring our ability to experience a world of universal variation (immanence). Rediscovering this matrix of the movement-image is one of Deleuze's philosophical goals. Deleuze also discovers the potential of the image to affect the sensible world, including ourselves. Images have their own being and force, which means that, rather than representing reality, they can transform it. This accounts for Deleuze's interest in the intersection of art and philosophy; as creative rearrangements of sensible elements, or configurations of force, they proliferate new affects (blocs of sensation) and new images (blocs of space-time), which, in turn, affect how and what we perceive. Thus, artworks can be fundamental encounters that disrupt routinised pathways of desire (social hegemony) and confound ease of consumption (consumerism).

In fact, Deleuze directly links the aesthetics of the image to material transformations of the brain.[13] In *What is Philosophy?* Deleuze and Guattari offer a neurological conception of aesthetics that builds upon the observations concerning the relationship between the image, materiality and the brain. As I have explained, Deleuze conceives of matter itself as a multiplicity or aggregate of images. Perception of matter consists of the same images oriented by the action of a particular image upon others, a centre of action or a body. In this schema, the difference between living organisms can be measured by the extent of delay between stimulus or perception and action. In more advanced organisms, there is more of a delay between a stimulus and response, culminating in the complexity centre of the brain. In *Matter and*

Memory, Bergson explains the mechanism of the brain as a network of links, routings and delays, which creates zones of indetermination. These gaps or intervals are where thought or reflection occurs: 'what fills the cerebral interval, these "zones of indetermination" that are the indices of life and what interposes itself [there] are affections, body-memories, and pure recollections' (Grosz 2000: 21). As a relation between affecting body and affected body this interval is also given another name – affect (Deleuze and Guattari 1994: 173).

For Deleuze, exploring and widening these gaps is what introduces creativity into this world and provides the possibility of resisting the inevitability of the overbearing present. Deleuze's philosophical (and political) aim, to make these gaps resonate, is both the process by which thought emerges (from the dis-alignment or discord that such an interval would suggest) and also marks the beginnings of a social act, as the rendering visible of force through this discordant interruption (gap) releases a new irruption of desire within the social field.[14] This gap is expressed as affect, which can be shared and can form the basis for new political subjectivities, or the catalyst for new political action. Finally, this interval is also where we have the possibility of encountering the vibratory being of movement and force (immanent life), which is generally bypassed by our need to selectively encounter reality (perception). It is this experience that necessarily opens us to the impersonal, inhuman forces of the universe, which I connect to the possibility of liberating desire from its fascistic tendencies. Indeed, everything does happen in the middle (see Deleuze 1995b: 161).

Deleuze's specification that the unique power of the artwork is to preserve affect addresses the problem of affective evanescence (Deleuze and Guattari 1994: 163, 166), in that the interval is held open through the artwork itself; in fact, we could say that the artwork is the space in which this in-betweenness is explored, and in which affects, which move and motivate us, are enlivened or intensified. Thus, the power of these images is that they offer a space of encounter that makes a break or cut in the normal flow of our affective and perceptive lives,[15] which is particularly profound because of the possibility of longevity. It is my intention to develop the concept of the artwork as a space for renegotiating spatio-temporal dynamics to address the contemporary political and social condition of simultaneous fascination with and oppression from images of violence and affects of terror.

Schizoanalysis of Affect, Desire and the Social Body

Deleuze and Guattari's method of schizoanalysis is crucially important here, as it is the means through which we can grasp the role of affect in both producing and unhinging the social body and explore its relation to the circumstances of the capture of desire. In *Anti-Oedipus*, they develop a novel theory of desire resulting from their critical engagement with Freudian psychoanalysis. Analysing Freudian case studies, they notice Freud's tendency to reduce the group character of fantasy to familial reproduction, from which they draw several conclusions, among them the observation that the resistance of the schizophrenic to this oedipalisation indicates that there is a kind of desiring-production that is connected to the whole social field, which is immanent and irreducible. Also, the psychoanalytic tendency to locate libidinal desire within individual subjects as 'lack of X' obscures the pre-individual, positive nature of desire. This leads Deleuze and Guattari to posit the unconscious as a pre-personal desiring-machine; that is, a process of production, for which desire is an immanent energetics of auto-production that causes flows and breaks flows in a cycle of production and product. Deleuze and Guattari argue that Freud discovers this domain of free synthesis of the unconscious but draws back in order 'to restore order' by fitting the coordinates of Oedipus over desiring-production, thereby capturing desire in a set of idealistic, transcendent structures that limit and obscure its productive capabilities (Deleuze and Guattari 1983: 24, 54, 333). Schizoanalysis involves denouncing the illegitimate (reductive) manifestations of the immanent processes of desiring-production and exposing the derivative nature of the transcendent illusions that come to determine (capture) it (Deleuze and Guattari 1983: 75, 342). These destructive tasks prepare the way for revealing other modes of desire and proliferating new syntheses on the basis of this liberation (Deleuze and Guattari 1983: 322).

The other trajectory of schizoanalysis involves the analysis of how desiring-production relates to social production and, particularly, to its repressive forms. Deleuze and Guattari explain that the late capitalist social formation is characterised by a radical decoding of desire, but always in the service of the mechanisms of capitalist production. This is a paradoxical situation in which capitalism appeals to the libidinal energetics of constant production while simultaneously performing a repressive binding of those energies into its own axiomatic. In other words, desire is enticed by deterritorialising flows, so long as it is bound to the body of capital itself. To understand how desire becomes captured in this way, we must understand the dual tendencies of desire, fascistic and revolutionary, *and* the way that social determinates impose themselves. The product of desiring-production, the Body without Organs, desires its own stasis, and thus comes to see production as something to be repelled, which means that desire maintains a desire for its own repression, a kind of counter-productivity that is an alternate, yet fundamental, pole of desiring-production (Deleuze and Guattari 1983: 9). Because the unconscious already exercises its own primal repression of desiring-production (Deleuze and Guattari 1983: 120–1), libidinal investments can be collectively routed according to dominant social, economic and class interests. To transform repressive or fascistic desire into a revolutionary desire, we must first be able to distinguish unconscious libidinal investment from the pre-conscious investments of interest (Deleuze and Guattari 1983: 347).

With respect to the transformative potential of art, this digression allows us to understand the stakes involved in moving to a Deleuzian model of image and affect. Since our interests and perceptions are generated from prevailing social determinates which invoke underlying unconscious libidinal desire, art which remains at the representational level and merely engages us at the level of perception, interest and signification cannot undermine the regime from whence it comes. Indeed, Deleuze and Guattari claim that 'Capitalism can endure so many manifestations of interest, but not one manifestation of desire' (1983: 379). So, the issue is not how art appeals to perception or transforms representation, but how art operates at the level of forces and intensities, affects and desires, and can therefore make us more aware of our immanent connection to the transcendental plane of machinic desire as well as liberate desire from its fascistic tendencies, those which keep it enthralled by spectacles of violence and the glut of affective production. Creative affect, as a form of critical intervention or resistance, must correspond to the tasks of schizoanalysis: destruction, revealing modes of desire and creation.

First, art, as a form of creative destruction, would need to be directed towards 'explod[ing] the organizing structure of the dominant system' (Carson 2003: 25), parallel to the destructive task of schizoanalysis of cleansing the unconscious of transcendent illusions. This destructive and liberatory potential of the artwork becomes visible when we consider how Deleuze's ontology of art corresponds to the model of machinic desire. Accordingly, for Deleuze, the question for art is not 'what does it mean?', but 'how does it work?' And what art *does* is produce new combinations of force and intensity as self-sufficient sensations. Art conveys the raw and pure violence of sensation. Art *disrupts* captured desires and reroutes them in new directions, which means that, like desiring-production, art is inherently characterised by creating new connections (what connections does it make?). Affects are machinic operators that both interrupt and connect with various contexts to reconfigure the plane of immanence and our perception of the world. Art as a creative destruction destratifies material forces and flows and exposes immanent conditions of force and intensity (desiring-production), laying bare the illusory world of stratified objects that lulls us into complacency regarding the inevitability and certainty of the present order of things.

Second, schizoanalysis involves distinguishing unconscious libidinal investments, or the desires of the social field, from the pre-conscious investments of class and interest (Deleuze and Guattari 1983: 373–418). This division parallels that between the affective force of a work of art and its narrative or interpretative content. To reach the former, we must consider how artworks reveal and intensify different modes of desire. In 'Can Images Kill?' (2009), Marie-Jose Mondzain develops an account of the relation between images and desire that correlates with this requirement. Like Deleuze, who emphasises the artwork's capacity to convey the violence of sensation, Mondzain approaches the image through the 'movements communicated by the image' rather than its figurative content. She also relates the potency of the image, its ability to be a space of cohabitation for our desires, to this unmediated nature.

Mondzain's main question is, given our modern condition of exposure to gratuitous violence and spectacle, what is the power of the image and is it a power that results in violence? Beginning with the religious image and its connection to incarnation, she explains the image's ability to invoke a particular kind of communion. By constructing the spectator as part of a unity between the visible, the invisible and the gaze, the image induces a fusional communion, evidencing a deep desire for similarity and identification. This desire for fusional communion sets a dangerous paradigm that she associates with the violence of the visible. It is also what renders the image an instrument of power and control (Mondzain 2009: 29–32). She claims that the production of univocal and mythical signs, which convey the fusion with totalising impersonal powers (2009: 45–6), is a form of manipulation meant to abolish thought and judgement indicative of forms of propaganda, religious imagery and advertising.

Mondzain proposes to analyse the 'types of visual productions that speak to destructive and fusional drives and those that are responsible for freeing spectators from a deadly tension' (2009: 26), similar to

Deleuze's division between fascist and revolutionary desire. Combining Mondzain's and Deleuze's analyses, we could say that three major affective components (desires) correspond to and exacerbate fascist desire: transcendence,[16] identification and fusion. Mondzain calls the fusional regime the murder of thought because there is no separation between the object and the spectator (2009: 39). Drawing on Deleuze's ontology of the image, we could say that it offers no interval in which freedom of thought can arise.

Mondzain also categorises the need for identification as one of the destructive, fusional drives. Identification is detrimental in that it inhibits the spectator's ability to recognise otherness and sets up an exclusionary politics (us/them). As Wilhelm Reich (1933) showed, when the desire for identification is engaged, images of violence or suffering can provoke unification with a hegemonic political order, even if that order is complicit in the production of these states of affairs. Simplified slogans would also comply with these desires, encouraging identification with a singular ideal rather than treating complex social realities. Deleuze and Guattari extend Reich's analysis by adding their formulation desiring-production (1983: 118–19), which allows them to explain this desire as a perversion of one immanent criterion of desiring-production, the disjunctive synthesis. Disjunctive synthesis is a process of selection related to the synthetic activity of desiring-production. It is a mode of designation (either/or). The perversion of disjunctions happens at the point where they cease to be inclusive (either/or/or) and become exclusive (it must be either this or that). Denouncing the illegitimate use of the synthesis is one of the primary goals of schizoanalysis, through which we can rediscover a transcendental unconscious and liberate desire from its perverse reduction.

Mondzain also contemplates what it takes to move from fascist to liberated images. She calls for strategies of the image that assign the spectator a place of mobility, so that the image does not become an object of passive communal consumption (2009: 34). To disrupt the fusion of the image and the spectator's desire for identification would also mean making a break or cut in the homogeneity of the image. This makes sense from a Deleuzo-Guattarian perspective, given that breaks characterise the production of desire as such; a machine's mobility and transformation occur through cuts (*coupage*) that disrupt the stagnant smooth space of the Body without Organs, which, as we have seen, is the object of the fascist form of desire.

This suggests a particular role for art. First, if, as Mondzain claims, 'every spectacle is measured by the yardstick of freedom that it grants'

(2009: 35), then aesthetic practices are central to our political and ethical being[17] and should be directed towards liberating desire from its fascistic tendencies, those which produce subjects ready and willing to submit themselves to a regime of sameness and homogeneity. Second, if desiring-production is always excessive to its captured forms, the potential for desire to break out of the social forms is fundamental. The role of the artist would be to impart mobility to the affective encounter, to facilitate the liberation of desire, its proliferation and escape, by putting images in relation to one another and inducing vibrations of pure matter (Deleuze 1997: 76). Deleuze likens this treatment of the image to a kind of delirium, significant in that he advocates transforming fascist desire into its revolutionary form by discovering desire *as* delirium, leading us to consider how the creative affect is related to the third task of schizo-analysis: to discover other possible modes of desire and functioning of desiring-machines. 'What are they, what do you put into these machines, how does it work' (Deleuze and Guattari 1983: 322). This demand corresponds to Deleuze's emphasis on experimentation, a role that he expressly bestows on art (Deleuze 1994: 68). Experimentation is both an imperative for the spectator, to engage with creative (new) affects, and the inherent nature of the artwork (see Zepke 2005).

Finally, it is necessary to ask what kinds of affects do we need, connecting this question back to the exigency for establishing community and temporal continuity necessary for effective action and social transformation. This question of need is a pivotal one, because it marks the transition between ontology and ethics, between indiscriminate desiring-production and addressing the need for new political and social relations that the contemporary condition of global terror demands.

Creative Affects: Exhaustion, Indeterminacy and Infinite Movement

Next, we shall consider how art could produce the kinds of affects and images needed to destabilise the hegemonic attitudes and fascist desires that feed upon the violence and terror pervading our communal horizon. Deleuze's goal has always been to provide us with concepts that resist totalising, immobilising frameworks and open us to a reinvigorated creative impulse. Warning of the capitalist/consumerist take-over of creativity, Deleuze called for resistance to the mere proliferation of more and more concepts as opposed to genuine thinking (Deleuze 1995a: 137; Deleuze and Guattari 1994: 108). This is even more difficult considering capitalism's model of constant deterritorialisation and production that, in effect, mobilises mobility *and* creativity for itself under the rubrics of 'innovation' and 'novelty'. Therefore, any simple recourse to the present model of creativity paradoxically reinforces the (consumerist/capitalist) desire for more cycles of 'innovation' and 'production'. To break with this cycle, we cannot merely proliferate more affects; we should consider affects that provide a counter-force to affective hyper-saturation and interrupt rather than accelerate these processes of overproduction and overconsumption.

When capitalism has spread itself over everything and even appropriated the creative for itself, it seems to me that we must resist this present, including the model of creativity it employs, and I propose that Deleuze provides the contours for a new model for creativity in this short statement: 'creation traces a path between impossibilities ... taking place in bottlenecks' (Deleuze 1995a: 133). Here, Deleuze suggests the need to reconsider the spatio-temporal dynamics of creation through a cartographic tracing of impossibilities and the experience of stoppage and delay.

Reaching the Impossible: Exhaustion through Inexhaustibility

The question then arises, how does one reach the *impossible*? Deleuze addresses this problem in a short piece dedicated to Samuel Beckett called 'The Exhausted' (1995c), in which he develops a very particular understanding of exhaustion as a method of relating to possibilities. Deleuze delineates two senses of exhaustion: the first, which he rejects, is to *realise* possibilities (a selection, which precipitates exclusion), while the second, which he associates with Beckett's work, is to combine the entire set of variables and inhabit contradictory imperatives. The possible, in the first sense, indicates the previously determined; in the second, it indicates the expansion towards a field of possibles as yet undetermined – the impossible. As Audrey Wasser explains, 'exhaustion invents the possible as it exercises it, and it is an affair not with future possibilities, but only with the impossible, which belongs to it as an essential determination and a limit to be displace' (2012: 128–9), which is evidenced in Deleuze's description of Beckett's *Quad* as a systematic exploration of the spatial potentials of space by the performers' repetitious tracings of variations within a quadrangular region which simultaneously creates the space itself. Exhaustion, in this case, intensifies the virtualities inherent in a space to move from repetition to creation, 'a precondition for reaching some other mode of the possible' (Pelbart 2015: 128). Rather than referring to possibilities inherent in a system, exhaustion has to be a kind of passage through catastrophe that breaks or interrupts the system. This helps us understand what is necessary for political change. The capitalist system, characterised by circulating concepts, forces, bodies and affects in ever-renewed combinations meant to generate and mesmerise our desires, operates by continuously proliferating new possibilities, but only as repetitive circulations of the same.

Following Deleuze, to break with the system requires the impossible. Given that Deleuze's fascination with the Event is its infinitude, that 'you never realize all of the possible' (Deleuze 1995c: 3), my proposal is that it is the *inexhaustible* which animates his notion of exhaustion and that *this* is what it means to 'trace a path between impossibilities'. Rather than exhausting all possibles *in a system*, inexhaustibility is the slowing down of the space, frustrating the smooth transition between possibles, opening a gap that cannot be immediately reclosed (all of those things that our discussion of Bataille led us to desire). On this reading, creativity is not just the invention of new things, but the recognition of the need to wrangle with inexhaustibility, and what we should really be talking about is what kind of aesthetic practices produce affects of inexhaustibility.

Taking our cue from Deleuze in 'The Exhausted', there are four ways of exhausting the possible: 1) form exhaustive series; 2) dry up the flow of voices; 3) extenuate the potentialities of space; and 4) dissipate the power of the image (the last two are most fully transformative). He discovers these as a result of his interest in Beckett's own strategies of exhaustion with regard to language. Though impossible to fully address here, Deleuze identifies three levels of language that Beckett systematically puts into crisis. The last of these is the language of the image, referring to a level of a-signifying, disembodied pure intensity. This language of image has 'nothing to do with things, words, or voices, but with immanent limits, hiatuses, holes and tears', revealing its non-linguistic materiality, the intensive. What we find is that the processes of exhaustion lead down a path of dissolution that puts the entire system of language and meaning into crisis, while revealing the true 'force' of the image. The dislocated image is thus a force that can defy 'language that imprisons and suffocates us' (Pelbart 2015: 124), opening us to new expressions of desire (the inexhaustible at the heart of exhaustion).

Elsewhere, I have offered an extended analysis of how certain artworks accomplish these modes of exhaustion, in particular the art forms of intermedia, the performance art of Fluxus and the musical experimentation of Cage (see Sholtz 2015; 2018). In each case, my argument was that these art forms express a kind of in-betweenness that extends and intensifies the spatio-temporal interval itself, extenuating the potentialities of space. Intermedial art, for instance, induces liminal states, establishing new zones of interaction, understanding, cognition and emotion through boundary crossing (Friedman 2012: 392). This transitivity produces a zone of indeterminacy out of which the affect of pure, *inexhaustible* mobility is born. Fluxus's 'event scores' extenuated the spatial dynamics of performance art by orchestrating situations meant to collapse the distance *between* artist and audience. Yoko Ono's iconic *Cut Piece* (1964) exemplifies this disruptive exploration of the potentialities of the performance space. Ono's instructions for the piece engaged the audience, inviting them to come on stage and cut pieces of her clothing while she sat silent and immobile. By ceding control to the audience, Ono dramatises their responsibility in producing the event-space and makes the spectator and spectacle relation visible in a way that Mondzain identifies as imperative for disrupting fusional, destructive desires. The interaction of the audience imparts mobility to the affective encounter, constituting the space as one of constant variation (the inexhaustible). Expressing Fluxus's esteem for principles of fluidity and contingency, Ono set minimal rules as to how or what should be cut and offered no indication of the duration of the event. The manner for the event's unfolding is open-ended and indeterminate.

The inexhaustibility of the performance (its mobility and indeterminacy) insinuates a process that is never finished and thus does not reside in the realm of the possible (Deleuze 1995c: 12). It is like the Deleuzian Event, never coincident with the actualised present moment, exceeding it on all sides, implying a field of infinite potentials that are, in effect, impossible. When an artwork occupies this between-space, it echoes the conditions of constant variation of the plane of immanence itself, and as such is a way of developing an affective connection to the immanent material flows and impossibilities that stratification fails to capture. This interruption of the possible is an extension of the spatio-temporal interval, which produces a kind of sensitised awareness by delaying or slowing down our ability to consume it, to designate it, or to comprehend it, *creating* the space (like *Quad*) as an encounter with this imperceptible spatio-temporal flux.

Regarding the fourth criterion, 'dissipating the power of the image', Deleuze suggests that the image can approach 'exhaustion by its power to produce a void or create holes' (1995c: 9). In order to explicate how this could be accomplished, I will refer to the performance troupe Ueinzz Theatre Company, which was founded in 1997 in São Paulo by Peter

Pál Pelbart, schizoanalyst and philosopher. Of course, it is Pelbart who identifies the activities of this group as modes of exhaustion, 'straddling the fine line between construction and collapse' (Pelbart 2015: 133). Modelled on Guattari's practices at La Borde, the troupe members, 'lunatics, therapists, performers, maids, philosophers' (Pelbart 2015: 133), exchange positions among themselves with no explicit lead, writer, performer or even script. Moreover, the troupe explodes its own unanimity, connecting with various social scenes, incorporating new members, and generally practising a model of free and dynamic synthesis as it connects with heterogeneous scenarios, social spaces and scenes. It is a mad, machinic interplay of interruptions, connections and heterogeneity.

The performative methodology of the group is motivated by the same commitment to indeterminacy that animated the pioneering performance-based practices of Fluxus. Pelbart emphasises the fact that in Ueinzz, nobody knows what is coming: 'this kind of plasticity [is important], where the limits are not clear and the "space between" becomes more important than individual people' (Egert and Pelbart 2015: n.p.). The challenge is to create new means of interruption. Just like Deleuze's characterisation of the process of creation in painting as a matter of destroying clichéd images that already populate the blank canvas, exhaustion would have to begin as a disruption of the already populated present. Pelbart conceives the practices of his performance troupe as producing interruptions that break the complacency of the performance space and void the common meanings therein – creating holes and vacuoles that dissipate the images that comprise our overwrought and oversaturated society of the spectacle. Exhaustion is an operation of disconnection, an unbinding of what captures and imprisons us (Pelbart 2015: 128), the practice of which opens the possibility of new social and political modes of living. To accomplish this constructive task of schizoanalysis, to cause a delirium of desire, we must create new spaces that are characterised by heterogeneity rather than homogeneous fusion, emptiness rather than the glut of capitalist consumption, and inexhaustible indeterminacy and variation rather than captured and fetishised desire.

Conclusion: Intervals of Resistance

Before political efficacy, before institutional change, something subtler, more ontological, must happen. As Deleuze insists, 'The problem is no longer getting people to express themselves but providing little gaps of solitude and silence in which they might eventually find something to say' (Deleuze 1995a: 129) – these are what I call intervals of resistance. To address the spectacles of violence, the overbearing constrictions of control and power, we must practise creative resistance by creating and inhabiting new spatio-temporal intervals, those which let in a modicum of indeterminacy and freedom, breaking the present through their inexhaustibility. The tacit acknowledgement of the undetermined multiplicity of possibilities within each moment (this inexhaustibility) opens a space in which they can therefore arise. Creative affects are those that create and maintain these spatio-temporal openings. These are the cracks and the fissures *within* the present which disrupt the present. This is the place of resistance: a gap, a wound, a space of deferral, where fate does not prevail and in which the future arises. These are intervals of resistance, and it is our communal responsibility to cultivate these kinds of affects that fundamentally move us forward rather than those that celebrate negativity and keep us mired in a repetition of the present.

Notes

1. Mondzain (2009: 21) suggests that in the orchestration of the spectacle of 9/11 the attackers were powerfully aware that their attack on symbology (the image) struck at the heart of America, as the empire of the visible.
2. Violence is habituated in multiple ways: sensationalist images for entertainment neutralise violence and produce an anticipated desire for staged violence which displaces moral responsibility and sentiment; shock-value is commodified as pleasurable; pleasure in the suffering of others (sadistic tendency) is encouraged through their dehumanisation; desensitisation and overstimulation prevail; the technologies of digital distancing put space between images and consequences; anxiety and fear are generated, leading to the acceptance of militarisation and relinquishing of agency (see Evans and Giroux 2015: 98–101).
3. Evans and Giroux (2015) have traced this cultural/historical phenomenon from Debord's critique of the society of the spectacle to Sontag's critique of the aesthetics of depravity ('fascinating fascism') as a conflation of war and spectacle in service capitalism.
4. See, for example, their analysis of the politicisation of imagery from the 1980s onwards, including the 'overt politicisation' of war imagery to justify political action and global interventions (Evans and Giroux 2015: 76).
5. Whereas Marcuse (1964) argues that cultural distractions render us too comfortable to revolt, now politicised spectacular displays of violence render us too petrified to revolt.
6. This can be connected to Deleuze's discussion of the difference between disciplinary control and control societies. Power is not disseminated through institutions but saturates the whole social field – what better way than through the manipulation of affect.
7. Adorno's critique of the culture industry, Marcuse's analysis of manufactured distractions and Benjamin's explanation of mass mentality have roots in the anti-fascist critiques of the Frankfurt School and their insistence on the power

of culture as a political tool, which is even more relevant today with the rise of Trumpism.

8. In *Frames of War* (2009), Butler also argues that photographic images have lost their power to enrage and incite. Her point is that the selective framing of violence serves to delimit the sphere of appearance, rendering some lives as visible and others as not 'lives' at all.

9. Superficially, this would seem to contradict Sontag's analysis, but it really marks a distinction concerning the way that the centrality and power of the subject has become hyperbolised. Though the classical view is to assume that reality can be represented, the subject must use its intellectual capacities to pursue an *external* objective truth. Sontag points to the added layer of metaphysical violence whereby reality is not only transparent to the subject, but the subject also frames it.

10. The 'partition of the sensible' divides bodies into categories, 'those that one sees and those that one does not see, those who have a logos—memorial speech, an account to be kept up—and those who have no logos' (Rancière 1999: 22). Sontag's description of the way that we are more apt to see images depicting the full extent of suffering and brutality inflicted upon those in remote or exotic places illustrates this idea. As she says, we are meant to understand that these sorts of things happen in these places, that tragedy and injustice is inevitable in 'backward', poor parts of the world (Sontag 2003: 70–1).

11. A series of photographs depicting *Lingchi* were published in Bataille's *Tears of Eros* (2001) (originally published in 1961). For a discussion of the Surrealists' fascination with *Lingchi* and their interest in transgression as a form of disruption, see Elkins 2004: 5–19.

12. Bataille emphasises the relational nature of the image; it exists as a mode of communication or communion that profoundly affects its spectator. This relationality is inherent to Deleuze's notion of affect as well.

13. 'We can consider the brain as a relatively undifferentiated mass and ask what circuits . . . the movement-image or the time-image trace out, or invent, because the circuits aren't there to begin with' (Deleuze 1995a: 60; see also Deleuze 1997). For a detailed discussion of the emphasis on the brain, see Murphie 2010.

14. Ruddick (2010) focuses on the productive possibilities of the scream in Deleuze's work, but its characteristics as an affect can be extrapolated.

15. It is even more profound, in that Deleuze claims that the aim of art is to reach pure sensation denuded of subjectivity, wresting affect from affection and percepts from perceptions. Thus, the experience of artworks is to take us outside ourselves, making us enter relations with inhuman and cosmic flows or intensities, where affects and percepts exist for themselves (Deleuze and Guattari 1994: 167).

16. We have already discussed how Freud's imposition of a transcendent structure on to desire is a perversion of desire.

17. Daniel Smith's (2007) position that greater attunement to immanent conditions and eradication of desire for the transcendent are the fundamental criteria for ethics give credence to my claim, as I have argued that art accomplishes both.

References

Barthes, R. (1980), *Camera Lucida: Reflections on Photography*, trans. R. Howard, New York: Hill and Wang.

Bataille, G. (2001 [1961]), *Tears of Eros*, trans. P. Connor, New York: City Lights.

Bataille, G. (2011), *Guilty*, trans. S. Kendall, New York: SUNY Press.

Bataille. G. (2014), *Inner Experience*, trans. S. Kendall, New York: SUNY Press.

Benjamin, W. (1969 [1935]), 'The Work of Art in the Age of Mechanical Reproduction', in *Illuminations*, ed. H. Arendt, trans. H. Zohn, New York: Schocken Books, pp. 217–51.

Bergson, H. (1988), *Matter and Memory*, trans. A. Mitchel, New York: Random House.

Bly, J. (2016), 'The First Snapshots of the Last Things: Kracauer and Benjamin on Photography and History', <https://hyleticdiscontinuity.wordpress.com> (last accessed 28 October 2016).

Butler, J. (2009), *Frames of War: When is Life Grievable?*, New York: Verso.

Carson, B. D. (2003), 'Towards a Postmodern Political Art: Deleuze, Guattari, and the Anti-Culture Book', *rhizomes*, 07, <http://www.rhizomes.net/issue7/carson.htm> (last accessed 3 May 2022).

Colebrook, C. (2011), 'Earth Felt the Wound: The Affective Divide', *Journal for Politics, Gender, and Culture*, 8 (1): 45–58.

Danto, A. C. (1983), *Transfiguration of the Commonplace*, Cambridge, MA: Harvard University Press.

Deleuze, G. (1994), *Difference and Repetition*, trans. P. Patton, New York: Columbia University Press.

Deleuze, G. (1995a), *Negotiations: 1972–1990*, trans. M. Joughin, New York: Columbia University Press.

Deleuze, G. (1995b), *The Fold: Leibniz and the Baroque*, trans. T. Conley, Minneapolis: University of Minnesota Press.

Deleuze, G. (1995c), 'The Exhausted', *SubStance*, 78, 24 (3): 3–28.

Deleuze, G. (1997), *Cinema I: The Movement-Image*, trans. H. Tomlinson and B. Habberjam, Minneapolis: University of Minnesota Press.

Deleuze, G. (2003), *Francis Bacon: The Logic of Sensation*, trans. D. W. Smith, New York: Continuum.

Deleuze, G., and F. Guattari (1983), *Anti-Oedipus: Capitalism and Schizophrenia*, trans. R. Hurley, M. Seem and H. R. Lane, Minnesota: University of Minnesota Press.

Deleuze, G., and F. Guattari (1994), *What is Philosophy?*, trans. H. Tomlinson and G. Burchell, New York: Columbia University Press.

Egert, G., and P. Pál Pelbart (2015), 'Sharing Distance: On the Precarious Assemblage of Singularities and the Art of Collectivity. An Interview with Peter Pál Pelbart', *Inflexions*, 8: 239–49.

Elkins, J. (2004), 'The Very Theory of Transgression: Bataille, *Lingchi*, and Surrealism', *Australian and New Zealand Journal of Art*, 5 (2): 5–19.

Evans, B., and H. A. Giroux (2015), *Disposable Futures: The Seduction of Violence in Age of the Spectacle*, New York: City Lights.

Flusser. V. (1984), *Towards a Philosophy of Photography*, London: Reaktion.

Friedman, K. (2012), 'Freedom? Nothingness? Time? Fluxus and the Laboratory of Ideas', *Theory Culture Society*, 29 (7/8): 372–98.

Grosz, E. (2000), 'Deleuze's Bergson: Duration, the Virtual and a Politics of the Future', in I. Buchanan and C. Colebrook (eds), *Deleuze and Feminism*, Edinburgh: Edinburgh University Press, pp. 214–34.

Jameson, F. (1984), 'Postmodernism, or The Cultural Logic of Late Capitalism', *New Left Review*, 146: 59–92.

Kracauer, S. (1993 [1927]), 'Photography', trans. T. Y. Levin, *Critical Inquiry*, 19 (3): 421–36.

Marcuse, H. (1964), *One-Dimensional Man: Studies in the Ideology of Advanced Industrial Society*, Boston: Beacon Press.

Massumi, B. (1998), 'Requiem for Our Prospective Dead (Towards a Participatory Critique of Capitalism Power)', in E. Kaufman and K. J. Heller (eds), *Deleuze and Guattari: New Mappings in Politics, Philosophy, and Culture*, Minneapolis: University of Minneapolis Press, pp. 40–64.

Mondzain, M. (2009), 'Can Images Kill?', trans. S. Shafto, *Critical Inquiry*, 36: 20–51.

Murphie, A. (2010), 'Deleuze, Guattari, and Neuroscience', in P. Gaffney (ed.), *Deleuze, Science and the Force of the Virtual*, Minneapolis: University of Minnesota Press, pp. 330–67.

Pelbart, P. P. (2015), *Cartographies of Exhaustion: Nihilism Inside Out*, trans. J. Laudenberger and F. Rebolledo Palazuelos, Minneapolis, MN: Univocal Publishing.

Rancière, J. (1999), *Disagreement: Politics and Philosophy*, Minneapolis: University of Minnesota Press.

Rancière. J. (2005), *The Politics of Aesthetics*, London: Continuum.

Reich, W. (1970 [1933]), *The Mass Psychology of Fascism*, New York: Farrar, Straus, and Giroux.

Ruddick, S. (2010), 'The Politics of Affect in the Work of Negri and Deleuze', *Theory, Culture & Society*, 27 (4): 37–40.

Sholtz, J. (2015), *The Invention of a People: Heidegger and Deleuze on Art and the Political*, Edinburgh: Edinburgh University Press.

Sholtz, J. (2018), 'Deleuzian Creativity and Fluxus Nomadology: Inspiring New Futures, New Thought', *Evental Aesthetics*, 7 (1): 102–37.

Smith, D. (2007), 'Deleuze and the Question of Desire: Toward an Immanent Theory of Ethics', *Parrhesia*, 2: 66–78.

Sontag, S. (2001 [1977]), *On Photography*, London: Picador.

Sontag, S. (2003), *Regarding the Pain of Others*, New York: Farrar, Straus, and Giroux.

Wasser, A. (2012), 'A Relentless Spinozism: Deleuze's Encounter with Beckett', *SubStance*, 127, 41 (1): 124–36.

Zepke, S. (2005), *Art as Abstract Machine: Ontology and Aesthetics in Deleuze and Guattari*, New York: Routledge.

Chapter 4

The Inhospitality of the Global North: Deleuze, Neo-colonialism and Conflict-caused Migration

Don Johnston

Even in the recent violent and wretched history of Iraq, the year 2014 stands out. As DAESH[1] forces swept through parts of Iraq, seizing the second largest city, Mosul, in early June, an estimated 500,000 people fled their homes to escape ethnic and sectarian persecution, murder and enslavement (OCHA 2014). As overwhelming as that movement of people was for both the people and government of Iraq, that was not the worst of it. The nadir was to come in the first days of August when DAESH forces attempted to wipe the Yezidi[2] people from the pages of history. Holding Yezidi communities in the area of Sinjar under siege for weeks, DAESH forces first abducted the women and girls. Those who remained in the besieged communities had the options of either converting to DAESH's jihadist, Salafist version of Wahhabi Sunni Islam, or being killed. Those who could, fled. Seeking safety in the Kurdistan region of Iraq, tens of thousands of families made for the city of Dohuk. Thousands of others became trapped on the rocky massif of Mount Sinjar by encircling DAESH forces. On Monday, 4 August 2014, and for several days thereafter, a weary stream of people filed from horizon to opposite horizon along the road leading into the Kurdish region of Iraq as Nineveh province was being emptied of humanity. Some walked. Some families drove. Many more sat packed in the backs of lorries or pick-up trucks, their hands clutching small children and the few belongings they had managed to bring with them. Others pushed their failed cars across the bridge over the Tigris at Faysh Khabur.

As if in the midst of some slow-moving, apocalyptic marathon, Iraqi Red Crescent volunteers handed out sandwiches and bottles of water to the hungry hands moving past them. After crossing the bridge over the Tigris many families stopped and sat on the berm. Their faces showed relief, anguish, confusion. Having escaped the violence behind them, they now faced an uncertain future. Their plans had not extended past reaching safety. That accomplished, they did not know what to do, or where to go. Eerie calm reigned.

This belied the frenzy of the residents of the nearby city of Dohuk, some of whom were speaking by mobile phone to those trapped on Mount Sinjar. With no shelter and little food or water, as day after scorching[3] day passed, reports of deaths among the very young and the very old came in over the failing mobile phones. A few more each day. And then the phones began to go silent. In Dohuk, we were filled with the certitude that we were working on the margins of a genocide in progress. Then, unexpectedly, the US military re-entered Iraq and together with the Kurdish Peshmerga forces drove DAESH back from the massif.

A call went out over the local radio as families slowly began to make their way off Mount Sinjar. With many eager to help the roads quickly became choked with vehicles. Returning to their homes, the people of Dohuk installed thousands of the displaced families – many who had been displaced multiple times over the past months – in their homes alongside their own children, parents and grandparents. Less fortunate families sought refuge under bridges or overpasses, in the concrete shells of unfinished buildings and in schools and mosques. Some found a space in UN- or NGO-operated camps. Soon it was reported by city officials that the displaced outnumbered the residents of the city. Having arrived with only that which they could carry, all soon came to depend upon the kindness of their host families, as well as on the food, water, hygiene parcels, kitchen sets, bedding, jerry cans and small allotments of cash provided variously by the Kurdish government, UN agencies, the Iraqi Red Crescent Society, as well as national and international NGOs.

A year later a similar sea of greeting hands met hundreds of thousands of mostly Syrian refugees as they exited the overloaded, makeshift rafts that had transported them over the uncertain waters of the Mediterranean and on to the safety of Greek soil. In the early days of what has become the largest refugee crisis the world has seen since the Second World War (UNHCR 2016b), many were fortunate enough to transit quickly from the islands to mainland Greece. They continued travelling north along what became a migration route through Macedonia, Serbia, Croatia and Slovenia opening on to Austria, Germany and beyond. However, as the months passed and the stream of people seeking haven in northern Europe continued unabated, later arriving families did not encounter the safe passage and the corridor of warm hands offering clothing, water, medication, food, shelter and basic sleeping and hygiene items that had been extended to those who had preceded them. Rather, increasingly they found barbed razor wire and cold refusal as the exit point from Greece to Macedonia at the hastily erected border crossing in the rural hamlet of Idomeni was closed. There, as the winter months set in, where previously up to ten thousand people a day had passed northwards, now thousands sat for days on frosty and fallow fields. Some remained in the hundreds of buses that could be found idling at any one time on the side of the road or at the last service station leading into Idomeni. Many thousands of others squatted in draughty, canvas warehouse tents erected by the medical NGO Médecins Sans Frontières (MSF), on what months before had been quiet farmland. Others sought to keep their small children and elderly parents warm inside flimsy camping tents handed out to them by the United Nations High Commissioner for Refugees (UNHCR).

As they waited for the barrier to a better life in northern Europe to be lifted, their meagre resources diminishing daily, again thousands of people depended on the kindness of strangers and the efficiency of UN agencies, the Red Cross and other humanitarian organisations for sustenance and shelter. When the border to Macedonia opened, which it did less and less frequently, only refugees from Afghanistan, Iraq and Syria were allowed through. And only after the previous lot of those who had been permitted to enter Macedonia had crossed into Serbia; and those in Serbia had passed into Croatia; and so on along the humanitarian corridor. When the Austrian border closed, as it increasingly did during those winter months in 2015 and 2016, in quick succession, like barriers to medieval castles or some giant exclusionary dominoes clanging down one after another, the borders into Slovenia, Croatia, Serbia and then Macedonia closed. None of these smaller, poorer, recently war-torn countries wanted to get stuck with a population of refugees in their land.

One day the border at Idomeni into Macedonia did not reopen. The gates to 'Fortress Europe' had been shut. Northern Europe would take no more refugees. A deal had been struck between the European Union and Turkey whereby Turkey would begin actively preventing immigrants from leaving Turkish soil and accept the return of refugees apprehended on land (in Bulgaria and Greece) and at sea (some 49,500 people in 2016). Unable to proceed north, unwilling to return to homes and communities that no longer existed, thousands of families were stuck on the wrong side of the razor wire. With the corridor through Greece to northern Europe closed, at the 'behest' of northern Europe, Turkey and the long-teetering, cash-strapped Greek state (along with Jordan and Lebanon) have become the de facto wardens of a significant mass of humanity. Almost 63,000 refugees remained trapped in northern Greece in 2017; Turkey held three million (UNHCR 2016a; 2016c).

There are few in the Global North who are unaware of the scale of the current refugee crisis. Most are aware of the conflagrations in the Middle East and Afghanistan that have forced millions of people to abandon their homes and former lives. In 2016, with one-third more people dying trying to reach Europe by crossing the Mediterranean than in any previous year, the perils of the voyage, too, are well known (Cumming-Bruce 2016). The uncertain and limited welcome those who did make it to northern Europe received, and the fact that millions upon millions of people are living lives of squalor in makeshift camps not only in Greece and Turkey, but in Iraq, Jordan and Lebanon, is likewise well known. Yet in 2017, as heavy snow hit the Balkans and Greece, people were dying in makeshift camps erected before the gates of Europe (Squires 2017).

Deleuze and Guattari's philosophical work provides no ready answer to this most pressing of intertwined, apparently insoluble, political problems. Yet their concept of 'becoming-democratic' enables us to take measure of just how inadequate the Global North's response to the contemporary refugee crisis has been.[4] And as I shall suggest over the following pages, the asymptotic incorporation of Derrida's conceptualisation of 'unconditional hospitality' into the concept of becoming-democratic enables us to better appreciate the extent of the welcome given to those who arrived unannounced – *en masse* and in need – on Greek and Kurdish doorsteps. Incorporating Derridean hospitality – even while being, strictly speaking, impossible to realise in its 'pure' or 'unconditional' state – as a basin of attraction into the concept of becoming-democratic opens the concept to a 'more cosmopolitan and globally egalitarian becoming-democratic' (Patton 2017). In a related vein, a consideration of the humanitarian relief sustaining this flood of humanity indicates that even as terror increasingly becomes the norm in much of the world, the world may also be experiencing a counter becoming, a 'becoming-humanitarian'. Such a becoming – uncertain, imperfect and perilous as the humanitarian endeavour is – could be seen as civil society's ethical response to the violence of global terror. As such, it stands in direct counterpoint to the life-negating violence of terrorism.

Deleuze considered concepts to be dynamisms that convey real force without ceasing to be ideal. Bringing a particular concept to bear on an actual problem 'enables us to see [it] differently', 'as [it] might become rather than as [it is]' (Patton 2010a: 155). Such an encounter might produce something new, new relations of force or becomings. The concept of 'becoming' is a cornerstone of Deleuze and Guattari's philosophical work. Operating against the West's static conception of identity and being, 'becoming' refers to 'the very dynamism of change' inherent in all aspects of the cosmos. 'Becoming' indicates that neither a person's nor a society's being and identity are fixed, but rather should be 'conceived as [. . .] constantly changing assemblage[s] of forces'. 'Becoming' as a philosophical concept indicates that being and identity are 'epiphenomen[a] arising from chance confluences of languages, organisms, societies, expectations, laws and so on', which tend towards 'no particular goal or end-state' (Stagoll 2010: 26). It refers to the transformations and 'non-linear dynamic process of change' (Parr 2010: 30) occurring around, through and in each of us.

Though Deleuze and Guattari wrote of several specific becomings, the concept of 'becoming-democratic' did not figure prominently among the becomings they considered in depth.[5] However, Paul Patton has proposed several 'vectors' that might fill out the concept of becoming-democratic: 1) 'a more just distribution of material social goods'; 2) 'minoritarian becomings'; and 3) 'the opening-up of decision-making procedures throughout society' (Patton 2010a: 157–9). Patton's work suggests that these vectors may provide areas of consonance between Deleuzian thought and aspects of more normative political theory. It also would seem to suggest that the concept 'becoming-democratic' could consider contemporary political issues and connect with and act upon processes at work in contemporary democracies. As the first and third vectors of what becoming-democratic might consist of are relatively straightforward, I shall focus on bringing the vector of minoritarian becomings to bear on the world's varying responses to the global refugee crisis.

Patton explains Deleuze and Guattari's concept of minoritarian becomings against the 'majoritarian' constant in contemporary European-derived societies, namely what Deleuze and Guattari have identified as the priority of the 'average adult-white-heterosexual-European-male-speaking a standard language' (Deleuze and Guattari 1987: 105). Patton explains:

> [t]he adult, white, etc. male is majoritarian not because he is numerically in the majority, but because he forms the standard against which the rights and duties of all citizens are measured. Minoritarian becomings are defined as the variety of ways in which individuals and groups fail to conform to this standard [. . .] [B]y their nature, processes of minoritarian-becoming will always exceed or escape from the confines of any given majority. They

carry the potential to transform the affects, beliefs, and political sensibilities of a population in ways that amount to the advent of a new people. (Patton 2010a: 157–8)

The feedback from processes of minoritarian becomings in a society are politically significant. As the events of May 1968, along with the civil rights, anti-war, ecological, second-wave feminist and lifestyle movements that occurred throughout the world in the 1960s demonstrated, changes to the 'character of the majority' do occur.[6] As we know, these minoritarian becomings 'forced changes in the [. . .] identities and forms of organizations' (Patton 2010a: 158) in political communities around the world; the effects of these minoritarian becomings continue to be felt everywhere in the world.

There is no doubting that the capitalist democratic systems prevalent in the Global North have evolved into ingenious if inequitable systems by which both to accumulate wealth and control the dissatisfaction of the many who live more precarious and vulnerable existences in what have become prosperous, stable countries. I will suggest here that there is an overlap between those who thrive in this system and globalisation's 'fortunate sons' – the 'one per cent' made infamous by the Occupy movements. Both are the inheritors, directly or indirectly, whether in manners genetic, structural, ideological, political, economic or socio-geographical, of prior centuries of imperialist and colonialist successes. Under globalisation we have seen, as Habermas argues, an already inequitable world society further divided into winners, beneficiaries and losers (Borradori 2003). Yet many of those thriving in this yet-evolving world system feel it to be inherently unstable, and fear that with the slightest (minoritarian) nudge the system could come to rest at another, less propitious, angle of repose. Much (majoritarian) effort is expended to maintain their favourable position in the contemporary world system.

The voices of those who would welcome becoming-minoritarian in the Global North and are actively engaged in envisioning and trying to bring about post-nationalist sociopolitical spaces (Braidotti 2006) are not heard in contemporary, mainstream political debates. It is rather the stridency of anti-immigration voices that resounds. Fearing that changes might alter the social, economic, cultural and political equations that balance with them being more capable of living the lives they value than others, and convinced it is a zero-sum game, many resist any process or movement that could transform their sociopolitical space. Whether expressed using racist, xenophobic, antisemitic, neophobic or nationalist discourses, the ascendant political parties in the Global North share a common molar identity that sees reasons for preventing minoritarian becomings or anything that might usher in 'the advent of a new people'.

The Global North's response to the refugee crisis has taken place within what has long been a highly contested environment. From Jean-Marie Le Pen in France in the 1990s to most recently Donald Trump in the United States, limiting the number and type of immigrants allowed into a country, even suggesting the wholesale deportation of those who are in a country illegally, or the erection of walls along national borders, has long been a pressing issue for those on the right in many democratic societies. Given this, the Global North's response to the current refugee crisis, which has moved from permitting a limited number[7] to enter its territories, to denying them entry, to returning them – at times forcibly – to their countries of origin (Nordland 2016), does not seem so unexpected.

In 1991 François Mitterrand infamously stated that France had reached its 'threshold of tolerance' on immigration (Riding 1991). Giovanna Borrodori explains that the term 'threshold of tolerance' describes the 'limit beyond which it was no longer decent to ask a national community to welcome any more foreigners', regardless of whether they are migrants or refugees. 'As is true with organ transplants and pain management', Borradori continues, 'the threshold of tolerance designates tolerance as the extreme limit of the organism's struggle to maintain itself in balance before collapse' (Borradori 2003: 16).

This raises a few questions. With regard to the current refugee crisis, might 'maintain itself in balance', 'collapse' and 'threshold of tolerance' be affectively and politically charged euphemisms for an imagined tipping point? That being the point at which the presence of a certain number of foreigners in a country would become a transformative vector altering the balance of the system that favours the position, opportunities, future and lifestyle available to those majoritarian few? Are we not seeing those in power in the Global North numerically determine the number of refugees that can 'safely' be allowed into their societies within a determined period of time such that their deviations from the majoritarian standard can be titrated out within the larger population and their potential for sociopolitical transformations dissipated? That is to say, are these numbers not set so low so as to prevent a tipping point being reached at which that country could no longer maintain the established system in balance, and processes of minoritarian becomings might begin to transform the political sensibilities of that country?

In 'The Becoming-Minoritarian of Europe' Rosi Braidotti identifies the immanent possibility for a post-nationalist sociopolitical space to exist within the European project. Written a decade before the refugee crisis, Braidotti's project envisions a becoming-ethical taking place by which Europeans come to identify and strategically relocate their privileged whiteness. This becoming-minoritarian would empower alternative becomings and enable multiple, post-national 'ecologies of belonging'. Noting the pain involved in such collective social reimaginings, given that one's sense of identity is built on identifications such as race, nationality, class and so on, Braidotti asks, 'how do changes of this magnitude take place?' (Braidotti 2006: 91).

Deleuze and Guattari developed the concept of deterritorialisation to describe the 'movement' or processes 'by which something escapes or departs from a given territory', as well as the 'correlative [concept of the] processes of reterritorialization, which does not mean returning to the original territory but rather the ways in which deterritorialized elements recombine and enter into new relations' (Patton 2010b: 72; Deleuze and Guattari 1987: 508). Fundamental societal change happens all the time. Sometimes change occurs gradually, 'by degrees'; occasionally it occurs quickly, through 'the eruption of events which break from the past and inaugurate a new field of social, political, or legal possibilities' (Patton 2010b: 73). Certainly, the largest number of refugees the world has seen since the Second World War living and dying in tattered tents erected on the pitches of football stadiums, empty schools, former army barracks and community centres in the shadows of the gates to Fortress Europe has the potential to be a vector for societal change. It is not difficult to imagine that the sudden entrance of a large number of foreigners, each with their different languages and ways of living, loving, worshipping and being, might catalyse processes of deterritorialisation and becoming-minoritarian that could in turn change the balance of the existing democratic systems in the countries that compose the Global North. Braidotti asks, 'can one be European, Black [or Arab, Persian, or Asian] and Muslim?' (Braidotti 2006: 82). By 'fail[ing] to conform to the majoritarian standard' the increasing enfranchisement and participation of such a number of minority citizens into the society of a country could have the effect of 'extend[ing] the scope of the standard and thereby broaden[ing] the subject of democracy', both in qualitative and quantitative terms. This would have corresponding effects on both the 'institutions' and distribution of 'rights and duties' in the functioning of that society (Patton 2010a: 158).

Certainly the majoritarian political right in the Global North has had no problems envisioning this scenario. And so the Global North has either ignored, prevented, impeded or discouraged refugees and asylum seekers, regardless of their country's obligation to those who have fled persecution in their countries and cannot avail themselves of the protection of that country under international law. The practice of maintaining control over who is permitted through a nation-state's borders has long been a way in which even the most democratic of countries have historically exerted sovereignty over their territory. There is an important caveat, however: each of the 142 nations that are signatories to the 1951 United Nations Convention Relating to the Status of Refugees and its 1967 protocol are legally obliged to provide refugees with certain civil, political, economic, social and cultural rights and services, such as assistance and shelter. The principle of *non-refoulement*, which is at the heart of the Refugee Convention, prohibits the return of a refugee to a territory where his or her life may be threatened. Moreover, this principle means that a refugee seeking protection may not be refused entry to a country; this, despite being current policy in countries such as Australia, would amount to *refoulement* (UNHCR 2011: 5).

Thus, the shift that began in 2015 in naming those endeavouring to enter northern Europe 'migrants' rather than 'refugees' was not incidental. Neither 'migrant' nor 'refugee' is a neutral term. The term 'refugee', not unlike the term 'genocide', carries with it certain, very specific, very powerful legal obligations for most nation-states in the world. The act of naming those seeking asylum in northern Europe as 'migrants' releases a state from the obligations it would have to them as 'refugees' under international law. Migrants, or those who leave their countries of their own volition and for reasons other than to escape persecution, do not have the right to such protections.

Naming them migrants (the world now speaks of 'conflict-caused migration'), regardless of the term's dubious validity, changes the entire tenor of the problem from one of the Global North's legal obligation to refugees under international law to that of national responses to European immigration policies under the existing Schengen protocol. The effect of this appellative move is apparent when examining the discrepancy between Greece's wholesale reception of refugees on to its soil and the Global North's growing reluctance to allow these economic or conflict-caused 'migrants' on to theirs. Two further tactics succeeded and buttressed this renominative strategy: the determination of who was a 'worthy' refugee, and the deployment of the 'security' card.

In late 2015, in an attempt to stem the flow of refugees northward, northern Europe decided that only refugees from Iraq, Afghanistan and Syria would be allowed through the razor wire at Idomeni. Without processing refugee applications, how were they to determine that someone from South Sudan, or Somalia, Tunisia, Yemen, Libya or the Central African Republic is less deserving of refugee status than someone from Syria, Afghanistan or Iraq? Yet those who were not of the select three nationalities were not permitted to pass north into Macedonia. As it has done before, the spectre of an increasingly insecure future for all, where acts of mass violence might result from permitting refugees-cum-migrants-cum-foreign terrorists to enter their countries, was raised by many in the Global North. Subsequent terrorist attacks in Belgium, France and Germany were touted as proof of the correctness of this assertion. Angry calls went out from northern foreign ministers blaming Greek incompetence and negligence for putting them and the system in which they lived at risk. The beleaguered Greek minister of migration, Yiannis Mouzalas, responded: 'Greece can guard its borders perfectly and has been doing so for thousands of years, but against its enemies. The refugees are not our enemies' (Stamouli 2015).

Derrida admits that the unconditional hospitality he writes of, which 'is in advance open' to 'whomever arrives', to an 'absolutely foreign visitor' whose arrival is not foreseeable, who is neither expected or invited (Borradori 2003: 162), exposes the host to risk. As such, he believes it can have no conceivable juridical or political status; hospitality without conditions 'is irreconcilable with the very idea of a sovereign state' (Borradori 2003: 163). The hospitality that the signatories to the 1951 Convention on Refugees and its 1967 protocol extended, in advance and universally, to all who lack the protection of their own countries and are forced to flee in order to escape persecution is not unconditional hospitality. Admirable though these practices may be (even if often honoured in the breach), they are rather less conditional or more closely approaching unconditional hospitality than being examples of unconditional hospitality itself. Neither are the rights extended to refugees by the 1951 Convention and its 1967 protocol the actualisation of the rights of visitation included in Derrida's concept of pure hospitality. Applying exclusions – such as defining what counts as a refugee rather than an immigrant, or excluding those who have committed a grievous crime, pose a considerable security threat, or carry the threat of disease – signifies less than completely unconditional hospitality (Patton 2017). As such, it must be noted that the 1951 Refugee Convention and the 1967 protocol, even as they extend hospitality to many vulnerable people in the world, are also codifying forms of limited hospitality.

Even the hospitality that the first waves of refugees and the few whose asylum applications have been successfully processed enjoy should not be considered unconditional hospitality. Allowing only a small number of the total set of all existing refugees into their countries reveals the limits to the hospitality the Global North has extended. These low numerical limits reveal and further entrench existing thresholds of tolerance. They show the hospitality offered to be 'one-sided' and 'paternalistic'. They reveal the 'kernels of intolerance' (Borradori 2003: 41) upon which such limited hospitality is founded.

This was not the case in either the Kurdish region of Iraq or Greece. The unqualified welcome that the citizens of Dohuk and the Kurdish de facto state extended to the unannounced arrival of the persecuted Yezidis and to the massive influx of Syrians and Iraqis of all ethnicities, tribes, religions and regions shows that the Global North's insufficient and meagre offer of conditional hospitality to today's refugees is not the only option. In the months I worked there with the Iraqi Red Crescent Society, we saw a change in those needing assistance. It was not uncommon for one family in Dohuk to host twenty-five people. I visited one site behind a large housing project in the hills above Dohuk where one person, the property manager, was hosting over one hundred people. He was effectively running a small camp by himself. Paying close to a thousand dollars a week out of his own pocket to feed and shelter a community of people he had never met before, he approached the Iraqi Red Crescent Society seeking both technical and financial assistance. Refusing to evict the families they had taken in even though it meant that they and their families would go with less, as the months passed, soon Kurdish host families, as well as those displaced by DAESH alike, came to depend on external assistance for their survival.

Likewise, even though battered and impoverished by recent political events, the Greeks I worked alongside in the early months of 2016 (many of whom had not received a pay cheque in well over six months) who waded into the sea to meet thousands of boats of refugees, caring for and assisting them in their journey north, showed similar hospitality. Those who arrived on Kurdish and Greek soil were 'neither expected nor invited'; their arrival was 'unforeseeable' (Borradori 2003: 129). Asking no questions, regardless of the families' and states' relatively limited means and uncertain future, countless Kurds and Greeks gave 'the new arrival[s] all of [their] home[s] and [themselves] without asking a name, or compensation, or the fulfilment of even the smallest condition' (Derrida and Dufourmantelle 2000: 77).

Annabel McConnachie, specialist in human rights and International Relations at Sydney's Macquarie University, wonders if the comparisons between the Kurds who sheltered the Yezidis and the largely less welcoming response in Europe to the mass movement of people has more to do with the issue of identity. McConnachie notes that the Kurds are under attack from the same forces that are displacing the Yezidis. This imminent threat links the two groups and puts them on the same side of the conflict (McConnachie 2017). The sense of an identity based on having a common enemy may also heighten the sense of wanting to care for those displaced as a result of the conflict. The Yezidis are also Internally Displaced People, rather than asylum seekers or refugees. Although the Kurds control an area in northern Iraq, it has (at the international level) remained an autonomous area of Iraq rather than being recognised as a separate country (such as South Sudan, previously part of Sudan). Not only does this make a difference to the legal definitions, but McConnachie wonders if this means that situations are not so close as to be able to draw conclusions based on a comparison:

> The Yezidis form a coherent cohort of people facing a common plight. They are all facing the same form of persecution. Therefore, if you are able to identify (as a Kurd) with that persecution, you are able to identify with each and every Yezidi within the group. On the other hand, the situation in Europe is more complex. There are multiple states of origin: Syria, Afghanistan, Iraq, Yemen . . . And thus multiple sources of persecution or reasons for their exodus. The issue of 'mixed migration' is one which is increasingly being acknowledged as a complicating factor when there are mass movements of people. (McConnachie 2017)

McConnachie's observations are on target. And, were it not for the hospitality exhibited by the Hellenic state, which possesses none of the similarities or common identity with the refugees that the Kurds shared with the Yezidis, I might be inclined to alter my evaluation of Kurdish hospitality. Even if being able to identify with the Yezidi people does explain the unwavering hospitality the Kurds extended to the Yezidis (and to many Shia families who had previously fled the sectarian violence in other parts of Iraq), the Greek example stands as a paragon of hospitality. Some could argue that as few if any of the refugees wished to stay in Greece, seeking rather only to transit through to a better life in the North, this made it easier for Greece to be so hospitable. This might be true, but Greece's immediate neighbours along the route to the North which were not final destinations did not show such hospitality.

Perhaps the value of the concept of hospitality does not come only from the 'critical perspective' (Borradori 2003: 163) it gives on the tolerance and conditional hospitality being extended to a limited number of refugees today. It is important to highlight that the Kurdish and Greek examples show that wholesale hospitality can and is being extended to the unexpected foreigner – the wholly other. It is true that the nature of the becomings that an event, whether occurring by degree or suddenly, engenders in a society cannot be known in advance. Once unsettled, societies can potentially resettle, become reterritorialised, in a variety of ways. Instead of bringing about a more inclusive becoming-democratic in the countries of the Global North, the event of the global refugee crisis seems rather to have energised the right and catalysed the coalescence of pre-existing, formerly marginal, hyper-nationalist, xenophobic, racist, protectionist and insular factions into the mainstream. For those who can envision and strive to bring about post-nationalist sociopolitical spaces, such as Rosi Braidotti and Simone Bignall, the outlook appears much more grim than it did in 2014.

Combining a Derridean-infused sense of hospitality with the vectors that Patton suggests could fill out Deleuze and Guattari's concept of becoming-democratic would open not only the conceptual way, but the minds, hearts, doors and borders that are currently keeping millions of refugees out of the Global North. So combined, a becoming-hospitable could contribute to bringing about a becoming-minoritarian and thus a becoming-democratic in the Global North. Two million conflict-displaced persons are living in Kurdistan (*Rudaw* 2016) and more than a million refugees passed through Greece in 2015–16, all of whom arrived 'unannounced' and 'unforeseen'. It seems conceivable that the practices of hospitality that the Greeks and Kurds have extended to so many foreigners could contribute to processes of becoming-minoritarian that could alter or transform the 'affects, beliefs, and political sensibilities' of both the Greek and Kurdish population and institutions. Certainly, the extremely limited hospitality the Global North has shown to date suggests that those on the right in countries such as the United States, Australia and Denmark can see the potential for processes leading to societal transformation that providing an unlimited welcome to today's refugees might bring.

However, with a concept of hospitality that more closely approaches unconditional or pure hospitality as a fourth or supplementary vector, the concept of becoming-democratic may be more capable of acting upon the kernels of intolerance found in the conditional hospitality of current refugee policies. Introducing hospitality as a vector of becoming-democratic shifts the concept from a domestic sense of democracy in a cosmopolitan direction. It may better equip the concept of becoming-democratic as a dynamism to convey force to and produce changes in the political sensibilities of the conservative, mainstream citizens of the Global North whose 'will' is being expressed through their government's policies. Even though unconditional hospitality is impossible to realise, it could serve as a 'pole or basin of attraction' that could call for or support claims to make existing forms of hospitality less conditional than they currently are. Put thus, it reads as 'functionally equivalent', albeit in a very different 'conceptual frame', to a Deleuzian idea of becoming-hospitable (Patton 2017). The changes that a more cosmopolitan concept of becoming-democratic would bring to current refugee policies would be felt immediately, especially by those who are living in off-shore 'processing' centres such as Nauru or Manus Island, or camped in the shadows of northern Europe's gates. The concept of becoming-democratic does not only help us quantify and qualify the ways in which the global refugee crisis has catalysed a becoming-less democratic in the Global North. If a concept of becoming-democratic that included a sense of hospitality more closely approaching unconditional hospitality were brought to bear on this ongoing event it could inform 'the perceptions and therefore the actions' (Patton 2010a: 155) of both citizens and the processes in the Global North concerned with the global refugee crisis. This in turn could precipitate a becoming-minoritarian, and thus a more cosmopolitan becoming-democratic, in the world.

Braidotti's project to construct a post-nationalist sociopolitical European space calls for a European becoming-ethical (Braidotti 2006). I would conclude this essay by proposing that such a becoming-ethical, in the form of international humanitarian action, has been occurring for the past century and a half. Arguably, a becoming-humanitarian began on a June day in 1859 when the Swiss businessman, Henry Dunant, came upon thousands of wounded soldiers on the battlefield of Solferino. Together with nearby townspeople, Dunant spent the next days tending to the wounded with no regard as to which side of the Franco-Sardinian/Austrian conflict they had fought on (Dunant 1986). This event led to the formation of the International Red Cross and Red Crescent movements; and later to the various Geneva Conventions, and to bodies of international humanitarian, refugee and human rights laws; as well as engendering what we know today as humanitarian action. Though the actualisations of humanitarianism (for example, organisations, agencies, their personnel and actions) are commonly misrepresented as charity and regularly (and at times rightly) flayed in the press for their inefficiencies and failures, I contend that humanitarian action and humanitarianism are a form of becoming-ethical that share much in common with Braidotti's post-nationalist vision.

Humanitarianism is not only an expression of international solidarity, it is an ethics that assesses disaster- and conflict-affected people's situations and ways of being in the world and actively works to save lives and prevent and alleviate suffering. Humanitarianism endeavours to protect the lives and health of vulnerable peoples around the world, and to do so voluntarily, neutrally, independently, with no discrimination as to nationality, race, religious beliefs, class or political opinions. Guided solely by the needs of those affected by disaster or conflict, priority is given to the most urgent cases of distress. Importantly, becoming-humanitarian is an 'ethics of refusal': humanitarianism refuses to accept the world system as it is currently ordered and endeavours to mitigate the effects of its most egregious failings. Affirming the value of all human life equally, humanitarian action expresses civil society's refusal to accept either political failures or 'active or passive assault[s] on the other' (Orbinski 1999). Acting often in spaces of political failure, humanitarianism refuses to displace the responsibility of states, but rather calls on states both to assume their responsibilities and to transform their ways of being.

Composed of a 'messy' assemblage of principles and actions, actors and activities, treaties and laws, individuals, states, institutions and civil society organisations, governmental, non-governmental and inter-governmental organisations, humanitarianism is both a network and a system. The becoming-humanitarian occurring in the world – that is, the growing sensitivity to disaster- and conflict-affected people's distress and the corresponding endeavours to prevent and alleviate their suffering neutrally, independently and impartially – like all becomings, has not been 'deliberately engineered'. It has been evolving 'organically', heterogeneously, over the past century and a half (Stoddard et al. 2015). Humanitarianism operates in a contradictory sociopolitical space. Contradictory, because it operates precisely because the post-national sociopolitical space Braidotti calls for does not yet exist; and because it operates in that space as if it did exist. As a concept, becoming-humanitarian connects with the people and processes seeking to assist those in distress in much the same manner that the concept of becoming-democratic can link up with and inform the perceptions and actions of those involved in existing processes of deterritorialisation (Patton 2010a: 155). In the context of refugee movements,[8] the affirmation of the equal value of all lives expressed through humanitarian action can effectively be read as extending the domestic egalitarianism of contemporary liberal democracies into the international sphere (Patton 2017). This shows a certain cosmopolitanism to be common to both concepts.

By providing shelter or protection or food, humanitarians establish a human's right to be sheltered, to be safe in home and body, to be nourished. . . Becoming-humanitarian creates, calls into existence, particular, context-specific rights and ways of being in the world that maximise the power and possibilities of life. Acting in a post-nationalist sociopolitical space that does not exist – because it does not exist – becoming-humanitarian, much like the becoming-minoritarian Braidotti calls for, is actively engaged in bringing this space into existence. Whether expressed in Cox's Bazar, Bangladesh, the Greek island of Lesvos, or Dohuk, Kurdistan, humanitarian actions show the connection between humanitarianism and egalitarian, hospitable cosmopolitan versions of democracy. In response to the question 'What it means to be on the Left?' Deleuze noted that, as 'justice doesn't exist, [the] "rights of man" do not exist'; being on the left means to 'act for freedom' in response to particular 'abominable cases' (Deleuze and Parnet 2004: 39). The areas of consonance common to humanitarianism and egalitarian, hospitable and cosmopolitan versions of democracy are visible when UN agencies, international and national NGOs, the Red Cross movement and governments alike act to ensure and protect each and every life equally. Indeed, I would argue that these are acts of cosmopolitan jurisprudence on the part of international civil society. The community-based, participatory approach to consulting with disaster- or conflict-affected people as to what is most needed and involving them in every stage of programme design and delivery exemplifies the case-by-case 'jurisprudence' favoured by Deleuze. Expressed in every humanitarian action, the humanitarian imperative effectively establishes the 'rights of life' of each and every life equally.[9] Humanitarianism, as an extension of international civil society, effectively brings those 'rights of life' into existence, thereby creating, inventing the law. By acting impartially, neutrally, independently and with little regard for borders, humanitarianism is in effect extending an egalitarian, hospitable and cosmopolitan version of democracy to the most vulnerable.

Though its end-state is unknown, the becoming-humanitarian that has taken place in the world can be identified by the distance travelled and the changes in processes, systems, attitudes and actions that have occurred since the event of Solferino. The becoming of becoming-humanitarian is evinced in a greater concern throughout the world for the well-being of the most vulnerable. Becoming-humanitarian is the mounting processes in the world that endeavour to remove that which most negatively impinges the material and affective capacities of disaster- and conflict-affected people. It does so, so that they can more fully realise what Spinoza via Deleuze might term their *vis existendi* and *potentia agendi*, their force of existing and power of acting (Deleuze 1988: 97–104): their capacity to affect the world and be affected by the world. Becoming-humanitarian is the change in those humanitarian processes so that they are more impartial, less influenced by foreign policy, more respectful of culture and custom; so that humanitarians build on local capacities, and to a greater degree hold themselves accountable to, recognise the dignity of, and involve beneficiaries in programme development and management of relief aid (IFRC 1998). This becoming-humanitarian causes people not only to actively and voluntarily seek out those living unseen, precarious existences (regardless of whether they are located in the plains of Darfur, the mountains of Afghanistan, or camping before the gates of Europe or in the depths of Calais), often at great personal risk and with few customary comforts. It seeks to enhance the power, capacities and possibilities of life of people they have never met – the 'wholly other'. For this, some policy analysts consider that 'humanitarians are the last of the just' (Rieff 2002: 333).

Like all becomings, becoming-humanitarian is fraught with perils both individual and collective. Acts against the very space that humanitarianism is striving to create, such as the bombing of an aid convoy in Syria and of hospitals in Afghanistan, Yemen and Syria, and the murder of Red Cross volunteers in the Central African Republic, are actively eroding the right to give and receive humanitarian assistance even while international humanitarian aid workers are trying to protect and create that right. Even the success of humanitarian interventions contains the spectre of possible failure. This is evident today as the Global North endeavours (with some success) to co-opt humanitarian organisations into co-managing the misery (Orbinski 1999) of millions of refugees along with them. Contested as it is, if this becoming even partially succeeds in making this a more just world, it will represent the legitimacy of international civil society, informal but no less real, and the global role it can play in creating the very human rights it is seeking to defend.

Humanitarianism and philosophy have the not unrelated and equally Sisyphean task of bringing new, more just ways of being into a world affected by and in the thrall of global terror. Incorporating hospitality as a vector in the concept of becoming-democratic shifts the concept in a cosmopolitan direction and into proximity with both egalitarian and hospitable versions of democracy and international humanitarian action. Applying the concepts of becoming-democratic and becoming-humanitarian to the people, practices and conflicting processes engaged in the global refugee crisis could positively change the reality and future of the millions of people living in refugee camps before the gates of the Global North. It also could bring about a becoming-hospitable, becoming-minoritarian and ultimately a more cosmopolitan becoming-democratic in societies whose doors, instead of opening to the foreign others who are arriving, are rather slamming shut. The increased spread of becoming-humanitarian and the practices of hospitality being extended to so many strangers throughout the world shows us that though it is running short, there is yet time. *Alea nondum iacta est . . .*

Notes

1. DAESH is the Arabic language acronym for the Islamic State of Iraq and the Levant (ISIL), also known as the Islamic State (IS) and the Islamic State of Iraq and Syria (ISIS).
2. The Yezidis are an ethno-religious Kurdish group living principally in the Nineveh province of Iraq. Their religious practices have links with Zoroastrianism, among other ancient Mesopotamian religions.
3. It was commonly 47° Celsius/116° Fahrenheit at 7 p.m., with midday temperatures in excess of that.
4. I use the term 'Global North' to refer to and incorporate the responses of the United States, Canada, Australia and New Zealand to the global refugee crisis with that of northern Europe. Though non-contiguous with Europe, each of these four countries could host many refugees and would be acceptable destinations to most. The term Global North indicates the unequal divide in prosperity and well-being that exists between former colonial and former colonised countries, which has been continued, albeit in a different form, and exacerbated by globalisation. Global North indicates that the divide these refugees seek to traverse is almost an exact replica of the colonial divide, and thus could be considered a neocolonial divide. With the semi-exception of Canada, which has welcomed approximately 39,000 refugees (with much fanfare), these countries, given the scale of the refugee crisis and their capacities, have allowed a relatively paltry number of refugees into their countries. Australia has received approximately 3,500 refugees, the US has received approximately 10,000 refugees, New Zealand has increased the number of refugees it will take every year from 750 to 1000, while Germany has taken in over one million refugees, and 163,000 sought asylum in Sweden in 2015. As these numbers indicate, the response to the refugee crisis has not been homogeneous between countries. Grouping them into the Global North risks papering over the very real differences in response to the refugee crisis that exist among European countries and the US, Canada, Australia and New Zealand. That being said, the term 'Global North' also indicates, despite the variation, the general and overwhelming insufficiency of the response of these countries given their capacities. See Kirk 2016; Migrationsverket 2016; Garza 2015; Board 2016; Lum 2016.
5. Deleuze and Guattari refer to becoming-democratic only once, in *What is Philosophy?* (1996: 113).
6. Deleuze refers to such intrusions of becoming as 'gust[s] of the real in its pure state' (Deleuze and Parnet 2004: 41).
7. That is not to say that the number of refugees allowed into some countries in northern Europe has been insignificant, especially not in the case of Germany or Sweden.
8. An example is the humanitarian assistance and protection provided in 2017 to over 420,000 Rohingya people who fled 'ethnic cleansing' in Myanmar and sought refuge in neighbouring Bangladesh.

9. The humanitarian imperative extends the principle of humanity (to prevent and alleviate human suffering wherever it may be found) to include the right to provide and receive assistance.

References

Board, E. (2016), 'America Has Accepted 10,000 Syrian Refugees. That's Still Too Few', *The Washington Post*, 2 September.

Borradori, G. (2003), *Philosophy in a Time of Terror: Dialogues with Jürgen Habermas and Jacques Derrida*, Chicago: University of Chicago Press.

Braidotti, R. (2006), 'The Becoming-Minoritarian of Europe', in I. Buchanan and A. Parr (eds), *Deleuze and the Contemporary World*, Edinburgh: Edinburgh University Press, pp. 79–94.

Cumming-Bruce, N. (2016), '"Worst Annual Death Toll Ever": Mediterranean Claims 5,000 Migrants', *The New York Times*, 23 December.

Deleuze, G. (1988), *Spinoza: Practical Philosophy*, San Francisco: City Lights.

Deleuze, G., and F. Guattari (1987), *A Thousand Plateaus: Capitalism and Schizophrenia*, trans. B. Massumi, Minneapolis: University of Minnesota Press.

Deleuze, G., and F. Guattari (1996), *What is Philosophy?*, trans. H. Tomlinson and G. Burchell, New York: Columbia University Press.

Deleuze, G., and C. Parnet (2004), *L'Abécédaire de Gilles Deleuze, avec Claire Parnet*, Paris: DVD Editions Montparnasse.

Derrida, J., and A. Dufourmantelle (2000), *Of Hospitality: Anne Dufourmantelle Invites Jacques Derrida to Respond*, Stanford: Stanford University Press.

Dunant, H. (1986 [1862]), *A Memory of Solferino*, Geneva: International Committee of the Red Cross.

Garza, F. (2015), 'Germany is Taking in More Refugees in 2015 than the US Has in the Past 10 Years', *Quartz*, 7 December, <https://qz.com/567469/germany-is-taking-in-more-refugees-in-2015-than-the-us-has-in-the-past-10-years/> (last accessed 6 June 2022).

IFRC (1998), Code of Conduct, International Federation of Red Cross and Red Crescent Societies.

Kirk, S. (2016), 'New Zealand Refugee Quota Upped to 1000 – "stinks of a Government that doesn't care" say advocates', *Stuff*, 13 June, <https://www.stuff.co.nz/national/politics/81001002/new-zealand-to-take-1000-refugees-each-year> (last accessed 6 June 2022).

Lum, Z.-A. (2016), '"Pay It Forward": Canada Resettles Nearly 39,000 Syrian Refugees', *The Huffington Post*, 24 December, <https://www.huffpost.com/archive/ca/entry/syrian-refugees-in-canada_n_13822554> (last accessed 6 June 2022).

McConnachie, A. (2017), personal communication, 29 March.

Migrationsverket (2016), 'Nearly 163,000 Sought Asylum in Sweden in 2015', Migrationsverket, <https://www.migrationsverket.se/English/About-the-Migration-Agency/Statistics/Asylum.html> (last accessed 6 June 2022).

Nordland, R. (2016), 'Afghanistan Itself is Now Taking in the Most Afghan Migrants', *The New York Times*, 4 November 4.

OCHA (2014), 'Iraq: Humanitarian Dashboard (as of 29 July 2014)', Office for the Coordination of Humanitarian Affairs, <https://reliefweb.int/report/iraq/iraq-humanitarian-dashboard-29-june-2014> (last accessed 6 June 2022).

Orbinski, J. (1999), 'Médecins Sans Frontières – Nobel Lecture', The Norwegian Nobel Committee, <https://www.msf.org/nobel-peace-prize-speech> (last accessed 6 June 2022).

Parr, A. (2010), 'Becoming + Performance Art', in A. Parr (ed.), *The Deleuze Dictionary: Revised Edition*, Edinburgh: Edinburgh University Press, pp. 29–31.

Patton, P. (2010a), *Deleuzian Concepts: Philosophy, Colonization, Politics*, Stanford: Stanford University Press.

Patton, P. (2010b), 'Deterritorialization + Politics', in A. Parr (ed.), *The Deleuze Dictionary: Revised Edition*, Edinburgh: Edinburgh University Press, pp. 72–4.

Patton, P. (2017), personal communication, 6 August.

Riding, A. (1991), 'French Right Hits a Nerve with Immigration Plan', *The New York Times*, 24 November.

Rieff, D. (2002), *A Bed for the Night: Humanitarianism in Crisis*, New York: Simon and Schuster.

Rudaw (2016), 'KRG Rejects Iraqi Minister's Data on IDP Numbers in Kurdistan', *Rudaw*, 12 November, <https://www.rudaw.net/english/middleeast/iraq/1211 2016> (last accessed 6 June 2022).

Squires, N. (2017), 'Refugees and Migrants are Dying at the Gates of Europe as Heavy Snow Hits the Balkans and Greece, UN Warns', *Daily Telegraph*, 13 January.

Stagoll, C. (2010), 'Becoming', in A. Parr (ed.), *The Deleuze Dictionary: Revised Edition*, Edinburgh: Edinburgh University Press, pp. 25–7.

Stamouli, N. (2015), 'Greek Minister Rejects Criticism over Allowing Transit of Migrants', *The Wall Street Journal*, 25 October.

Stoddard, A., A. Harmer, K. Haver, G. Taylor and P. Harvey (2015), *The State of the Humanitarian System*, London: Active Learning Network for Accountability and Performance (ALNAP).

UNHCR (2011), *The 1951 Convention Relating to the Status of Refugees and its 1967 Protocol*, Geneva: United Nations High Commissioner for Refugees.

UNHCR (2016a), 'Europe Refugee Emergency: Daily Map Indicating Capacity and Occupancy (Governmental Figures)', Geneva: United Nations High Commissioner for Refugees.

UNHCR (2016b), *Global Trends: Forced Displacement in 2015*, Geneva: United Nations High Commissioner for Refugees.

UNHCR (2016c), *UNHCR Turkey: Key Facts and Figures, November 2016*, Geneva: United Nations High Commissioner for Refugees.

Chapter 5

Suicided by *A Life*: Deleuze, Terror and the Search for the 'Middle Way'

S. Romi Mukherjee

The Interval

Any critical assessment of a philosopher must begin with the question of what they are afraid of. What constitutes the traumatic core that the thinker registers and repudiates (*Verleugnung*), only to evacuate from the site of the writerly? The oeuvres of Deleuze and Guattari enchant and enthrall in their indefatigable commitment to a politics of radical affirmation, one which aspired, in a systematic manner, to rid philosophy of its dark spot, of dialectics and of negativity *tout court*. Yet in the protracted line of flight that shoots through their corpora, one evinces how they inexorably strained, with the grimmest of determination, to occupy the plane of immanence (the axiomatic concept) and joyously proliferate its landscapes with all that emphatically proclaimed 'yes' to 'A Life'. However, forever poised to pervert the plane of immanence and its pre-subjective singularities is the hauntology of the negative – those ambient traces of psychic, epistemological and all too real forms of terror (all that which 'makes tremble'). Stated otherwise, a death is a death and much more than, to pastiche Deleuze's reading of Spinoza, a mode of decomposition, or rest, in the flux of the composite assemblage of simple bodies and substance.

Deleuze's desire to liberate us from the cult of death and the sad passions is among the noblest of contemporary philosophical enterprises. But it was one which was ill equipped to engage with all that resonated under 'A Life', or rather the tragic dimensions of life itself, our lives and 'theirs'. As Maria Nicheterlein and John R. Morss remark, 'for Deleuze May 68 was an example of how reality cuts through the ideologies' (2017: 5). What interests us is how, on the one hand, recent cycles of terrorism and violence demonstrate how 'ideologies' invade and obliterate 'reality', and, on the other hand, how transcendental empiricism, desiring politics, schizoanalysis et al. must grapple with innocent suffering, and the realities of the catastrophe and the catastrophe to come. Nonetheless, we remain Deleuzian. We too side with 'A Life'. We too side with becoming over Being. We too refuse to join the ranks of those who Terry Eagleton excoriates as those 'acolytes of the Real . . . liminal creatures, pure incarnations of Thanatos' (2009: 152). But one need not be an incarnation of Thanatos to recognise the presence of the Real, that which 'remains in the shadows' (Lacan 2006: 31), but is always there, 'returning to the same place' (Lacan 1966: 25). Hence, we aspire to temper the bliss achieved in pure immanence with a dose of pessimism, one which does not foreclose the possibility of 'A Life', but attempts to understand the journey there as one bound up in, following Winnicott, our 'going-on-being' or our capacity to withstand and outlast the fear of annihilation, from within and beyond.

Some see correspondences between Deleuze's conceptual landscape and that of Buddhism. According to Sylvère Lotringer, if French theory were to have a religious unconscious, one would surely find Derrida as the Jew, Lacan as the Catholic (with Bataille hovering in the wings) and Deleuze as the Buddhist (Lotringer 1999; see also O'Sullivan 2014; See and Bradley 2017). But Buddhism was never 'pure immanence'. Indeed, the corpse, the accident, the malady and the catastrophe are precisely where Buddhism begins in its march towards 'no-self' and 'no-thing'. For Timothy Morton, the dilemma in thinking Deleuze-Buddha is found in Deleuze's sealing off of the plane of immanence, where 'there is no lack: there is "not even nothing" in such a world' (Morton 2015: 201). Terror is the traumatic kernel that resonates underneath being's 'going on' and also the 'excess' that flanks the habitus of the bourgeois liberal lifeworld. Terror introduces lack and untenability into 'the system'. It is the intractable threat of the accident . . . a sustained *il y a*, the broken Other, broken object and broken world. Deleuze's sealing off of the plane of immanence valiantly tries to shut out this outside (from where death comes). As such, Deleuze's crypto-Buddhism and refusal of no-thing and lack betray, perhaps, the most important of Buddhist precepts, namely that of the 'Middle Way'. Here, Nāgārjuna refuses both ontology and nihilism: '"It exists" is an eternalist view: "It does not exist" is an annihilationist idea. Therefore the wise one should not have recourse to either existence or nonexistence' (Nāgārjuna 2013: 16). We are thus compelled to ask what it would mean to occupy the space, or Middle Way, between 'pure immanence' and terror or the undulations of the Real. What implications would this gap or interval have on Deleuze and Guattari's disavowal of no-thing, lack and violence (sacrificial, suicidal, symbolic etc.)? Is there a Middle Way between the affirmations of 'A Life' and the substrate of death and anxiety that traverse contemporary geopolitics and the everyday? In taking these questions as our point of departure, we attempt to reread and recast the Deleuzo-Guattarian *dispositif*, its historicity, its personae and its images of thought, not with a view to bringing its authors any sadness (as Deleuze would never want that. . .), but rather in order to open up 'the middle' as a space of possibility for new Deleuzian theoretical interventions, interpellations and vexations.

Shadows

The lives of Deleuze and Guattari were both marked by death and litanies of personal terror. In addition, they were symptoms of the most harrowing of generational traumas. Born respectively in 1925 and 1930, they were the children of the crisis of civilisation that marked the *entre deux-guerre*, children of its rabid reactionary politics, and children of an epochal twilight, whose paroxysm was Vichy. Their future union and the incarnation of what François Dosse calls 'The Third Man' was an intrepid melding and line of flight out of the tremors of private and sociopolitical brushes with finitude. Plenum against lack, affirmation against the dialectic, schizflux machinics against the ossifications of the oedipal, the rhizome against the tree, immanence against transcendence, joy against the sad passions – all themes and variations on the Third Man's intransigent counter-blitz against the vicissitudes of impermanence and the misfortunes of history. The Third Man may have been an osmotic composite of various philosophical *surhommes*, but he was also shadowed by anxiety, poor health and decidedly non-Dionysian moods. Perhaps they never ceased in their entirely justified assailing of the bad faith of certain strains of psychoanalysis, but the conceptual topography that they imagined and inhabited was where they searched for 'home'. It was also a domain of implicit auto-analysis and therapy.

Deleuze's father would frequent the Croix de Feu, an extreme-right Catholic league of First World War veterans. They played in the hazy interstices between radicalised nationalism and 'French fascism'. And as Deleuze recounts in *L'Abécédaire*, following the Blum government's 1936 tabling of a bill granting every French worker, employee or apprentice 15 days of paid holiday per year, his father recoiled at the site of the proles on the beach. Another shadow was cast, that of Deleuze's older brother: George Deleuze was a member of the French Resistance. He was arrested by the Gestapo, only to die while being transported to a concentration camp. Deleuze's family would mourn by creating a veritable cult around the older brother, thus relegating the younger Gilles to the 'not good enough son'. As Dosse observes, George would 'disappear from the horizon', but remain all too present in Gilles' nascent inferiority complex (Dosse 2007: 112). In surmounting the complex, Deleuze would respond to his brother's heroism with the heroes of affirmation who glided across the plane of immanence, forever in combat against death and the dialectic.

Guattari was not immune to the spasms of death and dying either. According to Dosse, from an early age he was besieged by oedipal anxieties and a constant feeling of homelessness. Furthermore, in 1939, just as France began to prepare for war, Guattari would witness the accidental death of his grandfather, which, following Dosse, was nothing short of a 'brutal contact with death', a trauma that it would take years to confront, a seism, instilling in Guattari 'a severe crises of anxiety, a sharp sense of finitude and the futility of things' (Dosse 2007: 36–7). Guattari would eventually find a home at La Clinique de La Borde and in the nascent environs of institutional psychiatry. He would further 'work through' his anxieties in his dual-pronged attack on the oedipal onslaughts of capitalism and psychoanalysis. Yet even as he matured, he remained haunted by paternal imagos (Dosse 2007: 41) and found himself, once again, prone to anxiety and 'political depression' after the betrayals of Mitterandism and the French left. And so commenced the 'winter years', when the once tireless political militant found himself in a catatonic state, slumped before the TV, with a pillow on his stomach as if to protect himself from the outside world (Dosse 2007: 489). Perhaps, death, real or political, does really come from the outside. . .

May 68, for both Deleuze and Guattari, was the delirium of history or the moment when the material conditions of society and a collective social dream merged. The political had been rediscovered. May 68, 'an irruption, a becoming in its pure state', was Deleuze's initiation into politics (Deleuze 1990a: 230–1). For Guattari it was the birth of 'a politics of the molecular which constituted a dimension of interrogation of the relationships between subjectivity, the body, time, work, sexuality and the problems of daily life' (Guattari 1995a: 3–4). *La Pensée 68* was, however, also haunted by what we could call *La Pensée 38* (with the Munich Pact as allegorical image). Yet in the 'becoming', a tabula rasa presented itself. May 68, a liberating ritual and the desublimation of social energies, was intent on returning the modern subject back to a domain of unmediated desire, one which the students simultaneously likened to the pre-Symbolic of Lacan, the Eden of Rousseau and the pre-oedipal of Marcuse. *Anti-Oedipus*, of course, was May 68's intellectual apotheosis, but despite the vectors of the new desiring politics, one wonders if the 'paternal' *and* 'fraternal' imagos could ever really be overcome?

Situating Deleuze and Guattari intellectually and historically requires that we acknowledge their desire also to seal off the latent psycho-political content of the 1930s, which they were born into. Or, to put it otherwise, 1938 is the sombre political unconscious of the effervescence of May 68. According to Jean-Louis Loubet del Bayle, the children of the 1930s were bearers of 'international instability, interior difficulty, economic, social, and spiritual disorder – these were only signs of the much more general and more profound *crises of civilization*' (Loubet del Bayle 1969: 269). The crisis was therefore not understood in purely economic or political terms, but rather as a crisis of Man, his conscience, his mastery, his will and his, potentially arbitrary, institutions. Civilisation at its modern apex was understood as a state of deprivation – the deprivation of dreams, the deprivation of desires and the deprivation of destiny – all of which would be rediscovered in 1968. Negativity is not simply a philosophical category, but also a historical one. And 1968 is also beleaguered by the negativity of the future (Paris, 2015). This is not say, of course, that history is dialectical. Perhaps it is a movement of dark and light, and darker and lighter, in a demiurgic going to the end, wherein affirmation is but a natural and needed response.

Persona non grata

The antinomy between 1938 and 1968 is also the antinomy between two radically divergent theoretical loci and two absolutely dissonant thinkers: in the genealogy of contemporary French philosophy, Bataille and Deleuze emerge as the great purveyors of immanence, the dissolution of the self and its ontologies, the breakdown of subject/object, the ultimate razing of the all-too-burdensome categories of Being, and the concomitant neurosis of analogical thought. Deleuze had little time for Bataille and, in private, he never ceased to lambast the reproduction of death and the erotics of violence that typified the work of 'The Priest'. As Etienne Turpin remarks, Bataille, for Deleuze, was 'conceptual persona non-grata'. In *Dialogues* Deleuze would more soberly assess Bataille's legacy and remark,

> transgression, a concept too good for seminarians under the law of the Pope or the priest . . . Bataille is a very French author. He made the secret the essence of literature, with a mother within, a priest beneath, and an eye above. It is impossible to emphasize the harm that this phantasm has done to writing. . . (Deleuze and Parnet 1987: 47)

Done with the dialectic of law/transgression/*jouissance*, Deleuze would rhapsodise on flows, fluxes and the infinity of desire. To French 'depth', Deleuze would sing the praises of Anglo-American surfaces. Contra the priest, one would learn the overman. Against mummy–daddy–me, an emancipated nomadic subject would auto-create a New Earth. And beyond the eye above, we would be reconciled to the horizontal smoothness of the Body without Organs and the oscillations of imperceptible affect. The phantasm, though, was not simply Bataille's syphilitic and blind father, left to burn in the childhood home, nor the witnessing of the destruction of Notre Dame de Reims, its spire plunging into the ground. For Bataille, the phantasm was the truth of our animality, inner violence and longing for orgiastic annihilation. The phantasm was immanence, the experience of death before death. It was terror and the fiery opacity of the sacred as total negativity. Bataille and Deleuze both searched for the pre-subjective and the pre-symbolic. Both rallied against transcendental morality. But they had different ways of getting to immanence, different 'techniques' for its achievement. Deleuze would return to the earth as a space to be decreated and recreated. Bataille would take us to the chthonian forces that rumbled underneath. Deleuze's temporality of the virtual and odes to Aeon projected us to a space outside the dialectic (a time beyond time). Bataille plunged us back to the archaic trace that forms the substrate of human project(s), the violence always/already there and ready to explode in a time before time, labour and reification. And de facto, the battle against Lacan was also a battle against the true progenitor of the Lacanian Real – Bataille.

Following from this, immanence, as the dissolution of the 'I', can be tragic and terrifying or life-affirming and productive. Stated otherwise, we must contrast he who confesses that

> my own actions annihilate me, opening a void within me, a void *to which I am subordinated*. Nevertheless, I survive this alteration by binding ties of immanence . . . I have shown nothing except the necessity of forming these connections, to shatter the limit of *the possible* in one moment. A bond of immanence demands a preliminary laceration from the transcendent system of activity: such as stripping someone bare, childbirth, putting to death. . . (Bataille 2001: 87–8)

from he who he says that immanence

> is A LIFE and nothing else. It is not immanence to life, but the immanent that is in nothing is itself a life. A life is the immanence of immanence: it is complete power, complete bliss . . . it is absolute immediate consciousness whose very activity no longer refers to a being but is ceaselessly posed in

life ... What is immanence? A life ... the life of the individual gives way to an impersonal and yet singular life that releases a pure event freed from the accidents of internal and external life, that is, from the subjectivity and objectivity of what happens. ... (Deleuze 1995: 4)

Hence, with Bataille, we glimpse a non-dialectical nature/totality which drains, expends and becomes unemployed negativity. However, what characterised these currents of unemployed negativity were their strict rapport with trajectories of loss and death – or the culmination of erotic (religious) desire as dissipation, and religion as the liminal passage between the human and the inhuman. For Bataille, immanence is that which never happens. While, with Deleuze, we apprehend 'a plane', 'A Life' and a pure power (bliss) that know nothing of terror. Perhaps, also that which never happens.

Is there a middle way? Perhaps not. But one could 'affirm', as Michael Eigen does, that 'Bliss catches up with torment, although torment never ends. Torment is a tunnel bliss passes through ... bliss and torment become part of each other, not split apart. Bliss ↔ torment. Separate ↔ interweaving. Rhythmic back-and-forth. States of fusion ↔ antagonism. Blocked ↔ flowing' (Eigen 2001: 45). This more nuanced psychoanalytic approach collapses Bataille's 'impossible' and all nostalgia for unmediated impossible animality and total fusion. It also problematises the Deleuzo-Guattarian injunction to unblock *all* the flows. The 'blocked' may become a paranoid site of self-control, but it may also simply 'hold us together'. Thus, if Bataille overcomes the antagonism in orgiastic dissolution and tragic laceration, Deleuze flees it in the nomad's escape out of 'the tunnel'.

Transmutations

Bataille was instrumental in coming to the rescue of Nietzsche during the interwar years. Deleuze too would go on to develop a left-Nietzscheanism following the Second World War, but one which was manifestly less subterranean, sacrificial and *acéphalic*. And disabused of the fascination with the sacred and the 'fiery', it was a 'left-Nietzscheanism' which would never flirt with the possibility of a 'left-fascism'. On the one hand, *Nietzsche and Philosophy* functions as a hagiographic account of quintessential Zarathustran topoi: the heroic overcoming of pessimism, interiority and the melancholic charm of the ascetic; the unravelling of the fictions of the self/human/identity within the infinite becomings of the eternal return; the exploding of stratified segmentarity (state, family, master, priest, school, job etc.); the revealing of the non-sense of suffering and pain; the dissolving of the forces of *ressentiment* and reactivity; the recoding of the will to power as affective *potentia* as opposed to desire to subjugate; and the rejecting of tragic fatalism in favour of chance and the dice-throw. On the other hand, the crucial intervention of the text is found in its relentless attack against Hegelianism and the dialectic as philosophical, political and psychic *dispositif*. Against these scourges of theory, Deleuze posits a 'non-dialectical negation' which is not really negation at all, but the entrance into the sovereign (dependent on nothing, existing in and of itself, for itself) reign of affirmation. Hence,

> only affirmation subsists as an independent power; the negative shoots out from it like lightning, but also becomes absorbed into it, disappearing like soluble fire ... there is no other power, but affirmation ... affirmation constitutes becoming-active as the universal becoming of forces ... at the moment of transmutation, negation is dissipated ... Nietzsche announces the Dionysian affirmation that no negation can defile. (Deleuze 1983a: 176–7)

Dionysos is this metamorphosis which bursts the dialectic itself and empties the plane of all traces of negativity and nothingness. The affirmative operation is total, totalising and beyond reification. There is no outside nor excess, or as Michael Hardt asserts, 'it must constitute an absolutely destructive negation that spares nothing from its force and recuperates nothing from its enemy' (Hardt 1990: 28). The plane is closed and thrust into a nether region which knows nothing of no-thing and affirms endlessly into the future. Here, we squint to see that distant bridge that pushes the human to overcome itself. However, in sealing off the plane, Deleuze refuses the duality or interval that marks the Dionysian, or the manner in which any invocation of the Bull God is the simultaneous reckoning with negativity *and* affirmation, with terror *and* bliss.

The task of Dionysos, Deleuze tells us, is to relate 'the negative to affirmation in the will to power' (1983a: 193) and produce 'negativity as negativity of the positive' (1983a: 198). While Dionysos does signify the alchemical process through which the spectres of finitude are transformed into ecstasy, he, like the ecstatic, also has another task. He is also the incarnation of the negative and the negative *as terror*, or the tensor between reason and madness, form and non-form, system and excess, masculine and feminine, dark and light, the city and nature, nomos and anomie, sobriety and intoxication, and pastoral bliss and annihilation. He is tearing and tearing apart. He goes to the end in his orgiastic dissolution, a mad cult leader revelling in blood and bile, bringing mothers to misrecognise their sons. Although he seeks recognition and integration, he is a radical negativity that cannot be absorbed. Savagely sublime and incalculable, he is the non-identity that haunts both the polis and the plane of immanence. He is that which both knowledge and intuition cannot account for – the stranger from the East. And resonating underneath the nexus of Dionysos-Crucified is also the sacrificial logic which maintains that the community can only be forged in and around the abject and ruined body. Next to Dionysos-Crucified is also Dionysos-Shiva, and the torrents of creative destruction which affirm only in their Thanatological tempests. Realer than Real, he is the return of the repressed, and neither Being nor Becoming – just polymorphous perverse indeterminacy. But always terrifying. Indeed, according to Eagleton, while Pentheus is a racist imperialist torn in his attraction/repulsion to the subterranean god, Dionysos is 'one the earliest terrorist ringleaders', and

> If he is the god of wine, milk, and honey, he is also a god of blood ... if Dionysos has all the fathomless vitality of the unconscious, then, he also has its implacable malevolence and aggression. He is the god of what Slavoj Zizek, after Jacques Lacan, has called 'obscene enjoyment or horrific *jouissance*'. His heart-warming, spine-chilling liturgy is a version of Hegel's Night of the World – that orgy of un-meaning before the dawn of subjectivity itself, in which bloodied stumps and mangled bits of bodies whirl in some frightful dance of death. (Eagleton 2005: 2–4)

The Dionysionology of certain strains of left-Nietzscheanism refuses to engage with the bloodied stumps and the larger truth concerning how all political, religious and social systems are born of dead bodies, sacrificial rituals and terror. It misunderstands 'health', which is not the foreclosure of negativity, but the existential tango with its riveting presence as absence. In addition, in its delirious flights of total non-negation it also refuses to engage with alterity *tout court*. And while Deleuze may be the great thinker of the multiple and difference, nowhere in his oeuvre do we seen any tangible confrontation with *L'autrui*, the Other or others. And is there not another 'task' of Dionysos – namely to bring the arrogance of reason that afflicts the city to account for that which exceeds it, to bring the Penthean obsession with the mono to make room for the poly, to bring masculinity to embrace its own femininity, and, most importantly to bring the Occidental ego to reach out to its phantasmatic Oriental id.

Dionysos is the stranger who returns to lay claim to the Europe that is rightfully his. Or, as Eagleton further notes, 'civilization must pay homage to its other, not least because there is a sense in which it lives off it' (2005: 15) or, more specifically, 'at the core of the self lies a power which makes it what it is ... the Other, the Real ... we come into our own through the Other, identity itself is a matter of self-estrangement' (2005: 24). Pre-subjective singularities swirl on the plane of immanence, but so too does the pre-subjective night of Dionysos. And he demands that we become strangers to ourselves, recognise the stranger – within and without – and paradoxically affirm that the pre-condition for ethical life, contra Deleuze, is not the refutation of the 'Dark side of the earth' and its 'becoming-reactive', but rather a serene and unflinching engagement with negativity, finitude and terror as the unfortunate substratum of 'this life', one where 'the impossible' becomes the locus of compassion and possibility, precisely that which Overman could not learn. 'To be done with judgement', among the most powerful mythemes of Nietzsche, Artaud and Deleuze, does not entail abnegating responsibility, but confronting suffering as the hallmark of this/our condition.

Nonetheless, *ressentiment* and reactivity do explode in the dark heart of the really existing terrorist. But the 'reactive' and the 'sad passions' that spill over into the terrorist's suspension of the ethical and passage to the gruesome act are not simply, as Deleuze would have it, products of the dialectic. All too often they are products of abjection, poverty and the loss of dignity and honour. These 'lacks' are then given a discursive and/ or theological framework through radicalised ideologies which canalise the experience of humiliation into the revolting triumph of sanguine ecstasy. Many of Arab and maghrebi descent were prevented from taking part in the events of May 68 (see Hajjat 2011). And some of their grandchildren, generations later, find themselves in the French *banlieue*, cordoned off from Paris by a series of real and symbolic barriers. Most go on to live their lives and get on with their stories, but some, stripped of all capital, succumb to the temptation of radicalisation, that other transmutation where on Monday you may have been selling weed on the corner only to find yourself, on Friday, a soldier of God, a celestial warrior in the apocalyptic cosmic showdown between the righteous and the wicked – with the latter often being transformed into the hallucinated figure of 'the West'.

The radicalised are by no means always products of the *banlieue* and we must be on guard against a certain 'sociologism' that explains terrorism solely in terms of the *ressentiment* born of social and economic poverty, lest we risk rendering the nefarious iterations of religion and political religion innocent. And of course, white 'domestic' terrorism, the specular double of its Islamist counterparts, is not an anomalous or minor phenomenon. Indeed, highly charged debates saturate terrorist studies, concerning whether it is Islam which radicalises the proto-terrorist or the proto-terrorist who radicalises Islam, and, *ibidem*, concerning whether it is MAGA that lays the ideological ground for alt-right inflected massacres, or the alt-right who instrumentalise MAGA as *raison d'être*. Yet, as Farhad Khosrokhavar observes, the radicalised in France and the UK are indeed plagued by 'sentiments of dehumanization' and the feeling 'that all doors are closed' (Khosrokhavar 2019: 103–4). And, in this isolation (physical, geographic, psychological), often delinquency and imprisonment, coupled with an overwhelming and incomprehensible rage, find an ideological support and sacralise themselves in the new articulations of apocalyptic Islam (Khosrokhavar 2019: 104). Feelings of inferiority and the most agonising experience of 'insect-like' alterity are transmuted into a revolutionary cult, virile, vital and deadly, against the injustices of the white world (Khosrokhavar 2019: 103–4). While perhaps not clearly identifiable as 'Dionysian' (this is not necessarily wine, honey and milk), as Khosrokavar also suggests, the radicalised, driven by the fury of the sacred, are bearers of a 'sublime joy', 'negative heroes' (or heroes of negativity) who mock the social contract of their co-citizens through ecstatic naturalisations of brutality (Khosrokhavar 2019: 108). The paroxysm of the reactive, radicalisation is lived by the jihadist as a means of surmounting indignity and valorising and transforming it in the nexus of the sacred (Khosrokhavar 2019: 109). Like Dionysos, then, there a quest for recognition and a vengeful alchemy wherein the experience of marginalisation is reconstructed in the death throes unleashed by the new heroes of the 'dark side'. They, mistaken for members of the infernal Oriental cult, 'return' to lay claim to the city where they were born, a city which their ancestors built. In the impasses of the post-post-colonial, the 'barbarians at the gates', the stranger-Other who is all too well known, rises to take back the honour and dignity of which they have been stripped.

Against the heights of non-dialectical negation, they surge from below with the most wrathful of total and absolute negations, where no traces of the affirmative can remain – only bloodied stumps. Hence, in this post-historical epoch, which perhaps Deleuze could have never imagined, the absolutely decoded *sur-homme* of the plane of immanence meets his daimonic rival in the *banlieue*, he who Fethi Benslama calls the absolutely overcoded '*sur-musulman*'. If the active *sur-homme* absorbs all negation in the play of affect and affirmation, the reactive *sur-musulman* outbids and amplifies the already existing negating injunctions of Islam. He is an 'explosive from hell' who sur-identifies with fever for death and concurrently sur-represents his perceived adversary. In these overdeterminations, the *sur-musulman* too moves beyond all-too-human recensions of good and evil and beyond the law, as his authority comes from something of a whole other 'plane' (Benslama 2016: 92–8). He is the 'post-subjective' singularity of pure negativity – a sordid incarnation of the Real.

Event Site/Event-Strike – Two Singularities

The plane of immanence is constituted by the free circulation of singularities which also surge forth in the advent of *l'événement*. Deleuze and Badiou remain the great thinkers of 'the event'. Whereas for the latter, the event refers to sociopolitical actualisations and/or materialist-messianic openings in history that violently alter both *doxa* and habitus, for the former, the event is the actualisation of the virtual and the apprehension of pure difference, which may be of this world, but is really of another (see Lecercle 2005). Where the two readings do overlap is in their respective understandings of the event as a dramatic rupture which shatters the contours of the phenomenal.

More specifically, for Deleuze, the event is a transmutation as well, one where the actual breaks down or is 'converted' into the plane of immanence and the circulation of singularities. In *What is Philosophy?*, he proposes, with Guattari, the existence of

> generic functions – scientific, artistic, political or doxic, and amorous or lived – to which production of 'truths' correspond . . . we then arrive at the conversion of immanence of the situation, a conversion of excess to the void, which will reintroduce the transcendent: this is the *event site* that sticks to the edge of the void in the situation and now includes not units, but singularities, as elements dependent on the preceding functions . . . the event appears (or disappears) less as singularity than as a separated aleatory point. . . (Deleuze and Guattari 1994: 151–2)

And in further stressing their disaccord with Badiou, they insist that the event 'eludes its own actualization in everything that happens. The event is not a state of affairs . . . [it] might seem to be transcendent because it surveys a state of affairs, but it is pure immanence' (1994: 156). And previously, in *The Logic of Sense*, Deleuze contends that the ideal event is a singularity or set of singularities, turning points and points of inflection (Deleuze 1990b: 52) , while also positing the singular and intrinsically revolutionary nature of the event:

> only the free man, can … comprehend all violence in a single act of violence, and every mortal event in a *single Event* … the revolutionary alone is free from *resentiment*, by means of which one always participates in, and profits by, an oppressive order. *One and the same event?* (Deleuze 1990b: 152)

The event is thus a cipher in which total univocity and the reconciliation with the One (which is multiple) are achieved and completed. It may surge from matter, but terminates in immateriality and always tends to the void and the virtual, while simultaneously being the site of inflection for 'the state of affairs' and the passive energetics that flow between bodies, milieu, encounters, sensations and apophatic language – the transition from the corporeal to the incorporeal. It unfolds on the plane of immanence, but is an embodied location of impersonal, 'singular' or 'inhuman' affect and interacting. It is also 'the cause', or precisely where the militant becomes politically disembodied and catapulted out of *ressentiment* into death beyond death where 'I do not die, I forfeit the power of dying … death turns against death: where dying is the negation of death … death loses itself in itself, and also the figure which the most singular life takes on' (Deleuze 1990b: 152–3). Hence, it is a quasi-Stoic concatenation and also the production of 'free men' who 'soldier on' against reactivity in the death of event where 'it dies in the same way that it rains' (Deleuze 1990b: 152). But, as Jean-Jacques Lecercle remarks, 'it is not the accident which is its corporeal double: it actualizes in the body, but escapes its proper actualization. Its time is Aeon, the time of the infinite division of past/future, without the present (while the violence of the Badiou-event bursts in the present of the epiphany)' (Lecercle 2005: 5).

Between infinity and the epiphany is also the dissonance between the time of Aeon and the time of the caliphate. In this antinomy we also find that which exists between the event and what Baudrillard describes as the 'event strike', precisely where excess does not rush towards void, but avenges itself upon the doxic and the generic functions of the political. The terrorist too becomes singular in the event-strike and, in his own unique way, also forfeits the power of dying in the act of martyrdom and 'the cause'. Moreover, reactive as he might be, he too understands himself to be battling against 'the oppressive order', which for many a jihadist is the neoliberal juggernaut itself. And, as is well known, those we call terrorists do not refer to themselves as such, preferring to think of themselves as 'freedom fighters' and architects of their own sordid vision of social justice. Between the *sur-homme* and the *sur-musulman*, between the event and the event-strike, are two negotiations of empire, the bodily, the 'outside', and the singularity.

Temporalities are always political and bound in narrative structures and communities which play within the interstices of the Golden Age of the past and the messianic promise of the future. What is of importance is the manner in which these polarities 'actualize' and (re)construct themselves in the present. For Deleuze, Aeon opposes Chronos and the normativity of the three dimensions of time. Or, in Aeon 'only the past and the future inhere or subsist in time. Instead of a present which absorbs the past and the future, a future and past divide the present at every instant . . . the instant without thickness and without extensions . . . Aeon is the locus of incorporeal events' (Deleuze 1990b: 164–5). This a-temporal temporality and post-bodily nexus is time without time, an 'empty form of time', and the extrication from causes and depths in the privileging of the effects/affects and surface. Aeon is one side of Chronos, but on the other 'darker side', one uneasily finds the temporal hallucinations of the caliphate.

Contemporary radical Islam makes use of hyper-modern technologies, media and institutions to return Islam back to its illusory pure point of origin – the fantasy of the caliphate, in the future to come. The paradox is glimpsed in how, in this chiasma of the pre-modern/radically modern, the diluting and profaning dimensions of globalisation are deployed to rebuild the pure point of the past in the future. Stated otherwise, the ideology of the caliphate insists on how the remotest rubbing up against the universes of modernity and post-modernity can only corrupt the sanctity of the founding moment. The sacrificial act, terror and martyrdom are not only spectacular instances of the new propaganda by the deed, but the means of accelerating the process to the ultimate break with Chronos, historical time and colonial and post-colonial time. As nostalgia for that which was never experienced, the caliphate functions as a critique of neoliberal temporality and habitus, and, like Sion, becomes a post-historical screen for the total resolving of all grievances. As a mythic supra-national Islamic polity, and the total achievement of the *umma*, it is the incarnation of the post-national global community of believers, one which offers a unique recension of globalisation's transformation of the nation-state (see Filiu 2008; Guidère 2016). Hence, between the *sur-homme* and the *sur-musulman* is also Aeon and the caliphate, or the a-historical and non-corporeal time of immanence *and* the post-historical regression qua event, where the body, the disciplined body, the purged body, the dogmatised body and the body that explodes introduce new untimely meditations.

However, these bodies are not singularities simply because they are, as Agamben remarks, 'whatever' and built as pure modalities of being that reject the determinism of language, identity and affinity, demonstrating an 'inessential commonality' or solidarity without essence (Agamben 1993: 17–19). Their post-personal singularity is forged in a fetishistic overdetermination of solidarity and commonality based on an ethical and transcendental ethos which opposes all traditional understandings of both the positive and negative community. Radicalisation may be rhizomatic in its organisational structure, but hyper-segmented in its ideological *obscura*. And if the Deleuzian singularity is alien, incorporeal, unable to be grasped in this world, the terrorist, as Matthew Noah Smith suggests, too is something of an 'ethical singularity', the bearer of 'values so totalizing and alien that they cannot be translated into one's own moral system, and, because they appear to be systemic, values whose gravitational pull threatens one's own moral system' (Smith 2010: 240). And here, following Badiou, we do find a remarkable 'fidelity to the event'. The terrorist's death asks you what you would die for. And the answer, for many of the comfy and coddled members of the bourgeois liberal lifeworld, is 'not much'. As an excessive and singular ethics, radicalisation completes itself in the excessive and singular event, the outside of the moral system and the system of ordinary liberal politics.

As universalism ceased to universalise and the internal antagonisms of liberalism revealed revealed themselves, 9/11 swooped down as the revenge of the Real on that lifeworld, desiccating any hopes of a cosmopolitan *ecumene* with Starbucks for all. The singularities produced the event as singularity or, for Baudrillard, the 'event-strike' as return of the Real, where we evince the restoration

> of an irreducible singularity to the heart of the system of generalized exchange. All the singularities (species, individuals, and cultures), that have paid with their deaths for the installation of a global circulation governed by a single power have their vengeance today through the situational transfer of terror . . . only symbolic violence is generative of the singularity. And in this singular event, this Manhattan catastrophe film, coalesces two elements of mass fascination in the 20th century: the white magic of cinema and the black magic of terrorism. (Baudrillard 2001)

The singularity of the sacrificial act and the pushing of 'the systems' to their limit-point through the recoding of the political as the exchange of death and counter-death unite the 'singularities' into the 'singular event', thus bringing the Real to overcome the virtual – with no hero of immanence in sight. Two singularities – one of the Deleuzian event and one of the event-strike. Two incorporealities – one of Deleuze's de-incarnated fluxes and flows, and the other of the dead bodies of the terrorist and his victims. Two recensions of death. Two 'free men'.

Buddhism also non-dialectically negates, but it is too world-weary and perhaps too wise to think that it could seal of the plane of immanence to the forces of impermanence and the Real. And so between immanent-singularity and terroristic-transcendental-singularity, we, the ordinary, members of the present and the real, stand to be eternally held hostage as we take our children to school and go to work. We in the middle, flanked by two singular and singularly opposed understandings of justice and emancipation – the ground of tragedy itself. We, in the middle, flanked between 'A Life' and the generalised global political economy of death.

Schizflux

Anti-Oedipus laid the groundwork for a new 'discipline' and field of experimentation called schizoanalysis – a politico-libidinal analysis, or modus operandi, which would examine the investments of desire in the social field and point the way to a liberation of desire through the pluralising and unblocking of 'Desire' and the desiring-machines. Such emancipation would be achieved through the realisation of 'successful schizophrenia'. Stated otherwise, through the progressive 'schizophrenisation' of subjectivities and the social field, tyranny and the totalising oedipal dynamics of capitalism, labour, the family and Lacanianism could be overcome. And here we encounter yet another 'conceptual persona', the schizo, whose revolutionary investments of desire oppose the paranoiac and oedipalising investments of the fascist and, for our purposes, the terrorist as well.

Both polarities are results of very particular social deliriums or 'deviations from the path of reason (from the main furrow)', the 'going off the tracks' (Diderot and d'Alembert 1777–79: 609). Delirium was always there underneath the axiomatic of capitalism and, according to Deleuze, 'everything is rational in capitalism, except capitalism itself . . . the rationality is always the rationality of the irrational. Underneath all reason lies delirium and drift. . .' (Deleuze, in Guattari 1995b: 54). Delirium's articulation takes two particular forms which span the spectrum between the molecular and the molar, the deterritorialised and the territorialised, plenum and lack, Reich and Lacan, and the machinic unconscious and 'the little Greek theatre'. Hence,

> every unconscious investment mobilizes a delirious interplay of disinvestments, of counterinvestments, of overinvestments. But we have seen in this context that there were two major types of social investment, segregative and nomadic, just as there were two poles of delirium: first, a paranoiac-fascizing (*fascisant*) type or pole that invests the formation of central sovereignty . . . and second, a schizorevolutionary type or pole that follows the *lines of escape* of desire. (Deleuze and Guattari 1983: 277)

The 'subject's' escape from psychic and sociopolitical oedipalisation can only be gained through 'becoming-schizo'. Yet, as is manifestly clear, when they speak of schizophrenia, they are not referring to the clinical or pathological condition wherein one suffers from an irreparable detachment from the world, but rather to a particular sociopolitical strategy which compels one to seek liberation in the constant suspension of fixed identity and overcoding. We are invited to embark on the line of flight where the desiring-machines may be perpetually reinvented, empowered, ceaselessly proliferating into creative cacophonous infinity. For Deleuze and Guattari, clinical schizophrenia signifies the thwarting of such a process, the interruption of the experiment: the schizophrenic only becomes pathologised or 'ill' when he or she is made to submit to Oedipus – her loss of reality is not a consequence of the schizophrenic process, but the forced effect of oedipalisation. Previously to being oedipalised, the schizo is in touch with too many realities, too many codes. He is always jumping from one to another, not blindly, but in the spirit of founding new worlds and joyous play – 'everywhere at once'. The schizophrenic strategy is organised around the logic of the 'neither/or', the occupation of *différance* and a fractal-like motion of becoming. The schizo asks the normal neurotic: Why exert so much control over yourself? Why labour to constantly 'put yourself together'?

They would celebrate the schizophrenic strategy simply because, clinically speaking, the schizophrenic is the most resistant to the oedipal triangle. He has no mummy–daddy–me and has ceased to place any stock in defensive structures of the ego and the 'I'. Schizos only say 'I' when they are forced to, when they are effectively pathologised. Deleuze and Guattari are thus quick to recall Freud's ambivalence towards the schizo: 'Freud doesn't like schizophrenics. He doesn't like their resistance to being oedipalized, and tends to treat them, more or less like animals. They mistake words for things, he says . . . they resemble philosophers – "an undesirable resemblance"' (Deleuze and Guattari 1983: 23). The question then becomes: Is the schizophrenic cut off from reality because she lacks Oedipus, or, on the contrary, is she disassociated because she has been forced to submit to oedipalisation, that which she cannot bear, that around which everything combines to subjugate her (social repression before psychoanalysis/psychoanalysis as extension of social repression)?

The schizophrenic not only resists Oedipus, but resists the social control and reterritorialisations of capitalism as well: escaping the symbolic and evading Oedipus means also escaping the structural organisations of domination that oppress the psyche in late capitalism, built as it is around the creation of good productive workers and mummy–daddy–me. The schizo's investments are no longer familial and his mode of being illustrates a transparency between the unconscious and the socius – war, class, revolt, race etc. The schizo's language and impulses are direct readings of the socius. He embodies the fluxes as nomadism at its limit point. He is mummy and daddy, yet none of these. He is dead or alive, not at once, but constantly gliding between the two, as he glides between everything. He is always establishing alternate alliances and deterritorialising every relation he comes into connection with. The schizo knows only becoming-rhizomatic and employs disjunctive syntheses as his technique of the fluxes and technology of the 'self', Yet disjunctive synthesis is not a simple juxtaposing of contradictory elements. Rather, Deleuze and Guattari characterise the process as affirmative:

> It would be a total misunderstanding of this order of thought if we concluded that the schizophrenic substituted vague syntheses of identification of contradictory elements for disjunctions, like the last of the Hegelian philosophers. He does not substitute syntheses of contradictory elements for disjunctive syntheses; rather, for the exclusive and restrictive use of the disjunctive synthesis, he substitutes an affirmative use. (Deleuze and Guattari 1983: 7)

The schizo, decidedly non-dialectical in his affirmations, is forever 'trans' and opens out on to the socius, allowing the desiring-machines to obtain their full potential, plunging head-first into the limits of deterritorialisation. In him every flux commingles as passage, nomadic movement and becoming. In the schizo's scramblings and wanderings is the limit of capitalism, the conflation of the 'demonaical' element of nature and the material processes of social production. Schizophrenia is social production extended to its farthest reaches: the codes that the schizo jumps between and scrambles are the manifestations of desiring production latent within social production. Only he knows the indices. He carries the socius in all of his pieces and drags it along with him at all times. In addition, as Deleuze and Guattari summarise, he is a free man, an overman:

The schizo knows how to leave: he has made a departure into something as simple as being born or dying. But at the same time his journey is strangely stationary, in place. He does not speak of another world, he is not from another world: even when he is displacing himself in space, his is a journey in intensity, around the desiring-machine that is erected here and remains here. For here is the desert propagated by our own world, and also the new Earth, and the machine that hums, around which the schizo revolves, planets for a new sun ... But such a man produces himself as a free man, irresponsible, solitary, and joyous, finally able to say and do something simple in his own name, without asking permission; a desire lacking nothing, a flux that overcomes the barriers and codes, a name that no longer designates an ego whatsoever. He has simply ceased being afraid of becoming mad. (Deleuze and Guattari 1983: 131)

Following from this, the schizo opposes the terrorist in his delirium. While both are, in their own way, liminal and limit figures of capitalism, the jihadist is not a free man (or his liberation paradoxically is only gained through the reactive). And his 'New Earth' is not really new, but just an extreme investment of the paranoiac-fascist pole of desire. He buckles under the oedipal phantasm of God and the Big Other and, in his quest to construct a moral code that beats back the desert of globalisation, an undisputable world, he is the fetishist of the barrier and the code. His sun is black and his desire driven by pure lack. Excluded from traditional modalities of masculine development (school, work, family etc.), he is often symbolically castrated and revirilised through the gun, the sword, the bomb. His desiring-machine, all too blocked, implodes, but with its own intensity. But he, too, does not ask permission insofar as his journey has been sanctified by the divine. On the contrary, the schizo's emancipation is a total break with the Thanatological: 'We say, on the contrary, that there is no death instinct because there is both the model and the experience of death in the unconscious ... [Freud] could no longer conceive the essence of life except in a form turned back against itself, in the form of death itself' (Deleuze and Guattari 1983: 332–3). The radicalised, on the contrary, as Benslama observes, are driven by 'the collective power of negativity in this world and beyond' (2016: 40), and the quest for meaning which is obtained in the *jouissance*, which extends beyond suffering to one's own proper destruction (2016: 39). Thanatos 'live'. In the fever of the death drive, and in the 'pushing of the limits of self', the radicalised transcends 'his own skin for a new one, risking actually leaving his skin' (Benslama 2016: 39). In doing so, he potentially becomes another singular affront to capitalism, for, in the purificatory *jouissance* of casting off the body, in the effacement of the frontier between life and death, he casts off and effaces his body as object of labour and reification, and his status as a consumer.

Terrorist violence is not necessarily spawned by mental illness, but one could hardly consider the radicalised to be in good health. It is, of course, infinitely preferable to dine with Deleuze and Guattari's Eros-driven schizo than with the radicalised. But we must still ask, to return things to the 'middle', if 'a schizophrenic out for a walk' is really 'a better model than a neurotic lying on an analyst's couch' (Deleuze and Guattari 1983: 2)? Moreover, is there not something fundamentally irresponsible in their mystification of mental illness (particularly in the context of Guattari's very real therapeutic commitments)?

Of course, this was the 1960s and early 1970s, the heyday of the anti-psychiatry movement. And as R. D. Laing never ceased to repeat, 'every breakdown was a breakthrough' – the truth of human existence, in its generative folly and crazy wisdom, was to be glimpsed in the schizo's delirium. Indeed, Laing and Cooper, informed by the anti-asylum critiques of Foucault and Thomas Szaz, were perhaps the most vocal in affirming a politics of madness which drew the fundamental rapport between mental alienation and widespread social alienation. Guattari, however, sought to distance himself from the LSD-laden counter-culture of his Anglo-Saxon peers, and never parted with the Ecole Freudienne de Paris. He insisted, always, that his criticism was of 'Lacanianism' and never Lacan himself. At the time he was an active member of the psychoanalytic team at the Clinique de La Borde, an experimental arena for 'institutional analysis' which stressed collective life, the radical revamping of the clinical setting and modes of analysis that were emancipated from the dogmatic constructs of Freudianism and the fatalism of Lacan. Crucial to 'Labordian analysis' were notions such as 'transversality', 'group fantasy' and the 'machinic unconscious'. According to Guattari, the team at La Borde proposed to combine and, if possible, surpass the diverse initiatives inspired by Laing, Cooper, Basaglia, Tosquelles et al. In addition, as Guattari added, 'we wanted to, above all, disengage ourselves from the almost mass-mediatized character of anti-psychiatry in order to launch a movement that effectively engaged mental health workers and patients' (Guattari 1995b: 199). This 'disengagement' was not to be, and after Guattari paired up with Deleuze, the former would invariably be referred to as the French Laing.

For Eugene Holland, the conundrum that Deleuze and Guattari found themselves in was located in how their 'utopian vision' seemed to 'outstrip real possibilities'. In addition, the 'exceptional forms that correspond best to the nature of desiring production seem to have little chance of transforming social conditions', and so 'no wonder Deleuze and Guattari insist that schizoanalysis has no political program!' (Holland 1999: 108). It had no real psychoanalytic programme either. If schizoanalysis is of little help with really existing politics, it also fails to engage with really existing schizos who, by and large, are not Dionysian prophets and overmen, but victims of immense pain, suffering and private forms of terror. It is not without irony that Deleuze had little tolerance for the mad and candidly admitted that he had never met a schizophrenic (Dosse 2007: 19). It is not without irony as well that Jean Oury, the veritable motor of French institutional psychiatry and director of La Borde, had little patience with Guattari's schizoanalytic deviations.

Two weeks after 9/11, I ventured to Blois to work as an intern and researcher at La Clinique de la Chesnaie (which, according to Danielle Sivadon, remained loyal to the spirit of Guattari's work and uncorrupted by Oury's ambivalence towards the 'schizflux'). I also conducted fieldwork at La Borde. My question: what rapport was there between 'schizoanalysis' and the reality of Guattari's institutional psychiatric practice on the ground? While many of Guattari's former patients revered him as a compassionate analyst, to my chagrin the response was very little. Indeed, there was something dynamic and liberating about breaking down the hierarchy between clinicians and patients (referred to in Blois as *pensionnaires* – those given room and board). And working in the circles of *la Grille* (the grid), where each and everyone rotated in their tasks, was a quasi-socialist experiment in collective auto-gestion: while cooking, dining and cleaning with the patients, many of whom told stories about Félix, there were moments of 'breakthrough', when the wall between the 'sane' and the 'mad' was, for a moment, broken – a joke, sweeping the floor together, the ritual of the cigarette, doing the dishes, playing music, and, yes, going out for a walk – all spaces where something both personal and political transpired. And certainly, a strange set of vectors of collective and group desire congealed among the staff and the patients as the result of sustained cohabitation in a world which was, for all practical purposes, set apart from the 'norm' and the 'normal'.

However, Oury's hesitations about the politics of the schizo-trip were not entirely unfounded. One simply cannot argue that these encounters, nor the 'schizos' themselves, were harbingers of a new revolutionary desiring politics, let alone 'successful' in their critique of domination and tyranny. The patients were not 'conceptual personae'. They were the victims of their own tyrannical psychic and psychiatric conditions, subjugated by things that were entirely out of their control – innocent victims. They were deserving of our care. And, perhaps, there was something ethically dubious in transforming them into screens for the political aspirations of the radical left. The reality of life at the clinic was the brute encounter with catanonic crawls, psychic and physical abjection, the tremblings of those sacrificed to shock treatment, the stooped gait and empty eyes, medication and more medication, and regular bouts of violence. On the night watch, no schizflux – just tears and howling. The interns and the staff were also prone to drug use and alcohol abuse. But who could blame them? Living in such close proximity to 'the mad' for a prolonged period of time inevitable breaks apart the super-ego, unravels the neurotic grip and plunges one into the radically interstitial. And while, in the beginning, this may have inspired a strange giddiness, for many of the interns, myself included, it quickly lapsed into a form of terror itself. At the end of my stay, I found myself pining for a bit of 'territory', a bit of 'ground' and a bit of my old super-ego. Alas, I was not a good enough Deleuzo-Guattarian and certainly no revolutionary superhero. Although I cherished many of those shared meals with the patients, I was more than happy to return to the drudgery and grind of graduate school and also to my rightful place on the analyst's couch. I needed to 'put myself back together'. There are worse things, no?

Aristocrats

As Badiou recounts, between 1969 and 1975 Deleuze became an unlikely mentor for

> that fraction of leftism for which all that mattered was desiring-machines and nomadism, the sexual and the festive . . . he was also the founder of a singular alternate genealogy in the history of philosophy whose work was never explicitly political: rather, it was politicized by virtue of the historical conditions in which Deleuze surged to eminence. (Badiou 1997: 95–7)

And in Deleuze's 'infinite repetition' and 'monotonous productions' (Badiou 1997: 7) we see nothing of a desiring revolution, but a philosophy which is ascetic, aristocratic and mystical. Aristocratic in its embrace of the highly cultivated, highly trained and largely luxurious heroes of 'the plane' (this is a genealogy which could not have been written in the late 1930s). Ascetic insofar as the pure immanence of these heroes is dependent upon the most rigorous of philosophical and spiritual exercises. And mystic insofar as the plane of immanence figures as an inverted (but certainly a-religious) form of transcendence – a line of flight up, down, away, outside traversed by gifted elites and masterful virtuosi of the One and the multiple. For instance, contra Deleuze, Yirmiyahu Yovel reminds us that Spinoza's 'adventures in immanence', his embrace of conatus, were not very practical and actually quite hard to embark upon:

> To reach this semi-mystical stage, we must therefore embark on a diversified program of study, aimed at knowing ourselves more and more as creatures of nature . . . I must know my specific place within the chain of being; the actual circumstances of my being in the world; the causes which explain my bodily situation, my personal biography, my structure, and the mental and social forces active within me; the hidden causes of my fear; my errors; the ignorance of which I am victim; my suffering, my ambitions, my covert motives, the powers that make me waver between fear and hope, joy and grief, and other unstable emotions that hold my life in bondage. All this requires a thorough scientific study not only of the body – through physics and other sciences of 'extension' (physiology, chemistry, climatology, etc.) – but also of psychology. (Yovel 1989: 149)

As is well known, the elitism of the 'semi-mystical stage' finds further iterations in the textual violence implicit in Nietzsche's 'philosophizing with a hammer'. Yet it also appears in the processual dynamics and durations of Bergson, whose community to come was, on the one hand, an 'open society', one 'which embraces the principle of all humanity', but also the province of 'elite souls' (Bergson 1932: 204). Deleuze goes further in *Bergsonism*, asserting that access to such a world, a place of the pure embodiment of cosmic memory and creative emotions, is only granted internally to privileged souls who will spread the message to lay people.

> It leaps from one soul to another, 'every now and then' crossing closed deserts. But to each member of a closed community, if he opens himself to it, it communicates a kind of reminiscence, an excitement that allows him to follow. And from soul to soul, it traces the design of an open society, a society of creators, where we pass from one genius to another, through the intermediary of disciples or spectators or hearers. (Deleuze 1991: 111)

But the open may actually be closed, and certainly closed to our drug dealer on the corner in the Parisian *banlieue*. There is a distinction to be made between the 'open society' and the conditions of 'really existing people' in 'really existing society'. Perhaps Deleuze is the inspiration for new modalities of micro-political *potentia*, virtuosity and the multitude itself. But against a certain reading of 'Deleuze and politics', one must grapple with the fact that immanence was never really democratised in the philosopher's oeuvre itself, unless democracy be understood as the collective aristocraticisation of *élan*, a spiritual force that traverses all being and matter. But does it traverse the world of the drug dealer? Perhaps where philosophy stops is where sociology begins.

Following from this, Deleuze offers us a mysticism of the virtual which embraces the Stoic all-cosmos as the Neoplatonic One (offering a sharp contrast to trenchant critiques of Platonism and representation found in *Difference and Repetition*). Yet Deleuze avoids the traps of Platonism in postulating the One as the frenetic movement of multiplicity and difference. In other words, the multiplicity is an ontology always to be fused back into the One-all and, as such, this monism (without monism) is strictly qualitative. Hence, can Deleuze really be hailed as the great thinker of non-dialectical negation or as a constructor of a positive ontology? If so, the critique of transcendence and the negative simply lapses into its overdetermined opposite. Peter Hallward shares this point of view:

> If Deleuze's radical philosophy of immanence entails the critique of transcendence just as it implies the refusal of negation, this very critique obtains only through a preliminary transcendence of what might be called the 'given' (relative, worldly, specific, human, significant) as opposed to the 'Real' (absolute, other-worldly, singular, inhuman, or impersonal, a-significant). (Hallward 1997: 6)

This may seem a facile critique of Deleuzianism, namely that the aristocratic consciousness and the work of non-dialectical negation leads to a 'spiritual' materialism and a type of redemption from the real/Real which becomes wrapped in the refrains of immanence. But, if true, one is inevitably compelled to problematise and call into question the substantive content of the 'and' which connects the coupling of 'Deleuze and terrorism', and the larger attempt to theorise a non-worldly theory of immanence which, nonetheless, claims to have implications and a basis in this world. Unlike Buddhism's enlightenment, Deleuze gets to immanence far too quickly, or rather does not embark on the agonising passage through the real, through trauma and terror. And repeating 'yes' to 'A life' does not make 'A Life' magically appear.

The problem, it seems, as Christopher L. Miller suggests, is that Deleuze and Guattari 'want it both ways', and ultimately posit a 'condition of *semi*-detachment between the virtual and the real . . . so, in the Deleuzian universe, the "derivation" of the philosophical and the virtual from the

real, and the historical, and the continuation of the contact between the
two, will come and go. Now you see it, now you don't' (Miller 2003:
132–3). Our core argument is that this contact should be rigorous and
sustained and, dare we say, anchored and embedded in the concrete
sociohistorical and material conditions of 'this world', fraught as they
are by negativity, negation and terror (all the while never ceasing to
seize the threshold of the impossible, which is not necessarily negativity,
but immanence). Soothed by the consolations of immanence, Deleuze
and Guattari admitted that 'the philosopher is only the envelope of his
principal conceptual personae and of all the other personae who are the
intercessors, the real subjects of his philosophy' (Deleuze and Guattari
1994: 64). And here, once again, they ducked, and ducked the question.

Three Children/Three Suicides

Some have referred to Deleuze's countenance as resembling that of a
'melancholic clown' (Eagleton 2011). And at his lectures at Paris VIII,
Deleuze himself would admit to having 'played the clown', but that's
'why everyone came to listen. . .' (Deleuze 1983b). The 'clown' cultivated
many personae. In this very particular theatre of philosophy, there could
be no identity in the conceptual modellisation and no identity *tout
court*. The time of the great Christian question – who/what am I? – had
long passed, as there was no longer any interiority to excavate. But, as
Deleuze and Guattari admitted, the horizontal proliferations of bliss
on the 'plane' were always haunted by the unwelcome figures of the
religious, representational and ideological 'figures of the plane', those
vulgar, vertical, transcendental ghosts and demons, always ready to
sweep down and calcify the flows and fluxes, and break the machines.
Indeed, in a moment of curious philosophical arrogance, they claimed
to be unfazed, for 'even illusions of transcendence are useful to us and
provide vital anecdotes – for when we take pride in encountering the
transcendent within immanence, all we do is recharge the plane of
immanence with immanence itself' (Deleuze and Guattari 1994: 73). Is
it really that simple . . . just recharge the plane?

There are three children: there are the children of immanence, who
'all resemble one another and have little individuality' as 'they are
singularities: a smile, a gesture, a funny face – not subjective qualities
. . . through all their suffering and fragility [they] possess an immanent
life which is pure power and even bliss' (Deleuze 1995: 4). But then there
are the 'figures of the vertical' or what Alan Bertho calls 'the children
of chaos', those children abandoned by the state, parents, collective

morality, those children who cultivate, not immanence, but the rage born of the experience at systemic injustice; delinquents and dealers in the lost territories of the Republic, ready to be mobilised, ready to be radicalised (Bertho 2016: 106–7). The third child is the former, now annihilated by the latter.

There are also multiple suicides: There is the suicide of the suicide bomber and terrorist-martyr – where death symbolically accosts 'the system' in the ultimate sacrifice that launches he who gives up his body into the vertical line to transcendence and immortality. There is also the suicide of the young newly minted college grad, on her first day of work on 9/11 in a Wall Street office – the young girl who jumped from the tower in a final act of agency. Then there is Deleuze's jump from his Parisian apartment, his own line of flight to the 'horizontal plane'. Suicided by 'A Life . . .'

He wanted to give philosophy a lung. He wanted to make it breathe and bring it back to good health. He wanted to release it from the stranglehold of the negative. But he was already a body without organs. Indeed, as a result of a bout with tuberculosis, Deleuze had one of his lungs removed at the age of 44. Nonetheless an unrepentant smoker, he would, after a tracheotomy, be 'chained like a dog' to a respirator. Two years after Guattari's death (a 'mutilation' for Deleuze), on 4 November 1995 Deleuze too would jump. What precipitated this? What were his final thoughts as he leapt, when he was, for several seconds, groundless? Did he repeat the mantra that 'death comes from the Outside'? Was this the performance of the line of flight? Did he, as André Pierre Colombat suggests, produce his own vitalism as force, his own 'event' and the transitions from the corporeal to the incorporeal (Colombat 1996)? But let us remember to call a death a death, and nothing more.

Deleuze always maintained that he was an empiricist exploring practical and pragmatic approaches to philosophy. He wanted nothing more than that we find a use for his theoretical landscape. Deleuze and Guattari would also go on to claim that *Anti-Oedipus* and *A Thousand Plateaus* were handbooks, and invite us to 'open to any page' to find a solution to our problems. But it is not clear, after 9/11, after 13 November 1995, after another school shooting, after the death of father, mother, grandfather or brother, after a suicide, after COVID, that any real answers could be found in their ruminations on desiring-machines and Bodies without Organs. You can, of course, look all you want and maybe find a 'concept'. As for terror, they knew everything about it and nothing about it. For better or worse, they could never resign themselves to the middle.

References

Agamben, G. (1993), *The Coming Community*, trans. M. Hardt, Minneapolis: University of Minnesota Press.

Badiou, A. (1997), *The Clamor of Being*, trans. L. Burchill, Minneapolis: University of Minnesota Press.

Bataille, G. (2001), *The Unfinished System of Knowledge*, trans. M. Kendall and S. Kendall, Minneapolis: University of Minnesota Press.

Baudrillard, J. (2001), 'L'esprit du terrorisme', *Le Monde*, 3 November <https://www.lemonde.fr/disparitions/article/2007/03/06/l-esprit-du-terrorisme-par-jean-baudrillard_879920_3382.html> (last accessed 20 October 2019).

Benslama, F. (2016), *Un furieux désir de sacrifice : le surmusulman*, Paris: Seuil.

Bergson, H. (1932), *Les deux sources de la morale et la religion*, Paris: PUF.

Bertho, A. (2016), *Les enfants du chaos: essai sur le temps des martyrs*, Paris: La Découverte.

Colombat, A. P. (1996), 'Deleuze's Death as Event', *Man and World*, 29: 235–49.

Deleuze, G. (1983a), *Nietzsche and Philosophy*, trans. H. Tomlinson, New York: Columbia University Press.

Deleuze, G. (1983b), 'Cinéma cours 22 du 02/11/83', *La voix de Gilles Deleuze*, transcription by V. Manifacier, <http://www2.univ-paris8.fr/deleuze/article.php3?id_article=124> (last accessed 20 October 2019).

Deleuze, G. (1990a), *Pourparlers*, Paris: Les éditions de minuit.

Deleuze, G. (1990b), *The Logic of Sense*, ed. C. Boundas, trans. M. Lester, New York: Columbia University Press.

Deleuze, G. (1991), *Bergsonism*, trans. H. Tomlinson and B. Habberjam, New York: Zone Books.

Deleuze, G. (1995), 'L'immanence: une vie . . .', *Philosophie*, 47/49: 1–9.

Deleuze, G., and F. Guattari (1983), *Anti-Oedipus: Capitalism and Schizophrenia*, trans. R. Hurley, M. Seem and H. R. Lane, Minneapolis: University of Minnesota Press.

Deleuze, G., and F. Guattari (1994), *What is Philosophy?*, trans. H. Tomlinson and G. Burchill, New York: Columbia University Press.

Deleuze, G., and C. Parnet (1987), *Dialogues*, trans. H. Tomlinson and B. Habberjam, New York: Columbia University Press.

Diderot, D., and M. d'Alembert (1777–79), *Encyclopédie ou Dictionnaire Raisonné des Sciences, des Arts, et des Métiers*, 2nd edn, vol. X, Geneva: Pettet.

Dosse, F. (2007), *Gilles Deleuze et Félix Guattari: biographie croisée*, Paris: La Découverte.

Eagleton, T. (2005), *Holy Terror*, Oxford: Oxford University Press.

Eagleton, T. (2009), *Trouble with Strangers: A Study of Ethics*, Chichester: Wiley-Blackwell.

Eagleton, T. (2011), 'François Dosse's *Deleuze and Guattari*', *Art Forum*, April, <https://www.artforum.com/print/201104/francois-dosse-s-deleuze-guattari-27817> (last accessed 20 October 2019).

Eigen, M. (2001), *Ecstasy*, Middletown, CT: Wesleyan University Press.

Filiu, J. P. (2008), *L'apocalype dans l'Islam*, Paris: Fayard,

Guattari, F. (1995a), 'Pragmatic/Machinic: Interview with Charles Stivale', *Pre/Text*, 14: 215–50

Guattari, F. (1995b), *Chaosophy*, ed. S. Lotringer, New York: Semiotext(e).

Guidère, M. (2016), *Le retour du califat*, Paris, Gallimard.

Hajjat, A. (2011), 'The Arab Workers' Movement (1970–1976): Sociology of a New Political Generation', in J. Jackson, A. L. Milne and J. S. Williams (eds),

May 68: Rethinking France's Last Revolution, New York: Palgrave Macmillan, pp. 109–21.

Hallward, P. (1997), 'Gilles Deleuze and the Redemption from Interest', *Radical Philosophy*, 81: 6–21.

Hardt, M. (1990), *Gilles Deleuze: An Apprenticeship in Philosophy*, Minneapolis: University of Minnesota Press.

Holland, E. (1999), *Deleuze and Guattari's Anti-Oedipus: Introduction to Schizoanalysis*, London: Routledge.

Khosrokhavar, F. (2019), *Radicalisation*, Paris: Editions de la maison des sciences de l'homme.

Lacan, J. (1966), *Ecrits*, Paris: Seuil.

Lacan, J. (2006), *Le Séminaire, Book IV: les formations de l'inconscient*, Paris: Seuil.

Lecercle, J. J. (2005), 'Il y a événement et évenement', *Polysémes: Les figures de la violence*, 7: 249–64.

Lotringer, S. (1999), personal communication.

Loubet del Bayle, J. L. (1969), *Les non-conformistes des annés 30: Une tentative de renouvellement de la pensée politique francaise*, Paris: Éditions du Seuil.

Miller, C. L. (2003), 'We Shouldn't Judge Deleuze and Guattari: A Response to Eugene Holland', *Research in African Literatures*, 34 (3): 129–41.

Morton, T. (2015), 'Buddhaphobia: Nothing and Fear of Things', in M. Boon, E. Cazdyn and T. Morton (eds), *Nothing: Three Inquiries in Buddhism*, Chicago: University of Chicago Press, pp. 185–266.

Nagārajuna (2013), *Nagārajuna's Middle Way: Mūlamadhyamakakārikā*, ed. M. Siderits and S. Katsura, Somerville, MA: Wisdom Publications.

Nichterlein, M., and J. R. Morss (2017), *Deleuze and Psychology: Philosophic Provocations and Psychological Practices*, Abingdon: Routledge.

O'Sullivan, S. (2014), 'Remarks on Deleuze, Badiou, and Western Buddhism', *Deleuze Studies*, 8 (2): 256–79.

See, T., and J. Bradley (eds) (2017), *Deleuze and Buddhism*, Basingstoke: Palgrave Macmillan.

Smith, M. N. (2010), 'Terrorism as Ethical Singularity', *Public Affairs Quarterly*, 24 (3): 229–45.

Yovel, Y. (1989), *Spinoza and Other Heretics: The Adventures of Immanence*, Princeton: Princeton University Press.

Chapter 6

What if, What One Needs to Cure Oneself of is the Cure? The Clandestine Complicity of Opponents

Anup Dhar

> How does one keep from being fascist, even (especially) when one believes oneself to be a revolutionary militant? (Foucault, in Deleuze and Guattari 2000: xiii)

> *Anti-Oedipus* develops an approach that is decidedly *diagnostic* ('What constitutes our sickness today?') and profoundly *healing* as well. What it attempts to cure us of is the cure itself. (Deleuze and Guattari 2000: xvii)

It would not be an exaggeration, perhaps, to suggest that a spectre is haunting the West: the spectre of the 'suicide bomber'. The 'un-beautiful' figure of the suicide bomber operating at what Freud calls the 'border of the knowable',[1] the uncanny and inexplicable ethic of such a figure[2] – an ethic that goes beyond the paradigmatic 'acting out' of legitimate violence: *war* – is putting into crisis the logic of pure reason, as also the simple division between an Ordered social and the unanticipated rupture: *terror*. 'Is there a crucial difference between someone *who kills in order to die*' – the suicide bomber – and someone '*who dies in order to kill*' – the soldier? Is there a need to think beyond the 'mythology of suicide as [mere individual] *pathology*', or as 'motivated irrationality' (see Lear [1998] for a discussion on *akrasia*)? Further, is the suicide bomber uncanny and inexplicable because it is 'not properly integrated' into the standard logic-language-ethos of, at times, 'liberalism', and at other times, 'Western civilisation', in general? Does this explain the *horror* – the horror Western societies experience when faced with images of suicide bombing, societies used to and complicit in the perpetration of unimaginable cruelties? Rose (2004) notes that suicide operations do not kill as many civilians as conventional warfare does, and yet people in the West react to them with exceptional horror.[3] Is it also because the suicide bomber is offering to a largely 'sick' context a form of 'cure' that is uncanny, that is neither the logic of war nor the logic of medicine, that is neither the logic of medicine that speaks the language of war (antigen/ antibodies) nor the logic of war that speaks the language of public hygiene or (ethnic) cleansing?[4]

What explains this horror? The 'unbearable intimacy' shared in their final moments by the suicide bomber and their victims; the 'passionate identification' with the 'enemy intimate'; the deadly deconstructive embrace; the fact that the perpetrator dies of their own *free will* at the very moment of their crime; the fact that crime and punishment are united; that punishment to the other and punishment to the self are joined in an uneasy/unholy embrace? Perhaps what horrifies is not just dying and killing (or killing by dying) but the 'violent appearance of something that is normally disregarded in secular modernity: *the limitless pursuit of freedom, the illusion of an uncoerced interiority*' (Asad 2007: 91), that can withstand the (naturalised-normalised) force of secret community Order and oedipalised institutional disciplines. Liberalism disapproves of the violent exercise of freedom outside the frame of law (what however is law; is it a delusional veil over the secret of community might?) (Dhar 2020). The suicide bomber is perhaps, like Schreber,[5] who forms the groundless ground for *Anti-Oedipus: Capitalism and Schizophrenia*, a figure and embodiment of, paradoxically, limitless freedom amid intense experiences of un-freedom at one and the same time.

Or is it uncanny because it is a new form of subjectivity (unknown to the ones modernity had engendered), with a 'culture of death' or 'death wish' *crypted* in the political (given that the extant discourse of the political is bereft of such a possibility)? How to account for contemporary suicide bombing not simply as an unsettling category of political practice, unknown once again to established idioms of political practice or protest, as Gandhian 'fasting unto death' was within the womb of colonialism? If *homo sacer*[6] is he who can be killed and *not* sacrificed, who then is the suicide bomber? Does he or she invert this relation to sovereignty, transforming themselves into the one who 'can be *sacrificed* but not killed'? Given the violence of community might masquerading as law, is this a 'this-worldly' endeavour of founding a just community, founding through 'religious sacrifice' (Latin: *sacri-ficium* – 'making holy')? Is it also uncanny because it (i.e. the act) puts to crisis the ubiquitous – ubiquitous in the 'whole discourse of modern Western philosophy' – and stereotypical perception and image of the *Muselmann* as the 'figure of the powerless, of extreme weakness and subjection' and of 'being the example par excellence of subjugation'; as also 'the terminal point of no return for *homo sacer*' (Agamben 1999: 63)? Hegel points out that 'both Jews and Muslims are thoroughly submitted, they are slaves. They are slaves to their god' and to the 'despot', and 'the terms of that submission' (Shaikh 2005) are precisely those that perhaps led to the redescription of the some of the more frail Jews (in extreme forms of physical inanition) in Auschwitz as *Muselmann* or Muslim; extreme powerlessness had, as it were, turned some of the Jews in Auschwitz into Muslims (Agamben 1999: 64; Shaikh 2005). Does 9/11 put to crisis this long-standing 'culture of stereotypes'?

The 'hauntology' of such a figure, problematising, on the one hand, the logic of the self-directed violence of suicide, and on the other, the other-directed violence of fascism, forms the context of the question this chapter asks: what is terror? (*What is terror*, and not the psycho-diagnostic question: *who* is the terrorist, or the question the security-state[7] asks: *where* is the terrorist, marked by the perpetual and endless search for the terrorist.) In other words, it also asks: what is *not* terror; where is the limit point of terror; and who is not perpetuating terror? This chapter argues that even oedipalisation *is* terror, albeit subtle. The oedipal family normalises us through loving terror; it terrorises us into *normalisation* (Foucault 2003); it normalises terror. The displacement of the simple (sexual) might of the father by the 'Law of the Father', the individual might of the sovereign by the (legal) might of the community, *is* sublime terror. The primordial *Urstaat*,[8] the eternal model of everything the state wants to be and desires, is terror.

Anti-Oedipus is 'The Other Side of Terror'. Foucault (2000) sees *Anti-Oedipus* as a book *of* (and not *on*) ethics. He sees *Anti-Oedipus* as a book of 'ethical action' and 'living', as a book of *praxis* and a book of *becoming*. It is a book that is not on ethics (which is usual in philosophy) but a book of ethics, a book that itself, in itself, exudes ethics. But how can a book be ethical? Be-*ing* anti-oedipal, becoming anti-oedipal is, for Foucault – who is standing at the threshold of foregrounding concepts such as Greek *askesis* (as against Christian asceticism) – a way of thinking (the ethical) as also (a form of ethical) living. The question of *Anti-Oedipus* or the 'anti-oedipal question' is: how does one keep from being fascist, even (especially) when one believes oneself to be opposing fascism? This chapter also marks a sharp distinction between *Anti-Oedipus* – the book – and 'anti-oedipus' – the subject/ schizo-position; between *Anti-Oedipus* – the written text – and 'anti-oedipus' – the process of becoming, the praxis, the art – not art as an object, but art as artisanal, art as the art *of*, art of becoming anti-oedipal or anti-fascist/anti-terror. This chapter argues that Deleuze doesn't just offer a theorisation of terror; by turning the table on the oedipalised/

neuroticised, he offers a possible praxis of anti-terror, which oedipalised psychoanalysis cannot. Deleuze and Guattari (2000: 45) designate oedipalised psychoanalysis as 'no longer a question of suggestion, but of sheer terrorism':

> Melanie Klein herself writes: 'The first time Dick came to me ... he manifested no sort of affect when his nurse handed him over to me. When I showed him the toys I had put ready, he looked at them without the faintest interest. I took a big train and put it beside a smaller one *and called them* "Daddy-train" and "Dick-train." Thereupon he picked up the train I called "Dick" and made it roll to the window and said "Station." *I explained:* "The station is mummy; Dick is going into mummy." He left the train, ran into the space between the outer and inner doors of the room, shutting himself in, saying "dark," and ran out again directly. He went through this performance several times. *I explained to him:* "It is dark inside mummy. Dick is inside dark mummy." Meantime he picked up the train again, but soon ran back into the space between the doors. While I was saying that he was going into dark mummy, he said twice in a questioning way: "Nurse?"'
> ... *As his analysis progressed ... Dick had also discovered* the wash-basin as symbolizing the mother's body, and he displayed an extraordinary dread of being wetted with water. 'Say that it's Oedipus, or you'll get a slap in the face.' The psychoanalyst no longer says to the patient: 'Tell me a little bit about your desiring-machines, won't you?' Instead he screams: 'Answer daddy-and-mommy when I speak to you!' Even Melanie Klein. (Deleuze and Guattari 2000: 45)

In an oedipalised framework, suicide bombing would be seen as 'phantasies of modern parricide' in a context of perhaps 'Muslim castration', precipitated in turn by the inescapable grip of the work of the 'death drive' in the powerless. In a standard Lacanian framework, it would be presented as 'desire stemming from *lack*' or as an unwelcome 'welcome to the desert of the *unrepresentable* Real' (Žižek 2002).[9] In one's search for 'suitably ordering explanatory paradigms' (Asad 2007: 44), and because of the 'absoluteness of the event, as much as its disorientating violence', one is often seduced by the 'gravitational pull of meta-identitarian narratives or orientalising platitudes that functionally *de-politicise* the suicide in suicide-bombing whilst inscribing it on various crudely psychological or purely instrumentalist milieus' (Michelsen 2012); and where political terms are invoked by psychologists or analysts, they generally mask structural or symptomatological understandings. How then does one not lose one's way into the dreary desert sand of a certain *psychologisation* of the 'subject' or the 'act'? How does one politicise without losing touch with the psychological?

The *a-politicism* of Psychoanalysis: The *a-psychoanalyticism* in Politics

Derrida (1998) invokes psychoanalysis's *a-politicism* as also *a-psychoanalyticism* in politics in the context of the question of 'torture' and human rights violation in Argentina. He asks: what is that form of violence that we call torture? Where does it begin and end? What is the status of the suffering inflicted or undergone in torture? What is the substance of torture? What is the phantasy structure of torture? What is the symbolic logic of torture? One can ask similar questions with respect to suicide bombing. Derrida asks:

> why is the International Psycho-Analytic Association unable to take up a position on certain kinds of violence in any other terms than those of a *pre-psychoanalytic* and *apsychoanalytic* juridical discourse, even then adopting only the vaguest and most impoverished forms of that traditional legal idiom, forms deemed inadequate by modern human rights jurists and lobbyists themselves? (1998: 76)

Derrida suggests: 'at present there exists no approach to political problems, no code of political discourse, that has in any rigorous way incorporated the axiomatics of a possible psychoanalysis' (1998: 76). In this chapter, we do not wish to be either pre-psychoanalytic/a-psychoanalytic or pre-political/a-political in our understanding of the suicide bomber. What, then, is it to put (not just someone [which is our usual understanding of psychoanalysis], but) something 'in analysis'; in this case, the question of torture (or the question of suicide bombing; avoiding all along oedipalised psychoanalysis)? What is it to put the 'political' (of suicide bombing) *in analysis*? The first 'concerns the neutralization of ethics and of the political realm, an utter dissociation of the psychoanalytic sphere from the sphere of the citizen or moral subject in his or her public or private life; and a consequent circumscribing of psychoanalysis within the realm of the "clinical"' (Derrida and Nicholson-Smith 1991). The other

> involves the retreat toward ethical-political positions whose neutrality is rivaled only by their seeming irreproachability; they lean, moreover, away from the political and toward the ethical ... It is in this context that a doctrine of human rights is evoked – a doctrine, what is more, itself ill-defined – the shelter is taken behind a language with no psychoanalytic content or pertinence, a language that takes no risks of a psychoanalytic nature and that should certainly satisfy no one present here today. What is an 'individual'? What is a 'legitimate freedom' ... what is the 'political' from a psychoanalytic point of view? (Derrida 1998: 77)

What is the psychoanalytic from a political point of view? What is it to politicise psychoanalytic concepts? This also relates to so many

> vast and pressing issues [such as philosophy of law, its history, the problem of its relationships to ethics, politics, ontology, and the value of the person or even of the humanity of the human individual – the possibility (or impossibility) of forming the notion of dignity, in the Kantian sense, which would transcend all values, all exchange, all equivalence, and perhaps even go beyond the idea of law itself, beyond judicial weighing-up] which the psychoanalytic problematic should no longer be able to evade and about which it ought to open a debate with Plato, Kant, Hegel, Marx, Heidegger, and several others, as well as with jurists and philosophers of law. A debate of this kind has never been more apropos, and when I say that psychoanalysis should no longer be able to evade it, this also implies, in my view, that psychoanalysis cannot itself in this respect be evaded. (Derrida 1998: 78)

What is the political from a psychoanalytic point of view? What is it to displace political concepts with psychoanalytic perspectives? Derrida shows how the Association 'dispenses with any properly psychoanalytic reflection upon human rights, upon what the meaning of "right" might be in a world where psychoanalysis is a contemporary reality' (1998: 78). One hence needs to look for the

> theoretical constructs best able to bring out the conceptual inadequacy of the axiomatics of human rights and of Western political discourse, and to show the way in which these are rooted in deconstructible philosophemes ... they indicate the necessity for a new ethics – not just for an 'ethics of psychoanalysis' [Lacan, 1997], but for another ethical discourse on ethics in general, another political discourse on politics in general, a discourse that would take into account deconstructive and psychoanalytic factors. (Derrida 1998: 81)

Derrida thus argues for a (deconstructive and) psychoanalytic rethinking of the political; however, this is possible only when, and if, there is a political rethinking, and why not, a political re-evaluation of the psychoanalytic corpus. Suicide bombing would thus require the Moebius of a psychoanalytic rethinking of the political and a political rethinking of psychoanalysis. Which kind of psychoanalysis and which kind of political would come to dialogue, or would come to interrupt each other, would, of course, be a question. This chapter is an invitation to the understanding of psychoanalysis (which is not psychoanalysis per se, but *schizoanalysis*: 'schizoanalysis ... does not hide the fact that it is a *political* and *social* psychoanalysis, a *militant* analysis' [Deleuze and Guattari 2000: 98]) and of the political that Deleuze and Guattari develop in *Anti-Oedipus*, the book.[10]

Rewriting the Lacanian Real

> Wouldn't it be better to *schizophrenize* – to schizophrenize the domain of the unconscious as well as the sociohistorical domain, so as to . . . rediscover everywhere the force of desiring-production; to renew, on the level of the *Real*, the tie between the analytic machine, desire, and production? (Deleuze and Guattari 2000: 310)

> the unconscious of *schizoanalysis* is unaware of persons, aggregates, and laws, and of images, structures, and symbols. It is an orphan, just as it is an anarchist and an atheist . . . The unconscious is . . . not structural, nor is it symbolic, for its reality is that of the *Real* in its very production, in its very *inorganization*. It is not representative, but solely machinic, and productive. Destroy, destroy. The task of schizoanalysis goes by way of destruction – a whole scouring of the unconscious, a complete curettage. Destroy Oedipus, the illusion of the ego, the puppet of the superego, guilt, the law, castration. (Deleuze and Guattari 2000: 311)

Deleuze and Guattari (2000; 2005) render the Lacanian registers *Marxian*: the three regimes – the primitive territorial regime, the despotic regime and the modern capitalist regime – are, as it were, made to correspond to the three points of Lacan's triadic mapping of the structure, namely the Real (primitive/primordial), the Symbolic (despotic/territorialised) and the Imaginary (deterriorialised) (Buchanan 2008: 89). While I do not get into the veracity of this 'translation', I would like to argue, building on Buchanan's incisive insight, that they thus ground the Lacanian concepts in *history*, answering in the process the question Lacan himself left unanswered, namely the question of the *genealogy* of his concepts:

> every subject is directly coupled to elements of their historical situation – the soldier, the cop, the occupier, the collaborator, the radical, the resister, the boss, the boss's wife – who constantly break all triangulations, and who prevent the entire situation from falling back on the familial complex and becoming internalized in it. (Deleuze and Guattari 2000: 96)

It is, as it were, a certain Foucauldisation of Lacan: 'what they aim to show is that it is capitalism itself that gives rise to Oedipus as the dirty little secret of desire. The aim isn't to exonerate desire and profess its innocence, however, but to show that it is primarily *social* [and political] in nature' (Buchanan 2008: 90).

Deleuze and Guattari, contrary to what Lacanians profess, argue that Lacan 'does not enclose the unconscious in an Oedipal structure'. For Lacan, according to them, 'Oedipus is imaginary'. It is nothing but 'an image, a myth' and this image is produced by an oedipalising structure:

> this structure acts only insofar as it reproduces the element of castration, which itself is not imaginary but symbolic. There we have the three major planes of structuration, which correspond to the molar aggregates: Oedipus as the imaginary reterritorialization of private man, produced under the structural conditions of capitalism, in as much as capitalism reproduces and revives the archaism of the imperial symbol or the vanished despot. All three are necessary – precisely in order to lead Oedipus to the point of its self-critique. The task undertaken by Lacan is to lead Oedipus to such a point. (Deleuze and Guattari 2000: 310)

Anti-Oedipus is directed against the reduction of the subject to a structured set of Lacanian questions: 'am I parent or child, alive or dead, man or woman, or am I desirable', as also to just the oedipal struggle:

> There is no Oedipal triangle: Oedipus is always open in an open social field. Oedipus opens to the four winds, to the four corners of the social field (not even 3 + 1, but 4 + *n*). A poorly closed triangle, a porous or seeping triangle, an exploded triangle from which the flows of desire escape in the direction of other territories. (Deleuze and Guattari 2000: 95)

The *real inorganisation of desire* stems from a schizophrenisation of the domain of the unconscious as well as the sociohistorical domain.

Deleuze and Guattari thus take us to 'The Other Side of (Lacanian) Psychoanalysis' – the 'reverse side' as a

> positive principle of *nonconsistency* that dissolves it: where desire is shifted into the order of production, related to its molecular elements, and where it lacks nothing, because it is defined as *the natural and sensuous objective being,* at the same time as the Real is defined as *the objective being of desire.* (Deleuze and Guattari 2000: 111)

It is the side of inorganisation, the side of schizophrenisation, as against the side of the *symbolic organisation* of the structure, with its *constitutive exclusions* that come from the function of the signifier. To be anti-oedipal is to be anti-organisation: anti-ego, anti-neurosis, anti-party, anti-repressive. To be anti-oedipal is to turn to the 'real' or the 'social-Real' (Deleuze and Guattari 2005: 215), to the psychotic phenomenon/experience, to non-party political formations, to the productive unconscious, to the group unconscious. It is to attack all reductive psychoanalytic and political analyses that remain caught within the sphere of totalisation, homogenisation and unification, in order to free the multiplicity of desire from the deadly neurotic and oedipal yoke (Deleuze and Guattari 2000: xx). Oedipus is not a mere psychoanalytic construct. Oedipus is the figurehead of imperialism, 'colonization pursued by other means, it is the *interior colony*, and we shall see that even here at home ... it is our intimate colonial education' (Deleuze and Guattari 2000: xx). This internalisation of man by man, this oedipalisation, creates a new meaning for suffering, *internal suffering*, and a new tone for life: the 'depressive tone'. The rupture with Lacanians is also in the way Deleuze and Guattari emphasise 'Lacan's admirable theory of desire' (2000: 27); a theory which has two poles: one related to the *objet petit a – objet petit a* as a *desiring-machine*, which defines desire in terms of a *real production* (or perhaps productions of the Real; because *objet petit a* is a fragment of the Real); and the other related to the big Other as a nodal signifier, which reintroduces a certain notion of *lack*.

Deleuze and Guattari show how depression and Oedipus are agencies of statism, agencies of paranoia, agencies of power, long before being delegated to the family. Oedipus is the *figure* of power as such, just as neurosis is the *result* of power on individuals. For anti-oedipalists, the ego, like Oedipus, is 'part of those things we must dismantle through the united assault of analytical and political forces' (Deleuze and Guattari 2000: xx). Oedipus is 'The Repressive Hypothesis' self-injected into the unconscious, it is what gives us faith as it robs us of power; *it* is what teaches us to desire our own *repression*: 'How could the masses be made to desire their own repression? ... Why do men fight *for* their servitude as stubbornly as though it were their salvation?' (Deleuze and Guattari 2000: xvi, 38).[11] One has been oedipalised and neuroticised at home, at school, at work; indoctrinated into disavowing the 'fascism in [the holier than thou in] us all', projecting it in turn on to others, with a reverse vengeance. Do the suicide bomber and the *Urstaat* come to pathological embrace (in a later section of this chapter I designate it, building on Massumi [2005], as the 'clandestine complicity of opponents') through, on the one hand, a mutual disavowal of one's 'inner fascism' and, on the other, a reciprocal diagnosis and condemnation of the Other's fascism? It's easy to be anti-fascist at the 'molar level', and not see the fascist inside oneself, the fascist one sustains, nourishes and cherishes at the micro-level, at the 'molecular' level, both personal and collective ... What makes fascism dangerous is its molecular or micropolitical power, for it is a mass movement: 'a cancerous body rather than a totalitarian organism' (Deleuze and Guattari 2005: 215).

Reversing the Freudian distinction between neurosis and psychosis[12] that measures everything against the former, *Anti-Oedipus* concludes: the neurotic is the one in whom the oedipal imprints take, whereas the psychotic is the one incapable of being oedipalised, even and especially by psychoanalysis. The first task of the revolutionary is to learn from the psychotic how to shake off the oedipal yoke and the effects of power, in order to initiate a radical politics of desire freed from 'The Repressive Hypothesis'. Such a politics dissolves the mystifications of power through the kindling of anti-oedipal forces – forces that escape coding, scramble the codes and flee in all directions: *orphans* (no daddy–mummy–me), *atheists* (no beliefs) and *nomads* (no habits, no territories, no membership). Schizoanalysis hence treats the unconscious as a *decentred* system, in other words, as a machinic network of automata (a *rhizome*), and thus arrives at an entirely different state of the unconscious: 'the unconscious itself is no more structural than personal, it does not symbolize any more than it imagines or represents; it engineers, it is *machinic*. Neither imaginary nor symbolic, it is the Real in itself, the "impossible real" and its production' (Deleuze and Guattari 2000: 53). Drives and part-objects are neither stages on a genetic axis nor positions in a deep structure; they are political options for problems, they are entryways and exits, impasses that the child lives out *politically*, with all the force of his or her desire.[13]

It is hence never enough to turn to psychoanalysis to make sense of the political. Which psychoanalysis, however, would be a question. What is the *nature* of the unconscious: *productive* not repressive; *group*[14] not individual; where desire is not emanating from individual lack but is social and political: 'the unconscious is directly related to a whole social field, both economic and political, rather than the mythical and familial grid traditionally deployed by psychoanalysis' (Deleuze 2015: 8). It is hence never enough to turn to the political to make sense of the psychoanalytic. Which understanding of the political; what is the nature of the enunciation of the political; is it marked by *ressentiment*; is it secretly nurtured by the 'fascism in us all', the fascism 'in our heads and in our everyday behavior, the fascism that causes us to love power, to desire the very thing that dominates and exploits us'; is it politics nourished in the broth of 'rural fascism and city or neighborhood fascism, youth fascism and war veteran's fascism, fascism of the Left and fascism of the Right, fascism of the couple, family, school, and office', where politics is defined by 'micro-black holes' that stand on their own and communicate with the others, before coalescing into a 'great, generalized central black hole' (Deleuze and Guattari 2015: 214)? Further, what is the need for introducing polities into psychoanalytic theory and practice and psychoanalysis into political theory and practice? Is not the 'real inorganization of desire' always already in the political? Is not politics always already in the unconscious (Deleuze 2015)?

Porcupine Peace

> One freezing winter day, a herd of porcupines huddled together to protect themselves against the cold by their combined warmth. But their spines pricked each other so painfully that they soon drew apart again. Since the cold continued, however, they had to draw together once more, and once more they found the pricking painful. This alternate moving together and apart went on until they discovered just the right distance to preserve them from both evils. (Guattari 2015: 112)

What was hitherto designated as a discrete porcupine 'self' in extant philosophies of the person is rewritten by Guattari as a short-lived and fleeting intensity *in-between* coefficients of 'pain' and 'cold', coefficients that are not just infinitely dynamic and shifting, but relative to relationships among entities. The self is one more thing Guattari dissolves. Guattari's formulation, 'the individual is also a group', 'we are all groupuscles', heralds, according to Deleuze 'the search for a new subjectivity, a group subjectivity, which does not allow itself to be enclosed in a whole bent on reconstituting a self (or even worse, a superego), but which spreads itself out over several groups at once' (Deleuze 2015: 7).

Guattari's dual interest in, on the one hand, desire (an issue rarely dealt with by Marxists) and psychoanalysis, and, on the other, the political (including a 'political analysis of desire') also led to, in a 'hospital setting' (i.e. a group setting, not the psychoanalytic dyadic setting), a rewriting of the Lacanian concepts in a collectivised context. Transference – which was hitherto dyadic (in 'object-relations') or quadratic (in Lacan's L or Z schema) – came to be seen as a *function of transversals* in a group context; fantasies were seen to be collective: desire was a problem of groups and for groups. With Guattari, transference becomes vehicular; it gets away from the dyad of the 'analyst and analysand' into group relations. The analyst is no longer the mirror or the screen; rather, it's the group. This places the group in the position of the analyst, thus making it an *analyser*.

Guattari thus helps us move from the methodological individualism of Freud and the dyadic hermeneutic to the question of groups. This chapter is thus about transversals that operate and manifest themselves in the suicide bomber's group 'structured like a language'. How does the group speak? Does it speak through the suicide bomber; is the suicide bomber the group unconscious's uncanny enunciation? To whom does the group speak? The *Urstaat* or the community might that confronts it? This takes us to a non-individualised non-psychologised understanding of the suicide bomber; s/he is one in the infinite numbers of (group) transversals. To make sense of the suicide bomber one has to make sense of the original multiplicity of transversals.

Deleuze (2015: 13–14) divides groups into 'subjugated groups' and 'group subjects'. The hierarchy, the vertical or pyramidal organisation that characterises subjugated groups, is meant to ward off any possible inscription of 'dispersal', to discourage the development of 'creative ruptures', and to ensure the self-preservation mechanisms rooted in the *exclusion* of other groups. Their centralisation works through structure, totalisation, unification, replacing the conditions of a genuine collective 'enunciation' with an assemblage of stereotypical utterances (around, say, friend/enemy, inside/outside, good/evil) cut off from the 'inorganization of the real'.[15] Group subjects, on the other hand, are defined by 'coefficients of transversality' that ward off totalitarianism and hierarchies.[16] Subjugated groups follow a path of reference received passively from the outside or the leader. Group subjects follow a path of self-reference (they have the ability to assume an internal law), that is, of interpreting their own position, with regard to their elaboration of projects and tools, and vocation in general.

Does the suicide bomber emanate from a subjugated group? Is suicide bombing the project, the tool, the vocation of a subjugated group? Deleuze shows how 'many groupuscles that as yet inspire only phantom masses already possess a structure of subjugation, complete with [a paranoid] leadership, a mechanism of transmission, and a core membership, aimlessly reproducing the errors and perversions they are trying to oppose' (Deleuze 2015: 14). This will, however, bring us back to the question of the clandestine complicity of opponents as also the terror group's own inner fascism.

The Secret of Community Might: 'the peace of generalized terror'

This section argues through the invocation of the idea of the *secret of community might* how the suicide bomber is face to face with the apparent and paradoxical peace of generalised majoritarian terror. Freud's reply (Vienna, September 1932)[17] to Einstein on 'war' works its way through the '(primitive) might' versus '(modern) right' dualism in much of the thinking on violence, and reaches, somewhat paradoxically, the question of the transition or the movement from the violence of 'primitive might' to first 'right' and then 'law'; according to Freud 'under primitive conditions, it is superior force – brute violence, or violence backed by arms – that lords it everywhere' (somewhat like Hegel's 'struggle to the death', it is brute power that determines who will be 'master' and who will end up being 'slave'; there is little space for either right/wrong, good/bad, beautiful/ugly, or a moral/proto-legal 'no', or even self-censorship). But 'in the course of evolution this state of things was modified, a path was traced that led away from violence to law'; to *law*? How? What was this path? '[I]t issued from a single verity: that the superiority of one strong man can be overborne by an alliance of many weaklings, that *l'union fait la force*. Brute force is overcome by union; the *allied might* of scattered units makes good its right against the isolated giant. Freud thus re-defines 'right' not in terms of 'might/right', but as the allied *might of a community*; 'right', too, 'is nothing else than violence, quick to attack whatever individual stands in its path, and it employs the selfsame methods, follows like ends, with but one difference: it is the communal, not individual, violence that has its way'. Freud adds: 'for the transition from crude violence to the reign of law, a certain psychological condition must first obtain'. Condition one: 'the union of the people must be permanent and well organized'. Condition two: 'it must enact rules to meet the risk of possible revolts'. Condition three: it must 'set up machinery insuring that its rules – the laws – are observed and that such acts of violence as the laws demand are duly carried out'.

Freud argues that this recognition of a 'community of interests' engenders in turn a psychology of 'unity' and 'fraternal solidarity'; it links up its members psychologically. Freud thus shows that the effort to replace brute might by right is at a deeper level the 'might of an ideal'; that right is also founded on force and needs violence to maintain itself needs to be kept in mind. While we have hitherto pitted right against might, law against force (force as irrational, as the [ab]use of power) and have assumed that it is the discourse of right(s) that counters the discourse of might and the perpetration of force, Freud shows how the discourse of right(s) is also premised on the *foreclosure* (i.e. repudiation) of a 'fundamental signifier': 'community might' and how subsequent transitions (i.e. revisions and humanisations) in the discourse of right(s) keep the signifier 'community might' *crypted* (i.e. hidden; see Abraham and Torok 1986; Derrida 1998).

Freud thus questions the assumed transformation from might *to* right; he shows that it is merely a transition from one kind of might (individual might) to another kind of might (community might). At times, such community might secretly, clandestinely crystallises into a macro-fascism. At other times, it floats along subtle and supple lines and suffuses every little social cell, every pore of life. The 'multitude of black holes' may not become centralised, become coagulated into a macro-fascism. 'Instead of the great paranoid fear', we may be trapped in a 'thousand little monomanias, self-evident truths, and clarities that gush from every black hole and no longer form a system, but are only rumble and buzz, blinding lights giving any and everybody the mission of self-appointed judge, dispenser of justice, policeman'; 'the system of petty insecurities . . . leads everyone to their own black hole in which to turn dangerous, possessing a clarity on their situation, role, and mission' (Deleuze and Guattari 2005: 228).

Clandestine Complicity of Opponents: Between the Devil and the Deep Blue Sea[18]

The real problem of 'politics' or the politics of the 'problem' is that, more often than not, the oppressor and the oppressed, the perpetrator and the victim, the colonised and the coloniser, are paradoxically united and clandestinely complicit in their respective enunciations of the logic of the oppressor or the language of the hegemonic; at times, the oppressed repeats, reiterates, mimes the 'drives' of the oppressor with uncanny vengeance; in the process, securitisation[19] and 'terrorism' become intimate enemies and are locked, intertwined in a deadly dyadic bond; they legitimate and justify, as it were, each other's steps; resistance and power are interlocked in a mutually constitutive relationship.

Building on Deleuze and Guattari's (2000; 2005) 'ontology of self-organizing processes and becoming rather than substance and being', conceptions of time as 'durations of intensity' rather than chronology or teleology, subject position as a 'dynamic process always in relation rather than an autonomous subject, and ethics (as premised on immanent criteria rather than transcendental ideals)', one could argue that there is no stable oppressor or oppressed; oppressor and oppressed are subject positions or relationships haunted by the 'inorganization of the real' or the real inorganisation of desire. The question of the ethico-politics of the oppressed or the suicide bomber is hence a charged question; ethics as a 'typology of immanent modes of existence replaces Morality' (Deleuze 1988: 23). Morality 'always refers to transcendental values'.

Morality 'is the judgement of God, the *system of judgement*'. Ethics 'overthrows the system of judgement. The opposition of values (Good–Evil) is supplanted by the qualitative difference of modes of existence (good–bad)' (Deleuze 1988: 23).

The question of *Anti-Oedipus* or the 'anti-oedipal question' becomes relevant here: 'how does one keep from being fascist, even (especially) when one believes oneself to be a revolutionary militant [or a liberator]'? *Anti-Oedipus* or the anti-oedipal becoming is thus, for Foucault, a 'tracking down of all varieties of fascism, from the enormous ones that surround and crush us to the petty ones that constitute the tyrannical bitterness of our everyday lives' (Foucault, in Deleuze and Guattari 2000: xiii). How does one refuse the pernicious invitation to participate in a Manichean politics that polarises the arguments: either one defends the 'victimised' or defends the war on terror? The anti-oedipal position is also about 'political practice as an *intensifier* of thought and analysis as a *multiplier* of the forms and domains for the intervention of political action' (Foucault, in Deleuze and Guattari 2000: xiii). It is an attack on 'what is all-too-human in mankind, on oedipalized [territorialities such as family, Church, school, nation, party] and oedipalizing analyses and *neurotic modes of living*' (Foucault, in Deleuze and Guattari 2000: xvii), as also on 'Christ, Christianity, and the herd'[20] or the 'masses' (Foucault, in Deleuze and Guattari 2000: xvii) (as against the 'pack' [of wolves] in *A Thousand Plateaus*). The crucial question for Deleuze and Guattari is hence not just what constitutes our sickness today, but more profoundly what constitutes *healing* as well. Which is why what *Anti-Oedipus* 'attempts to cure us of is [not just sickness but] the cure itself' (Foucault, in Deleuze and Guattari 2000: xvii); the purported cure that suicide bombing is, or is thought to be.

Notes

1. *Why* unknowable and *what* is so unknowable is a question this chapter shall explore; how is the register of the unknowable engendered in psychoanalysis? Is it engendered through the invocation of an inassimilable Lacanian *Real* (we shall see, in a later section, how the Lacanian Real is *rewritten* by Deleuze and Guattari in *Anti-Oedipus*)? Is it engendered as an outside or an exception in politics because the 'shoe' (of politics or of paradigmatic cures) is too tight-fitting and even the tiniest gravel of *différance* is found to be inhospitable? Is it also unknowable because we are looking for the cause in a wrong register: the individual unconscious; whereas we need to look at the group unconscious (we shall see, in a later section, how the Freudian unconscious is *rewritten* as 'productive' by Guattari in *Psychoanalysis and Trasversality*)?
2. Once again, *why* uncanny and *what* is so inexplicable; do Deleuze and Guattari (2000) help us make sense of the 'act' of suicide bombing by turning the

tables, by making *not* the proto-pathological 'acting out' but what Freud calls in *Why War* the *secret* of 'community might', and by default, the primitive or primordial *Urstaat*, the axis of inquiry? What the suicide bomber's group unconscious confronts is this *community might* crypted in the apparently law-like operations of the *Urstaat*.

3. According to the New America Foundation, 'jihadists' killed 94 people in the United States between 2005 and 2015, which, of course, is not acceptable. But during that same time period, 301,797 people in the US were shot dead, Politifact reports. At first blush, these numbers might seem to indicate that Donald Trump's temporary ban on immigrants from seven countries – a goal he said was intended to 'protect the American people from terrorist attacks by foreign nationals admitted to the United States' – was utterly misguided. But Trump was right about at least one thing: *Americans are more afraid of terrorism than they are of guns*, despite the fact that guns are 3,210 times more likely to kill them (Anderson 2017).

4. The question of 'cure' and the need to 'cure ourselves of paradigmatic cures' will recur in this chapter. What *Anti-Oedipus* 'attempts to cure us of is [not just sickness but] the cure itself' (Foucault, in Deleuze and Guattari 2000: xvii). What is the nature of the cure that the suicide bomber offers? *Dual death*; *double death* of both the 'sick' or the perpetrator of sickness, on the one hand, and the 'healer', on the other, *purportedly* the healer, the self-certified healer of social maladies, the healer who comes too close to sickness, *uncannily close*, so that s/he internalises the sickness of the sick and dies, in the last instance, of the shadow of the 'sick' or of 'sickness'? Or perhaps the philosophy of cure that drives the purported healer is that such sickness can only be cured by the death of both, by the doubling up of the dead. Does the radical intimacy with the enemy render intimate the enemy's principles; does the suicide bomber unknowingly live, reiterate and even perpetuate some of the enemy's principles; does the language of *opposition* paradoxically speak the language of the *proposition* (Nandy 2009).

5. Schreber's 'debilitating detachment from the world is a quelled attempt to engage it in unimagined ways. Schizophrenia as a positive process is inventive connection, expansion, rather than withdrawal . . . Schizophrenia . . . goes by many names. Philosophy is one. Not just any philosophy. A bastard kind. Legitimate philosophy is the handiwork of "bureaucrats" of pure reason who speak in "the shadow of the despot" and are in historical complicity with the state. They invent . . . [an] absolute State that effectively functions in the mind. Theirs is the discourse of sovereign judgment, of stable subjectivity . . . of rock-like identity, "universal" truth, and (white male) justice. Thus the exercise of their thought is in conformity with the aims of the real State, with the dominant significations, and with the requirements of the established order.' The schizophrenic, in contrast, is aligned to 'an orphan line of thinkers [Lucretius, Hume, Spinoza, Nietzsche and Bergson] affiliated only in their opposition to the State philosophy that would nevertheless accord them minor positions in its canon' (Massumi 1992: 2–3; Deleuze and Guattari 2000: 9).

6. *Homo sacer* is the paradoxical figure in ancient Roman law whose life was included in the political order only by way of its exclusion; it is a life judged unworthy of being lived; a life that could be ended with impunity and whose death therefore had no sacrificial value; the suicide bomber is also driven *by the fact that she would be put to death if the act did not already accomplish death*. The *homo sacer à la* Agamben (1995) could have been a standard way of reading the act and figure of the suicide bomber. Not any more. Because then we would read the 'what' and the 'who' of the suicide bomber. We would not

make sense of the *how*. Deleuze (and Guattari) (2000) take us to the 'how', to the *machinic*; not 'mother' and 'baby', not the baby at the mother's breast, but 'breast machine' and 'mouth machine' in 'desiring-production'. We shall hence come back to the suicide bomber on the question of the their 'group unconscious' confronting 'community might', group machine confronting community machine. We shall, however, first examine the hitherto *exempted* – that is, the oedipalised register of secret community might. Only then will we be in a position to examine the uncanny ethic of the suicide bomber.

7. Deleuze's essay 'Postscript on Societies of Control' (1992) indicates the ways in which he saw the security environment changing to one of modulated control and the management of flows and circulation, rather than the strict policing of identities. 'Unknown unknowns' determine the obsessive compulsive and paranoid logic of the radically interconnected post-Clausewitzean security-state. Such securitisation is unleashed in the name of what Massumi (2005) calls the 'spectre of the absent towers' (one remembers incessantly 'what one does not see'). War becomes conceived under the banner of 'pre-emption', where one acts to prevent something which has not occurred, which has not been experienced; one is on 'red alert'.

8. Deleuze and Guattari (2000: 217), contrary to received historical wisdom, argue that 'the State was not formed in progressive stages; it appears fully armed, a master stroke executed all at once; the primordial *Urstaat* . . . is the basic formation, on the horizon throughout history . . . Every form [of the State] that [looks to be] more "evolved" is like a palimpsest: it covers a [basic] despotic inscription: [the *secret of community might*].' The 'State itself' has always been formed 'in relation with an outside'; this exposes the warlike origin of all modern forms of civic ordering; the history of state/statist politics thus becomes the *continuation of war by other means*.

9. For Deleuze and Guattari, the Real is not unrepresentable. It is *non-representational*. It is not an unreachable limit. It is to be conceived as a *process* (Buchanan 2008: 50; Deleuze and Guattari 2000: 59–61). In their radical rereading of Lacan and the Lacanian Real, Deleuze and Guattari show how 'in Lacan, the symbolic organization of the structure, with its exclusions that come from the function of the signifier, has as its reverse side the *real inorganization of desire*' (2000: 328). They track this real *inorganisation* of desire (including the inorganisation that the Real institutes), its *productive* function in the psychotic phenomenon or experience. In the process, they *schizophrenise* the psychoanalytic field, though they themselves feel that it was Lacan 'who was the first on the contrary to schizophrenize the analytic field' (2000: 363).

10. See Dhar 2016 for a rethinking of psychoanalysis in terms of the rewriting of 'The Repressive Hypothesis' and the Wolf Man case in Bose (1921), Lacan (1997), Derrida in Abraham and Torok (1986), and Deleuze and Guattari (2000).

11. 'This is a question which the English and Americans are reluctant to deal with directly, tending too often to respond: "Fascism is a phenomenon that took place elsewhere, something that could only happen to others, but not to us; it's *their* problem." Is it though? Is fascism really a problem for others to deal with? Even revolutionary groups deal gingerly with the fascisising elements we all carry deep within us, and yet they often possess a rarely analysed but overriding group "superego" that leads them to state, much like Nietzsche's man of *ressentiment*, that the *other* is evil (The Fascist! The Capitalist! The Communist!), *and hence that they themselves are good* ("holier than thou"). This conclusion is reached as an afterthought and a justification, a supremely self-righteous rationalisation for a politics that can only "squint" at life, through

the thick clouds of foul-smelling air that permeate secret meeting places and "security" councils. The man of *ressentiment*, as Nietzsche explains, "loves hiding places, secret paths and back doors, everything covert entices him as *his* world, *his* security, *his* refreshment"' (Deleuze and Guattari 2000: xvi).

12. See Dhar 2017 for a rethinking of philosophy, psychoanalysis and the political from the experience and perspective of the 'psychotic phenomenon'. Our standard theories, our *neuroticised* frameworks, may not be enough to understand the figure of the suicide bomber, let alone explain the act.

13. Melanie Klein has no understanding of the cartography of one of her child patients, Little Richard, and is content to make ready-made tracings – Oedipus, the good daddy and the bad daddy, the bad mummy and the good mummy – while the child makes a desperate attempt to carry out a performance that the psychoanalyst totally misconstrues (Deleuze and Guattari 2000).

14. 'Freud tried to approach crowd phenomena from the point of view of the unconscious, but he did not see clearly, he did not see that the unconscious itself was fundamentally a *crowd* . . . he mistook crowds for a single person . . . and the shove of the crowd for daddy's voice' (Deleuze and Guattari 2005: 30).

15. The Lacanian Real can be understood as the register of the *inassimilable*, as also of the *foreclosed* (see Dhar 2015). Deleuze and Guattari rewrite the Lacanian Real as the register of *inorganisation*.

16. *Transversality* is inaugurated as a new concept replacing the ambiguous idea of institutional transference. 'The idea of transversality is opposed to: (a) verticality, as described in the organogramme of a pyramidal structure (leaders, assistants, etc.); (b) horizontality, as it exists in the disturbed wards of a hospital, or, even more, in the senile wards; in other words a state of affairs in which things and people fit in as best they can with the situation in which they find themselves . . . Transversality is a dimension that tries to overcome both the impasse of pure verticality and that of mere horizontality: it tends to be achieved when there is maximum communication among different levels and, above all, in different meanings' (Guattari 2015: 112–13).

17. This correspondence is available at <https://www.public.asu.edu/~jmlynch/273 /documents/FreudEinstein.pdf> (accessed 10 June 2022).

18. Gropp 2020.

19. 'State violence' is very difficult to pinpoint 'because it always presents itself as preaccomplished'; 'the mutilation is prior, preestablished' (Deleuze and Guattari 2005: 447). 'State policing or lawful violence is something else again, because it consists in capturing while simultaneously constituting a right to capture. It is an incorporated, structural violence distinct from every kind of direct violence. The State has often been defined by a "monopoly of violence," but this definition leads back to another definition that describes the State as a "state of Law". State overcoding is precisely this structural violence that defines the law, "police" violence and not the violence of war. There is lawful violence wherever violence contributes to the creation of that which it is used against . . . wherever capture contributes to the creation of that which it captures. This is very different from [the] violence [of the suicide bomber]. It is also why, in contradistinction to primitive violence, State or lawful violence always seems to presuppose itself, for it preexists its own use: the State can in this way say that violence is "primal," that it is simply a natural phenomenon the responsibility for which does not lie with the State, which uses violence only against the violent, against [he suicide bomber] in order that peace may reign' (Deleuze and Guattari 2005: 447).

20. Such a herd instinct is based on 'the desire to be led, the desire to have someone else legislate life. The very desire that was brought so glaringly into focus in

Europe with Hitler, Mussolini, and fascism; the desire that is still at work, making us all sick, today' (Seem, in Deleuze and Guattari 2000: xvi).

References

Abraham, N., and M. Torok (1986), *The Wolf Man's Magic Word: A Cryptonymy*, trans. N. Rand, Minneapolis: University of Minnesota Press.

Agamben, G. (1995), *Homo Sacer: Sovereign Power and Bare Life*, trans. D. Heller-Roazen, Stanford: Stanford University Press.

Agamben, G. (1999), *Remnants of Auschwitz: The Witness and the Archive*, New York: Zone Books.

Anderson, J. (2017), 'The Psychology of Why 94 Deaths from Terrorism are Scarier than 301,797 Deaths from Guns', <https://qz.com/898207/the-psychology-of-why-americans-are-more-scared-of-terrorism-than-guns-though-guns-are-3210-times-likelier-to-kill-them/> (last accessed 3 April 2020).

Asad, T. (2007), *On Suicide Bombing*, New York: Columbia University Press.

Bose, G. (1921), *Concept of Repression*, Calcutta and London: Sri Gauranga Press and Kegan Paul, Trench, Trubner.

Buchanan, I. (2008), *Deleuze and Guattari's Anti-Oedipus: A Reader's Guide*, London: Continuum.

Deleuze, G. (1988), *Spinoza: Practical Philosophy*, trans. R. Hurley, San Francisco: City Lights.

Deleuze, G. (1992), 'Postscript on Societies of Control', *October*, 59: 3–7, <https://www.jstor.org/stable/778828?seq=1> (last accessed 3 May 2022).

Deleuze, G. (2015), 'Preface: Three Group-Related Problems', in *Psychoanalysis and Transversality: Texts and Interviews 1955–1971*, trans. A. Hodges, ed. F. Guattari, Los Angeles: Semiotext(e), pp. 7–21.

Deleuze, G., and F. Guattari (1986), *Nomadology: The War Machine*, trans. B. Massumi, Los Angeles: Semiotext(e).

Deleuze, G., and F. Guattari (2000), *Anti-Oedipus: Capitalism and Schizophrenia*, trans. R. Hurley, M. Seem and H. R. Lane, Minneapolis: University of Minnesota Press.

Deleuze, G., and F. Guattari (2005), *A Thousand Plateaus: Capitalism and Schizophrenia*, trans. B. Massumi, Minneapolis: University of Minnesota Press.

Derrida, J. (1998), *Of Grammatology*, trans. G. C. Spivak, Baltimore: Johns Hopkins University Press.

Derrida, J., and D. Nicholson-Smith (1991), 'Geopsychoanalysis: ". . . and the rest of the world"', *American Imago*, 48 (2): 199–231.

Dhar, A. (2015), 'What if, the Hurt is Real', in R. Ramdev, S. Devesan and D. Bhattacharya (eds), *The State of Hurt: Sentiment, Politics, Censorship*, New Delhi: Sage, pp. 15–28.

Dhar, A. (2016), 'The Schizo-Political: Repression, Liberation and the Beyond', *CUSP*, 1 (2): 1–17, special issue 'Psychoanalysis and the Political'.

Dhar, A. (2017), 'Cryptonymy: Deconstruction, Psychoanalysis, Politics', in F. Manjali and M. Crépon (eds), *Philosophy, Language and the Political: Poststructuralism in Perspective*, New Delhi: Aakar Books.

Dhar, A. (2020), 'The Real of Law', in L. Vashist and J. Sood (eds), *Rethinking Law and Violence*, New Delhi: Oxford University Press, pp. 1–18.

Foucault, M. (2000), 'Preface', in G. Deleuze and F. Guattari, *Anti-Oedipus: Capitalism and Schizophrenia*, trans. R. Hurley, M. Seem and H. R. Lane, Minneapolis: University of Minnesota Press, pp. xiii–xvi.

Foucault, M. (2003), *Abnormal: Lectures at the Collège de France, 1974–1975*, vol. 4, trans. G. Burchell, London: Verso.

Gropp, L. (2020), 'Interview with Salman Rushdie: Kashmir, Paradise Lost', *Qanta ra.de – Dialogue with the Islamic World*, <https://en.qantara.de/content/interview -with-salman-rushdie-kashmir-paradise-lost> (last accessed 4 April 2020).

Guattari, F. (ed.) (2015), *Psychoanalysis and Transversality: Texts and Interviews 1955–1971*, trans. A. Hodges, Los Angeles: Semiotext(e).

Lacan, J. (1997), *The Ethics of Psychoanalysis 1959–1960: The Seminar of Jacques Lacan*, book VII, trans. Denis Porter, London: Routledge.

Lear, J. (1998), *Open Minded: Working Out the Logic of the Soul*, Cambridge, MA: Harvard University Press.

Massumi, B. (1992), *A User's Guide to Capitalism and Schizophrenia: Deviations from Deleuze and Guattari*, Cambridge, MA: MIT Press.

Massumi, B. (2005), 'Fear (The Spectrum Said)', *Positions: East Asia Cultures Critique*, 113 (1): 31–48. Revised and reprinted in B. Massumi, *Ontopower: War, Powers, and the State of Perception*, Durham, NC: Duke University Press, 2015, pp. 171–88.

Michelsen, N. (2012), 'Politics and Suicide in the Work of Gilles Deleuze and Felix Guattari', PhD thesis, King's College University of London.

Nandy, A. (2009), *The Intimate Enemy: Loss and Recovery of Self under Colonialism*, New Delhi: Oxford University Press.

Rose, J. (2004), 'Deadly Embrace', *London Review of Books*, 26 (21): 21, <https://www.lrb.co.uk/the-paper/v26/n21/jacqueline-rose/deadly-embrace> (last accessed 3 May 2022).

Seem, M. (2000), 'Introduction', in G. Deleuze and F. Guattari, *Anti-Oedipus: Capitalism and Schizophrenia*, trans. R. Hurley, M. Seem and H. R. Lane, Minneapolis: University of Minnesota Press, pp. xvii–xxiv.

Shaikh, N. (2005), 'The Muselmann in Auschwitz: Interview with Gil Anidjar conducted by Nermeen Shaikh of AsiaSource', <http://www.cambridgeforecast.org/MIDDLEEAST/MUSELMANN.html> (last accessed 26 February 2020).

Žižek, S. (2002), *Welcome to the Desert of the Real*, London: Verso.

Chapter 7

Terror and the Time-Image: How Not to Believe in the World

Clayton Crockett

What is terror? Terror implies and often mediates violence, but the crucial form of terror is a mode of visibility. Terror works by constituting an image, a spectacle. Terror works against a given state of affairs that is experienced as intolerable. The intensification of intolerability leads to a situation where visible violence is preferred to the hidden violence of slow death. Terror makes manifest something that is usually hidden. The difference between terror in general and what is called terrorism can be distinguished in relation to the state. The contemporary nation-state is threatened with violence from within and without, by peoples, weapons, economic and energy constraints, but it works to contain this violence in different ways. If the state possesses the monopoly on violence, which is only ever true in theory not in fact, then it sometimes resorts to terror to enforce and preserve state power. Terrorism is the name given to acts of terror that are used by non-state actors against supposedly illegitimate states and their people.

To engage with a Deleuzian perspective on global terror, I want to consider his treatment of the image. Specifically, Deleuze articulates the time-image in *Cinema 2* as a way to free the image from the spectacle that is aligned with terror. Here I endorse Paola Marrati's striking claim that '*Cinema 1* and *2* are the key texts in which Deleuze develops his political philosophy' (Marrati 2008: x). This claim is not intended to minimise the importance of Guattari, or the groundbreaking political thought of *Capitalism and Schizophrenia*, but much of the specific schizoanalysis of *Anti-Oedipus* and *A Thousand Plateaus* will remain in the background so that I can consider the nature and stakes of the image.

In his famous book *Society of the Spectacle*, Guy Debord presents the spectacle as the culmination of a world in which images have been detached from life and 'fuse[d] in a common stream' that constitutes 'the concrete inversion of life' (Debord 1983: §2). Here images mediate all of our social relations, replacing the directly lived experience of human beings. Debord's Situationism attempts to expose and counter the alienation introduced by the spectacle, whose ultimate content is capital. Our lives are more and more regulated by images that mediate commodities as objects, and the assemblage of these images into a whole composes a spectacle. This spectacle constitutes a universal world history and consciousness, but it is a false consciousness. Debord says that 'unified irreversible time is the time of the *world market* and, as a corollary, of the world spectacle, but this general world perspective that proceeds irreversibly from production to its goal of consumption is an illusion' (1983: §145). The illusion of the spectacle distracts us from our awareness of its separation from life, and we could argue that the situation in the twenty-first century is even more fully saturated with spectacular images.

This book was originally published in 1967, and it evinces the leftist hope that analysing the spectacle can give people the power to surmount it. For Debord, 'the very development of class society to the stage of spectacular organization of non-life thus leads the revolutionary project to become *visibly* what it already was *essentially*' (Debord 1983: §123). This visibility of revolutionary theory and practice works against the ideology that pervades our society of the spectacle. The only way to destroy the society of the spectacle is with 'the resumption of the revolutionary class struggle' that combines unified critical theory with unified rigorous practice (Debord 1983: §203). Such revolutionary expectation appears utopian, although it was much less so in the late 1960s in the context of Third World liberation movements as well as the insurrection that broke out in France in May 1968. In hindsight, we can see that what Debord and others glimpsed as a revolutionary possibility ended up becoming a transformation to a new 'spirit of capitalism'. As Slavoj Žižek explains it, 'the hierarchical Fordist structure of the production process was gradually abandoned and replaced with a network-based form of organization founded on employee initiative and autonomy in the workplace' (Žižek 2010: 355–6). The world economy shifted from a productive real economy to a speculative financial economy, and money and debt were used as weapons backed up by military force to ensure that revolutionary movements were contained, co-opted or crushed.

Our contemporary social media organises our lifeworld so completely that we do not know where life ends and non-life begins. Our experiences of the world are mediated primarily by the screens of computers and smartphones that stream images and text for our consumption. The society of the spectacle that Debord critiqued has metamorphosed to encompass the entire globe, constructing what Peter Sloterdijk calls the 'crystal palace' of contemporary global capitalism. The totalisation of the society of the spectacle leads to a 'gigantic hothouse of relaxation' that is 'devoted to a merry and hectic cult of Baal for which the twentieth century suggested the term "consumerism"' (Sloterdijk 2013: 170–1). The crystal palace is a vast spatial enclosure that prevents anything new from occurring, even as its reflective elements heat up the planet to dangerous levels.

This crystallisation is also a kind of visibility, a spectacle that draws us in and numbs us in its beauty and its banality. As Deleuze says in *Cinema 2*, 'it is because this world is intolerable that it can no longer think a world or think itself. The intolerable is no longer a serious injustice, but the permanent state of a daily banality' (1989: 170). We need reasons to believe in this world, whose link has become broken. The society of the spectacle is intolerable, because it substitutes the social relation of images for the real relations of life. And the intolerability of the society of the spectacle leads to terrorism, because the violent smashing of its images is seen by many as the only way to revolt against it. The problem is that such violence only feeds the spectacle, because the precise nature of terroristic violence is visible and spectacular. The way to operate in a terrorist mode is to make state violence and counter-state violence visible and spectacular.

The slow, crushing violence of capital is a subtle form of terror that operates as fear, including the fear of spectacular violence and terrorism. The daily banal intolerability of capitalism and neoliberalism is simply the flip-side of the spectacular violence of terrorism. As workers, whatever our situation of labour, we experience our situation as precarious and threatened, even as extremists threaten our being and way of life. The fear is palpable, and under the happy surface of pop psychology lurks this anxious dread. We are rendered schizophrenic from the demands to be productive, to be happy and to be successful, along with the brutal reality of the emptiness of our soulless lives that can measure satisfaction only in terms of material wealth. The banality of our daily existence cries out for some dramatic image to distract us or feed our narcissism, but this only intensifies the grip of the spectacle that holds us in place.

It is not just the sheer amount of images that overwhelms us, but also their *speed*. Here the work of Paul Virilio is relevant, and Virilio is an important influence on Deleuze and Guattari. In his book *Desert Screen: War at the Speed of Light*, written during and after the first Gulf War in 1991, Virilio anticipates many elements of the second Gulf War in 2003 as well as the ongoing conflict in Afghanistan as a response to the terrorist attacks of 9/11 and the ongoing global 'war on terror'. He argues that weapons of communication are even more important than weapons of destruction in this new situation of war. These weapons of communication 'are going to dominate, thanks to the development of a globalized news network and a generalized tele-surveillance' (Virilio 2002: 49). Technology and the military merge with the entertainment industry to produce war as a spectacle to consume, scripted and staged by corporate media.

We are constantly bombarded with new threats and new enemies: China, America, Russia, North Korea, Syria, IS, earthquakes, hurricanes and famines. It's a blur, as well as a shell game to confuse and distract the masses from the ongoing transfer of wealth from poor to rich. In his book Virilio calls for an ecology of the media that shows how this spectacle prevents thought. He says that 'no politics is possible at the speed of light. Politics depends on having time for reflection' (Virilio 2002: 43). In order to respond in real time we have to work faster and faster to keep us with our technologies. It is hard to conceive of democracy working under such conditions, because 'what defines democracy is the sharing of power. When there is not time to share, what will be shared? Emotions' (Virilio 2002: 43). Politics in the society of the spectacle is fundamentally based on triggering emotional responses, not rational discourse.

In his discussion with Giovanna Borradori in *Philosophy in a Time of Terror*, Jacques Derrida articulates his notion of autoimmunity to help make sense of the 'war on terror' in the wake of the 9/11 attacks. He argues that we need to interrogate our received concepts of war and of terror, and recognise that what we call the war on terrorism 'work[s] to regenerate, in the short or long term, the causes of the evil they claim to eradicate' (Borradori 2003: 100). The war on terror is an autoimmune response by the United States and its allies, because the nation is willing to attack itself in order to preserve its way of life. The relationship among important concepts such as *terra*, territory and terror 'has changed, and it is necessary to know that this is because of knowledge, that is, because of technoscience' (Borradori 2003: 101). This technology of technoscience fundamentally concerns the image and the spectacle of terror in terms of how it is produced, how it is recognised and how it is consumed.

In his discussion, Derrida cites the significance of Carl Schmitt's work on war and politics, although he does so critically. He says that we can learn from Schmitt's analysis of the different types of war, including classical war, civil war and partisan war. In his book *The Theory of the*

Partisan, Schmitt argues that partisan war constitutes a new type of war that is related to contemporary terrorism. Partisan war for Schmitt is a broadening of war beyond the traditional battlefield. Guerrilla wars are intensely political, in Schmitt's terms, because they are based on enmity towards the oppressor, who is a true enemy. These partisan wars extend war, but they do not absolutise it. As a realist, Schmitt was concerned with limiting and preventing the manifestation of war and its chaotic violence. He was not a fan of the partisan, but he recognised it as an important phenomenon, and saw it as both an intensification of war in some ways as well as a restraining of war in others.

In his analysis, Schmitt emphasises the connection of the partisan fighter to territory. This link is what prevents partisan war from becoming absolute, even if partisan war is totalising in its mobilisation. 'For at least as long as anti-colonial wars are possible on our planet,' Schmitt claims, 'the partisan will represent a specifically terrestrial type of active fighter' (2007: 21). This limiting of the nature of partisan struggle is used to develop a more explicit theory of the terrorist by the translator, G. L. Ulmen. Ulmen argues that 'Schmitt's theory of the partisan contains an implicit theory of the terrorist' (Schmitt 2007: xvi). The partisan is telluric, tied to the land in a specific way, whereas the terrorist is entirely ungrounded: 'his hostility is not spatially limited'. For Schmitt and Ulmen, the partisan has a genuine enemy, but 'the terrorist has an absolute enemy, who must be annihilated' (Schmitt 2007: xvii).

Schmitt agrees that 'the partisan has a real, but not an absolute enemy' (2007: 92). At the same time, Schmitt is keen to follow where and how the real enemy becomes the absolute enemy, and where the partisan slides into the terrorist. For Schmitt, Lenin's revolutionary ideology is the hinge towards a theory of absolute enmity towards an absolute enemy, even if he does not quite go all the way. And the development and proliferation of nuclear weapons provides the means to accomplish this absolute and total annihilation. According to Schmitt, only the acknowledgement of real enmity can prevent the outbreak of absolute enmity. Only the precise naming of the enemy can prevent the formation of an absolute enemy that requires total annihilation. And finally, terrorism is a way to name this process of designating an absolute enemy.

One implication of Schmitt's analysis of the partisan is that the terrorist is delinked from the ground of *terra* as territory or as earth, to which the partisan is still tied. The terrorist floats free, at least potentially, which is how terrorism becomes a spectacle in the sense of Debord's theory. Derrida points out that terrorism is not really even war, but rather a strange simulacrum of war, because it has no specific nation-state as enemy (Borradori 2003: 101). Part of the debacle in Iraq (and to a lesser extent Afghanistan) in the early twenty-first century was due to the attempt to shape the war on terror into a more conventional war against an evil aggressive nation-state. And the war ostensibly undertaken to prevent the proliferation of weapons of mass destruction was waged by the state with the most powerful of such weapons, which presumes it has the right to own and, at least potentially, to use them.

Terror and terrorism are ambiguous, scary phenomena that are uncanny precisely in their being unmoored from territory. The ubiquity of terror works in both directions: from the terrorist to the public, and in reverse, from the anti-terrorist measures and scaring of the people in its attempt to wage war on the abstraction of terror. The image of terror *is* terror, which does not of course prevent it from being violent and deadly on all sides. In Debord's terms, and also according to Deleuze's critique of the image of thought in chapter 3 of *Difference and Repetition*, there is something intrinsically terroristic about the image, due to its abstraction, distraction and mediation of violence by means of spectacle. But Deleuze doesn't stop there. In *Cinema 2*, he rehabilitates the image and tries to free it from representational violence as well as terror.

Before turning directly to *Cinema 2*, I want to follow some of Deleuze and Guattari's schizoanalysis in *Anti-Oedipus*, to show how they are working within a similar context to both Derrida and Schmitt. In Part 3 of *Anti-Oedipus*, 'Savages, Barbarians, Civilized Men', Deleuze and Guattari develop a historical analysis based on differential types of social organisation. They begin by considering the earth as a 'territorial machine', which means that it is 'the primitive, savage unity of desire and production' (Deleuze and Guattari 1983: 140–1). The earth is the ground of terrorism, because it is the original socius as savage and primitive. It is this territorial machine that is the underlying social formation of humanity prior to the advent of the state. In fact, the 'savage, primitive socius was the indeed the only territorial machine in the strict sense of the term' (Deleuze and Guattari 1983: 146).

Here we should note the parallels between Deleuze and Guattari's analyses and those of Schmitt in *The Nomos of the Earth*, even though they do not cite Schmitt but rather formulate their understanding in terms of Marx and Nietzsche. For Schmitt, the origins of human law lie in land appropriation. The earth as territorial machine indicates what Marx calls 'primitive accumulation', which is only possible by equating the earth with territory. However, Schmitt conflates Deleuze and Guattari's distinction between primitive and barbarian society. For Deleuze and Guattari, the barbarian socius is the emergence of the state, which they view in extremely negative terms. The barbarian socius is a despotic machine that fashions an empire with a king, ruler or despot at the top. Instead of the immediate co-emergence of territory and law as seen by Schmitt, Deleuze and Guattari disjoin territory from the creation of law.

Law emerges as a top-down process given by a despot who rules over the 'megamachine' of the state. Instead of a territorial machine, the state is 'a functional pyramid that has the despot at its apex, an immobile motor, with the bureaucratic apparatus as its lateral surface and its transmission gear, and the villagers at its base, serving as its working parts' (Deleuze and Guattari 1983: 194). Law is here the consolidation and compression of territory into a densely organised space ruled by a human or divine despot. The elements of the primitive territorial machine are 'taken into an immense machinery that *renders the debt infinite* and no longer forms anything but one and the same crushing fate' (Deleuze and Guattari 1983: 192). As a result, 'the earth becomes a madhouse'.

Terror emerges along with the state as the barbarian social machine. Terror is here the desire for territory, but not as territory. Terror replaces the desire for territory and incorporates this desire into its heart in the form of punishment as vengeance. Terror is an operation on primitive territory, but it is not the working of the savage territorial machine. According to Deleuze and Guattari, 'the system of terror has replaced the system of cruelty' (1983: 211). Cruelty characterised the savage territorial machine, but it persists in transformed fashion within the state apparatus because it is directed by the law of vengeance. The Sumerian state of Ur appears all at once, as 'the primordial *Urstaat*, the eternal model of everything the State wants to be and desires' (Deleuze and Guattari 1983: 217). Every later state or empire simply attempts to reproduce this model of Ur.

The fundamental transformation of the despotic barbarian machine comes with the transition to capitalism. Schmitt claims that 'the original terrestrial world was altered in the Age of Discovery, when the earth first was encompassed and measured by the global consciousness of European peoples. This resulted in the first *nomos* of the earth' (Schmitt 2003: 49). Again, Deleuze and Guattari tease apart the conflation of law with territory that Schmitt presumes, and set out three stages whereas Schmitt only sees two. In *Anti-Oedipus*, 'the capitalist machine begins when capital ceases to be a capital of alliance to become a filiative capital. Capital becomes filiative when money begets money, or value a surplus value' (Deleuze and Guattari 1983: 227). The surplus value that constitutes capitalism is generated by the 'discovery' and exploitation of the Americas by Western Europe, first by the Spanish and the Portuguese, and then by the Dutch, French and English. For Schmitt, the encompassing of the territory of the globe generates the first true nomos of the earth, and the nation that controls this nomos is the one that controls not the land, but the sea – Great Britain.

For Deleuze and Guattari, however, it is the ability of capital to reproduce itself that founds a new type of society. There emerges a fluctuation and differential relation of capital that 'expresses the fundamental capitalist phenomenon of *the transformation of the surplus value of code into a surplus value of flux*' (Deleuze and Guattari 1983: 228). It's the controlling – the coding and decoding – of these fluxes of capital in financial and commercial terms that distinguishes capitalism and modern society. Now terrorism is the name for anything that would interfere with or block the flows of capital, either as a regression to the violence of an imperial state, or the nostalgia for an original territorial machine that no longer exists. Every machine gets plugged into the capitalist machine, and all of desire is integrated into the monetary flows. Fundamentalism is a reaction against the intrinsic nature of these flows, a desire to stop or dam them. But it is impossible to return to any pure territorial machine.

Capitalism 'reproduces its immanent limits on an ever widening and more comprehensive scale' (Deleuze and Guattari 1983: 239), which means that everything becomes spectacle, image, virtual or simulacrum due to the intrinsic denial of transcendence by the capitalist machine. It is here that Deleuze and Guattari develop their experimental gambit: 'So what is the solution? What is the revolutionary path?' Rather than slow down or stop the process, what if we 'accelerate the process?' (Deleuze and Guattari 1983: 239–40). This is the strategy of absolute deterritorialisation. Capitalism works by deterritorialising territory, and then reterritorialising it in monetary terms. But would it be possible to push the deterritorialisation so far that it becomes absolute, and unable to be reterritorialised?

This potential is only possible because of the acute similarity and important difference between capitalism and schizophrenia. Schizoanalysis activates schizophrenia by pushing it beyond the limits of itself, and ideally beyond the limits of capitalism. Capitalism is the relative limit of every society, but schizophrenia is the absolute limit. 'Hence one can say that schizophrenia is the *exterior* limit of capitalism itself or the conclusion of its deepest tendency', Deleuze and Guattari suggest. 'Hence schizophrenia is not the identity of capitalism, but on the contrary its difference, its divergence, and its death' (Deleuze and Guattari 1983: 246). Schizophrenia completely inhabits capitalism, but if it can be liberated and activated, then it can lead to the end of capitalism.

How can schizophrenia reactivate belief? We do not believe in anything any more, and the fact that the world has become an illusion means that 'we have lost our beliefs that proceeded by way of objective representations. The earth is dead, the desert is growing ... We are along with our bad conscience and our boredom, our life where nothing happens: nothing left but images that revolve within the infinite subjective representation' (Deleuze and Guattari 1983: 308). The goal is to destroy these images, because schizoanalysis proceeds by way of destruction. We must go further with our processes of deterritorialisation: 'we cry out, "More perversion! More artifice!"—to a point where the earth becomes so artificial that the movement of deterritorialization creates of necessity and by itself a new earth' (Deleuze and Guattari 1983: 321). The problem is that this project of intensification and acceleration does not work – it does not create a new earth, despite the enthusiasm of *Anti-Oedipus*. I am not going to go into detail on *A Thousand Plateaus*, but the second volume of *Capitalism and Schizophrenia* is much more sober and pessimistic than the first.

The deterritorialisation accomplished by the war machine in the treatise on nomadology against the state is ultimately neutralised, or reterrorialised by the apparatus of capture by the state. A revolution based on territory is not possible, even though Deleuze and Guattari still celebrate absolute deterritorialisation in *A Thousand Plateaus*. Absolute deterritorialisation is here the earth itself. Deterritorialisation 'is the movement by which "one" leaves the territory. It is the operation of the line of flight' (Deleuze and Guattari 1987: 508). This is a more abstract analysis, based on abstract machines, even if they are always associated with concrete assemblages. There is a great deal to be learned from *A Thousand Plateaus*, but despite its brilliance it is politically a book of failure. Or at least, it comes up to an impasse that *Anti-Oedipus* imagined that it could push through.

Deleuze and Guattari want to give us a new nomos of the earth that differs from the one that Schmitt indicates. They argue that the earth is deterritorialisation *par excellence*, even 'to the point that D[eterritorialization] can be called the creator of the earth—of a new land, a universe, not just a reterritorialization' (Deleuze and Guattari 1987: 509). At the end of *The Nomos of the Earth*, Schmitt refuses such a nomos based on absolute deterritorialisation, and considers three possible realist alternatives. First, there could be a winner between the USA and the USSR that would then ring in a new nomos of the earth: 'The victor would be the world's sole sovereign' (Schmitt 2003: 354). This book was published in German in 1950, during the Cold War that succeeded the Second World War. The second possibility Schmitt foresees is a nomos that is similar to the older nomos of European hegemony that ruled during the centuries between 1500 and 1900. Here the USA would be the hegemonic power in its domination of sea and air, because it is 'the greater island that could administer and guarantee the balance of the rest of the world' (Schmitt 2003: 355). American domination here is not based on military victory, but something like what occurred during the second half of the twentieth century, and its economic might was just as crucial as its military strength.

The final option, which Schmitt appears to favour, is 'a combination of several independent Grossräume or blocs [that] could constitute a balance, and thereby precipitate a new order of the earth' (Schmitt 2003: 355). I think that Schmitt would have liked Germany, or possibly a larger European Union, to constitute such a Grossräume. One way to view the contemporary political situation is a balance of power that is based on a volatile relationship among the United States, China and Russia. This does not appear as a new nomos, however, but merely a continuation of the power dynamics that were set up in the twentieth century. The emergence of China as a world power in the wake of the Second World War and the Communist Revolution, and then its break from the USSR, gave us a precarious stability for the second half of the twentieth century, until the USSR broke apart.

Deleuze and Guattari are on the side of the revolutionary minorities who leave the plane of capital, becoming opponents of capitalism and its brutal war machine. The minorities do not compose a state, but their 'issue is instead that of smashing capitalism, of redefining socialism, of constituting a war machine capable of countering the world war machine by other means' (Deleuze and Guattari 1987: 472). The problem, however, is that this strategy is being thought and advocated based on movement. The new digital state controls the territory, and the explicit and implicit weapons of its control have made it virtually impossible to imagine a revolution against capitalism, as opposed to this or that state.

Terrorism is a false revolution, because it is based on the same false image of territory and movement, which is spectacularised in ways that reinforce the images of infinite subjective representation. Terrorism appears as a movement of absolute deterritorialisation, but this connection is false because terrorism and its response envisions a reterritorialisation, based on an old or new form of territory that does not exist. Terror is part of our global war, our global fear and our globalised communications networks that distribute and reinforce the very threats that they are supposed to be preventing. Terror is in the image, along with boredom.

In an essay on the Palestinian people, Deleuze argues that 'Israel thinks that it will defeat the militants by creating more refugees, thereby creating more militants' (Deleuze 2006: 162). The irony is that the struggle against terrorism exacerbates the conditions for the production of terrorists. And the Israeli-Palestinian situation is exemplary because it

> is a model that will determine how problems of terrorism will be dealt with elsewhere, even in Europe. The worldwide cooperation of States, and the worldwide organization of police and criminal proceedings, will necessarily lead to a classification extending to more and more people who will be considered 'virtual terrorists'. (Deleuze 2006: 162)

Deleuze wrote this essay in 1978, and its predictive value is clear: radical Islam based on the Palestinian refugee/militant is the model of the stereotypical terrorist, and it is produced by the conflicts of states and the militarisation of the Middle East.

How can we think otherwise? At the end of his career, Deleuze decides to go to the movies. His books on cinema are important works in terms of film studies and philosophy, but I argue that they are also profoundly political books. In the transition from the movement-image to the time-image, Deleuze sketches a resolution to the impasse that he and Guattari ran into at the end of *A Thousand Plateaus*. In *Cinema 2*, Deleuze delves deeply into thought, in an attempt to create a new brain for our species, which is an important political activity because it articulates a new nomos of the earth based not on territory but on time.

Cinema 1: The Movement-Image and *Cinema 2: The Time-Image* offer a sort of compressed schizoanalysis based on the transition from a cinema and philosophy based on movement to one based more directly on time. Here Deleuze also draws on his discussion of the third synthesis of time in *Difference and Repetition*, where the narcissistic ego is fractured by the internalisation of death. Death is 'the empty form of time', but it is also the point of transition towards a future, which Deleuze associates with Nietzsche's eternal recurrence (Deleuze 1994: 112).

Cinema 1 is about how the early twentieth-century history of cinema is associated with movement, the movement of the image and its action. The problem with movement is that it implies representation: the moving image is supposed to represent a pre-given reality. This representation forces the image into the form of a cliché. Here 'the image constantly sinks to the state of cliché: because it is introduced into sensory-motor linkages' (Deleuze 1989: 21) that work along prescribed lines of motion. At the same time, there is something revolutionary at the heart of the image, a real image, because 'the image constantly attempts to break through the cliché' (Deleuze 1989: 21).

At a certain point in modern cinema, after the Second World War, the cinematic image becomes associated more directly with time. The time-image is the pure and empty form of time that provokes a creative response on the part of the director (the *auteur*). The reason that the time-image is so important is that it functions for Deleuze as the locus for re-establishing belief in the world, rather than escaping from it. The vitality of the image in its revolutionary aspect is actualised in and through the time-image, which leads us not only beyond the movement-image, but beyond the entire association of the image with sensory-motor clichés and the spectacles of unreality, including boredom and terror.

It's about restoring the links of belief with the world, which are frayed and broken. Most of our thinking and our actions are reduced to the level of cliché and resemble a scripted movie. Their possibilities are prescribed and proscribed by the state. The time-image, however, is the restoration of the link between humanity and the world. 'Only belief in the world can reconnect man to what he sees and hears' (Deleuze 1989: 172). The power and possibility of modern cinema is its ability to restore our belief in the world, here and now.

The problem is not simply the loss of the world: we have lost our belief in ourselves, politically and ethically as a people. Deleuze says that 'if there were a modern political cinema, it would be on this basis: the people no longer exist, or not yet ... *the people are missing*' (Deleuze 1989: 216). Deleuze transfers his hopes to Third World cinema, a cinema of and for minorities, as a vehicle for inventing the people who are missing. 'Art, and especially cinematographic art, must take part in this task: not addressing a people, which is presupposed already there, but of contributing to the invention of a people' (Deleuze 1989: 217).

Action degenerates into cliché in the recent history of art, politics and cinema, because movement becomes automatic, and this automaticity undermines the integrity of movement as such, even as it makes possible a direct image of time. The time-image is composed of crystals of time that, following Henri Bergson, consist of peaks of the present and sheets of the past. Time is not exhausted by these peaks and sheets, however, because for Deleuze it's all about the generation of a future, something new. There are three essential forms of the time-image, and the first two concern the *order* of time, 'the coexistence of relations or the similarity of the elements internal to time' (Deleuze 1989: 155). The most important form of time-image 'concerns the series of time, which brings together the before and the after in a becoming, instead of separating them: its paradox is to introduce an enduring interval in the moment itself' (Deleuze 1989: 155). This interval is the pure and empty form of time, a kind of death that shatters the chronological succession of time and opens the image up to a new configuration, a new existence as body and brain that could be thought of as a new *nomos* of earth in a counter-Schmittian sense.

The time-image concerns the interval itself, that is seized and then linked up to other intervals and other becomings beyond the workings of neoliberal financial capitalism, the commodification and consumption of clichéd images, and the destructive spectacular explosions of terror and terrorism that hold us captive. Here I consider the two most important chapters of *Cinema 2*, 7 and 8, from the perspective of a politics of the image based on time. At the beginning of chapter 7, 'Thought and Cinema', Deleuze presupposes Walter Benjamin's famous essay, 'The Work of Art in an Age of Mechanical Reproduction'. He does not explicitly refer to this essay or name Benjamin, but he considers the idea that 'cinema as industrial art achieves self-movement, automatic movement, and it makes movement the immediate given of the image' (Deleuze 1989: 156). This automatic movement gives rise to a *'spiritual automaton* in us', and it is the shock of this automatic spiritual automaton that forces us to think, and ultimately to think time as such.

Deleuze is wrestling with Benjamin's famous distinction between the aestheticisation of politics in fascism (and terrorism) and the politicisation of aesthetics that Benjamin calls for in authentic communist practice (Deleuze 1989: 156). Deleuze relies on the Russian filmmaker Eisenstein to show how the experience of shock that is produced by the automaticity of cinema 'forces us to think, and to think the Whole' (Deleuze 1989: 158). This is the production of a conceptual montage in cinema, which strives to think the whole that is given in part as a shock to the nervous system by the spiritual automaton of material reproduction. In classical cinema, there is still a viable concept of action that expresses the natural 'relation between man and the world', which cinema films (Deleuze 1989: 161).

The problem with cinema is not just that there are so many mediocre films, which is also a consequence of mass production. The problem is that the art of the masses quickly became the art of intoxicating and manipulating the masses. The liberation of desire and the deterritorialisation of a nomadic war machine that would oppose the state were reterritorialised upon fascism in Europe. Deleuze says that

> the mass-art, the treatment of masses, which should not have been inseparable from an accession from the masses to the status of true subject, has degenerated into state propaganda and manipulation, into a kind of fascism which brought together Hitler and Hollywood, Hollywood and Hitler. The spiritual automaton became fascist man. (Deleuze 1989: 164)

We expect the processes and products of our technological civilisation to liberate us, but they serve rather to enslave us, and to make us at once master and slave of our own oppression. We could consider contemporary films that do the same thing with the war on terror, including the film *12 Strong*, which focuses on a heroic regiment of American Special Forces that entered Afghanistan shortly after the 9/11 attacks and helped one of the warlords, Abdul Rashid Dostum, in his fight against the Taliban. American military force and terror, including its drone killings and 'collateral damage' deaths against civilians, mirrors the spectacular terrorism of al-Qaeda, as it gets instantiated in the Afghan Taliban and adopts the image of the bloodthirsty Muslim terrorist.

Deleuze recognises the problematic essence of cinema and its spectacular images, but he continues to believe that it harbours revolutionary significance. Deleuze turns to Antonin Artaud, the originator of the 'theatre of cruelty' who shared the excitement of early cinema but then quickly became disillusioned. For Artaud, what is important is the 'powerlessness at the heart of thought' that shocks us into an awareness that we are not yet thinking (Deleuze 1989: 166). This shock is a kind of violence akin to terror, but it serves a more profound purpose for Artaud and Deleuze, who applies Artaud's insights to cinema. Deleuze says that with Artaud, 'the spiritual automaton has become the Mummy, this dismantled, paralysed, petrified, frozen instance which testifies to "the impossibility of thinking that is thought"' (Deleuze 1989: 166). Here the Mummy is the core or the navel of thought, which leads thinking beyond or outside itself, where it bumps up against a limit that later becomes a fault. The 'innermost reality' of cinema is not the whole, which thought cannot think without being manipulated and duped, but rather 'a fissure, a crack' (Deleuze 1989: 167).

The crack of thought at the navel of being is the gap that opens on to the time-image. If politics is based primarily on movement, any move we make is already predicted and prescribed, and the game itself is rigged.

To choose to play on the board and act based on selected options of movement – conform, protest, write, work, donate, campaign, legislate, etc. – is to lose because the alignment of capitalism and the state has sovereign control over your movements and even your desires. What is left? Only thought, but only in a negative rather than a positive sense. You can only think that you are stuck, that you are not truly thinking, but that thought opens up a crack and you can follow that crack into a time. The spiritual automaton is an idiot, a 'dummy', a 'Cartesian diver in us, unknown body which we have only at the back of our heads whose age is neither ours not that of our childhood, but a little time in the pure state' (Deleuze 1989: 169). Time in its pure state is the pure and empty form of time, and this time-image indicates the powerlessness of thought, which nonetheless has a strange potentiality or power.

Time comes to a standstill. The crisis of the movement-image and the deterioration of action into cliché dispossesses us of our world. Our inability to truly think in a world of images means our inability to think a genuinely sincere world, except as a fantasy or false world, a utopia. This means that the real world is unthinkable and therefore unlivable, which is why the world has become intolerable for us.

Cinema expresses the modern problem of belief for Deleuze: we do not believe in the world. 'We do not even believe in the events that happen to us, love death, as if they only half concerned us. It is not we who make cinema; it is the world which looks to us like a bad film' (Deleuze 1989: 171). Our own consciousness has been colonised such that we perceive and act as if we are the protagonist of a movie. Unfortunately, it is never a good movie, but usually an intolerably banal movie and at best a bad movie. The movement-image implies an organic whole of which it is a part. This movement-image runs aground when we lose our faith in our perception of the world and the value of our actions upon it. 'The link between man and the world is broken' (Deleuze 1989: 171–2). We still talk about the world as if we believe in it, but Deleuze thinks that we only half-believe it because our sensory-motor links between human perception and human action in the world have broken down. Furthermore, he does not think that these links can be restored in their original form, that the world can be put back together for us the way that it was as an object of faith. So what do we have left? 'Henceforth, this link must become an object of belief' (Deleuze 1989: 172). All we have are the links themselves, which still function even if they do not function representationally.

We need to be more thoughtful, more desperate and more creative. The power and potential of modern cinema is its capacity to restore our belief in the world by filming or thinking the time-image directly as transformative link. The link is not the organic link to a whole, but the *interstice* between two images. The time-image refers to this productive interstice. Referring to Jean-Luc Godard's oeuvre, Deleuze explains that Godard's method is not one of association but rather, 'given one image, another image has to be chosen which will induce an interstice between the two', which is an operation of differentiation (Deleuze 1989: 179). The time-image is the 'between two images', the interstice that produces an image as link, and this 'does away with all cinema of the One' (Deleuze 1989: 180).

We need to produce a new world with these fragmented links, a world that would not be another world or a new world, but this world, produced anew. That is the political and artistic challenge of the time-image, and what Paula Marrati calls 'an *immanent conversion* of faith' (2008: 86). Believing in the world means believing in the radically transformative and revolutionary power of thinking, precisely in its un-power. The images of terror and terrorism that saturate us are entirely unbelievable, even when they are deadly and deliver us to death.

Believing for Deleuze means believing in a body and in a brain. We must believe in the body, but as in the germ of life, the seed which splits open the paving stones, which has been preserved and lives on in the holy shroud or the mummy's bandages, and which bears witness to life, in this world as it is. We need an ethic or a faith, which makes fools laugh; it is not a need to believe in something else, but a need to believe in this world, of which fools are a part (Deleuze 1989: 173).

Given a body, how does cinema or the time-image help us build a brain? In chapter 8, 'Cinema, Body and Brain, Thought', Deleuze says that the body is no longer the obstacle to thinking, as in classical philosophy, but rather what thought 'plunges into or must plunge into, in order to reach the unthought, that is life' (Deleuze 1989: 189). It's not a question for Deleuze of opposing thought and bodies. In *Cinema 2*, there are two types of modern cinema, a cinema of body that he associates with Godard, and a cinema of the brain, associated with Alain Resnais (1989: 204). The event is what happens when body is linked to thought in a certain way, when the links of body are charged with building a brain, and the brain is literally and viscerally embodied. The two series, thought and body, form a kind of parallax, such that neither collapses entirely into the other, but they remain separated by an invisible cut, which is the synaptic gap or interstice of an event as time-image. The time-image is the event, the event of producing or creating an embodied brain, and this event is directly and importantly political.

Deleuze distinguishes between an inside (thought) and an outside (body), and shows how each aspect intensifies in modern cinema and in our scientific understandings of the brain. What we saw previously as an 'organic process of integration and differentiation' comes to indicate 'an absolute outside and inside, in contact topologically' (Deleuze 1989: 211). This topological cerebral space conjoins thinking and embodiment together, but they are conjoined by cuts or micro-fissures that define the brain as 'an acentered system' (1989: 211). These breaks or fissures take precedence over organic integration and association. It is the interstice, in neurological terms the synapse, that relates images together; 'it is the equivalent of an irrational cut, which determines the non-commensurable relations between images' (1989: 213). The cut 'relinks images on either side', absorbing them to become a 'membrane of the outside and the inside' (1989: 215). In this way, Deleuze affirms, 'the cinematographic image becomes a direct presentation of time, according to non-commensurable relations and irrational cuts' (1989: 214). The cut of the image and the fact that the image is unlinked from its organic connection or association with other images in the composition of a world as a whole means that the interstice is the link itself. *The link itself is the direct presentation of time*, because time cannot be directly presented as an image, but only composed *between* two or more images, and yet time is just as fully present in the film or the frame. *The time-image is an operation of time that constitutes belief in the world beyond terror.*

The time-image puts thought into contact with its outside, which is un-thought. A time-image shows the un-thought at the heart of thought as that which propels thought forward, to the creation of something new. Deleuze claims that Resnais is not just a cerebral filmmaker, but a great *political* filmmaker (Deleuze 1989: 215). Resnais is a great political filmmaker because he knows 'how to show the people are what is missing' (Deleuze 1989: 215). The problem with classical cinema is that the masses were pre-given or pre-supposed, and mass art and politics was to fashion them into a people. The masses were supposed to become a revolutionary subject, 'but a great many factors were to compromise this belief', including Hitler, Stalinism and 'the break-up of the American people', who were reduced by consumer capitalism (Deleuze 1989: 216). We can mourn the loss of the people and the failure of the promise of revolutionary mass art and politics, but that does nothing but give in to despair. Most of us no longer believe in meaningful political transformation, despite the insurrectionary and revolutionary movements all around us, in the squares, *Podemos*, Occupy, the Arab

Spring and many others. These links are what constitute a new image of thought because they generate the people who are missing on the world stage, even when they fail, fade and disappear.

Deleuze claims that 'if there were a modern political cinema, it would be on this basis: the people no longer exist, or not yet . . . *the people are missing*' (1989: 216). If the people are missing, then they need to be filmed, they need to be invented, and that is the task of contemporary cinema, which Deleuze associates with Third World or minority cinema. On the one hand, this conclusion appears negative, because we have to give up the dream of revolutionary politics on a classical grand scale. Deleuze is unequivocal. He says that 'there will no longer be conquest of power by a proletariat, or by a united or unified people' (Deleuze 1989: 220). We have to give up this impossible dream. But the alternative is not to simply surrender to the cynical realism of neoliberal capitalism. On the other hand, there is the consciousness that 'there were no people, but always several peoples, an infinity of peoples, who remained to be united, or should not be united, in order for the problem to change' (Deleuze 1989: 220).

According to Deleuze, there is a membrane, a double becoming, between inside and outside, private and public, I and world, and this membrane is a plastic membrane. Deleuze affirms a Third World or minority people, and today almost everyone is on the way to becoming minority at least in material terms. This is a planetary phenomenon in the context of the concentration of wealth and power, resource depletion and global warming. In terms of our membrane, 'it is as if the whole memory of the world is set down on each oppressed people, and the whole memory of the I comes into play in an organic crisis' (Deleuze 1989: 221). The I who assumes the role of actor, director or politician in a genuine sense, rather than a corrupt dupe of corporate capital, 'is in a situation of producing utterances which are already collective, which are like the seeds of the people to come, and whose political impact is immediate and inescapable' (Deleuze 1989: 221). Deleuze is experimenting with the political possibilities of the time-image, the direct presentation of time in its pure state, which stitches together humanity and world in an ethic or a faith that is post-capitalist, post-spectacle and non-terrorist.

The time-image is not a specific determinate image, but the way to think with and about images. We need to seize them and creatively deploy them against their organic logic that is given to us as spectacle and commodity. We need to see and work with the links between images to create a new nomos of the earth in the context of war, terrorism, resource destruction and global warming. We need to compose a new brain for our species, a new way of being a planetary animal if we want to live in this world.

References

Borradori, G. (2003), *Philosophy in a Time of Terror: Dialogues with Jürgen Habermas and Jacques Derrida*, Chicago: University of Chicago Press.

Debord, G. (1983 [1967]), *Society of the Spectacle*, Detroit: Black and Red.

Deleuze, G. (1989), *Cinema 2: The Time-Image*, trans. H. Tomlinson and R. Galeta, Minneapolis: University of Minnesota Press.

Deleuze, G. (1994), *Difference and Repetition*, trans. P. Patton, New York: Columbia University Press.

Deleuze, G. (2006), 'Spoilers of Peace', in *Two Regimes of Madness: Texts and Interviews 1975–1995*, ed. D. Lapoujade, trans. A. Hodges and M. Taormina, New York: Semiotext(e).

Deleuze, G., and F. Guattari (1983), *Anti-Oedipus: Capitalism and Schizophrenia*, trans. R. Hurley, M. Seem and H. R. Lane, Minneapolis: University of Minnesota Press.

Deleuze, G., and F. Guattari (1987), *A Thousand Plateaus: Capitalism and Schizophrenia*, trans. B. Massumi, Minneapolis: University of Minnesota Press.

Marrati, P. (2008), *Gilles Deleuze: Philosophy and Cinema*, trans. A. Hartz, Baltimore: Johns Hopkins University Press.

Schmitt, C. (2003 [1950]), *The Nomos of the Earth: In the International Law of the Jus Publicum Europaeum*, trans. G. L. Ulmen, New York: Telos Press.

Schmitt, C. (2007 [1963]), *Theory of the Partisan*, trans. G. L. Ulmen, New York: Telos Press.

Sloterdijk, P. (2013), *In the World Interior of Capital*, trans. W. Hoben, Cambridge: Polity.

Virilio, P. (2002), *Desert Screen: War at the Speed of Light*, trans. M. Degener, London: Continuum.

Žižek, S (2010), *Living in the End Times*, London: Verso.

Chapter 8

The Image of Terror:
Art, ISIS, Iconoclasm and the Question of the People to Come

Julian Reid

The work of Gilles Deleuze was dedicated in a fundamental sense to a particular political problem, that of the production of what he described as a new type of 'people to come'. This would be a people distinct from the historical peoples produced by nation-states, institutions, laws and social contracts; a people different to those dreamed of and made possible by the many different ideological projects of the modern era. It would be a people defined indeed by a positive destruction of the conditions of possibility for those various projects, brought together by a desire not to change the world in order to make it a better place, but to see the world for what it really is, in all its incoherence and brokenness. This would be a people, he argued, no longer concerned as such with the problem of how to act but precisely with how to see, and how especially to see the intolerability of the world as it is revealed to be, once we start to privilege sight over action, and open our perception to the poverty and forms of oppression that otherwise pass us by (Deleuze 2005; Deleuze 1989; Reid 2013). This new people, this 'people to come', expressed in effect, Deleuze argued, a new typology on which to base its struggle against poverty and oppression, that of 'the seer', and a new kind of imaginary on which to form political community, a community of seers possessive of the collective perception of the intolerability of present social relations and defined by a common will to destroy them and remake those relations anew (Reid 2013).

A community of seers possessive of the collective perception of the intolerability of the present; this is also a people that, Deleuze tells us, endures a particularly intense relation with images as such. A people that, as the second volume of the *Cinema* series tells us, does not simply know how to use images in order to render its movement efficient, by subjecting images to its bodily needs, but sees time in its images, and that, in seeing time, also suffers disorientation, losing that capacity for efficiency in movement within space that was the hallmark of the peoples of the past (Deleuze 1989: 44–7). It is the people that enables the shift, therefore, which Deleuze saw taking place throughout politics of the twentieth century, from a regime of the movement-image to one of the time-image. This was also a people, therefore, that in its emergence had to repress and, where it could, destroy that particular regime of images that had constituted those peoples of the past that now stood in the way of its becoming. It is, like every real political movement, a community of iconoclasts, which depends on the destruction of a given regime of images for the constitution of its imaginary in the real.

Where should we look, if we want to, to see the emergence, if there has been any, of this new people? Does it exist or is it still a fictional product of Deleuze's own imagination, which itself depended on the imaginal qualities of cinema to embellish its claims to potential? Certainly, when we consider the influence of Deleuze it is possible to conclude that it has been exerted mainly in the Western world. One can consider Occupy as a relatively recent example of an attempt to experiment deliberately and in a self-conscious kind of way in the constitution of such a people, as others already have to some extent observed (Nail 2013). What, however, about that other movement, which has in recent years offered the most spectacular and indeed terrifying attempt at the constitution of something like a people to come? Could we consider ISIS as an example of experimentation in the creation of such a 'people to come'?

Certainly its appeal to those who followed and joined up with the struggle for the creation of an Islamic State rested partly on its denunciation of present social relations and desire for the creation of a differently constituted world. The leaders of ISIS offered their very own apocalyptic narrative and prophecies, and denunciations of present world conditions, by way of which to recruit followers (Fromson and Simon 2015). Or would that be an affront to Deleuze, given what Jon Protevi has described as his 'gleeful anti-clericalism' (Protevi 2001)? ISIS was also a very explicit and deliberate attempt at the creation of a territorial state, something that many have argued is anathema to a Deleuzian political sensibility and his 'nomad science' (Lenco 2012: 100–5). Yet it is not clear that Deleuze considered the state form, based as it is upon a principle of unity and unification of a multiplicity of peoples, to be so irreconcilable with nomadism (Reid 2010). Indeed he argued for, precisely, a politics of 'nomadic unity' (Reid 2010: 424). The question he posed was that of how, on the peripheries of global order, 'communities embark on another kind of adventure, display another kind of unity, a nomadic unity, and engage in a nomadic war-machine'

(Deleuze 2002: 259). In this context it would seem repressive not at least to entertain the idea of ISIS as a somewhat ironic attempt at the fulfilment of a Deleuzian 'people to come'.

The Art of Iconoclasm

Rather than religious movements, Deleuze looked to art and movements within the arts for inspiration when trying to seed his own image of a people to come. Not only did he foreground the power of cinema but also a range of other arts, artists and fields of artistic production, for the purposes of understanding how new forms of collective political subjectivity are inspired and brought into being (O'Sullivan 2006: 69–97). Yet religion and religious movements of the twentieth century have themselves been shaped, arguably, by forces at work in avant-garde artistic practices, as much as the avant-garde within art has been shaped by forces at work in religion (Agamben 2019). Could ISIS not itself be seen and interpreted as an expression of the dual combination of these precise forces, and could the terror of ISIS not be understood precisely as a violence aimed at dissolving the boundaries between art and religion?

In order to explore these two questions I want to focus on the iconoclasm of ISIS. Their wilful destruction of images and idols, often on archaeological sites and in museums, notoriously at Palmyra and Mosul, is often depicted as a feature of their religious fundamentalism, their barbarism, their opposition to modernity and all the possibilities of pluralism that proceed once we learn to ironise belief. Yet the destruction of the image of the other, especially when it is a hateful and oppressive other, can as well be understood as a necessary and progressive feature of any political movement. Spinoza, that great inspiration for Deleuze's own wider philosophy, indicated as much: 'He will be saddened who imagines that which he loves to be destroyed' while 'he will be rejoiced who imagines the destruction of that which he hates' (Spinoza 1972: 99). Of course, there is a difference between making an image in one's imagination of the destruction of that which one hates and destroying an image of that other, but there is nevertheless an intersectionality between these kinds of images which implies the point.

The 'people to come' that Deleuze sought to fabulate into being was itself defined by its own iconoclasm. For its coming demands the destruction of a particular image, 'the movement-image' of its nemesis, which constituted the peoples of the past, and by way of which they moved seamlessly within their worlds of illusion (Deleuze 2005: 152). Their coming is consistent, also, with the broad remit of Deleuze's entire philosophy, which is an attack upon 'the classical image of thought', an attack of and for 'nomad thought' (Deleuze and Guattari 1988: 379). Deleuze's iconoclasm involves its own paradoxes, for the destruction of the movement-image requires itself an investment in another particular image, 'the time-image' (1989), and nomad thought itself, in its embodiment of Deleuze's first principles, has to be understood as not simply an attempt to emancipate thought from its capture within an image, but an attempt at the constitution of a new and different image. Images reign throughout Deleuze's iconoclasm.

The Image of Art

Art, of course, we tend to associate more often with the making of images. Images are what art creates and gives life to (Langer 1953: 47), and thus the destruction of images would seem to represent sheer hostility to art itself. We are taught to think of art as a practice of production, rather than destruction, rooted in the *poiesis* which is 'the gift of the original space of man' (Agamben 1999: 101). Yet when it comes to the avant-garde within art, we have to address it as a movement of destruction, as Agamben has well argued; and indeed a movement that aims at destroying that which works within itself to make it art, the foundations of its own productivity, the *poiesis* that precedes the *praxis* (Agamben 2019: 3). This is an argument concerning the nature of art, at least in its modern manifestations, that can be found in his earlier text, *The Man Without Content* (1999), as much as in the more recent *Creation and Anarchy* (2019). The foundations of the production of the work of art concern the image of art itself, its distinction from the illusory or imitative forms of non-art, the distinction of art from non-art; and so it is that art, in order to destroy the given image of art, has struggled for the destruction of that very distinction between *poiesis* and *praxis*. This is why so much avant-garde art has centred on fusing objects that otherwise would be considered too banal to be seen as art, or taken nature itself as its object, such that it has become increasingly difficult to distinguish art from either the natural or the banal (Agamben 1999: 50), without the intervening and regulatory power of museums to determine that distinction for us (Groys 2008: 22–42).

It is perhaps an obvious point that the production of the image of the new requires a parallel destruction of the image of the old. But there is more to it than that, in so far as art, in order to make a new image of itself, has sought to destroy the critical distinction between the image and the real, not so much in art as such, but in those fields of perception and discussion that concern the reception of art, which is to say critique. The enemy of art, at least in its avant-garde and modern manifestations, has been the critic and his or her policing function. Art, on Agamben's terms at least, would seem to abhor the distinction between the image and the real, which has come to it, not from within itself, but from the outside, and that particular critical outside that is expressed in the aesthetic field of judgement. But this struggle over the illusory boundary of the image to the real, and who polices it, is bigger than art. Is it not the task of imagination itself to dissolve it? Foucault expressed something of the complexity of this problem when he argued that imagination itself is fundamentally an iconoclastic power: 'the true poet denies himself the accomplishment of desire in the image, because the freedom of imagination imposes itself on him as a task of refusal. The value of a poetic imagination is to be measured by the inner destructive power of the image' (Foucault 1993: 72). It is not simply art therefore, in its modern and avant-garde manifestations, that seeks to make images that destroy existing boundaries between the image and the real, but the faculty of imagination itself, of which perhaps art is derivative.

Let us consider therefore the importance of this idea, that iconoclasm is as operative in art as much as we know it to have been in religion, and that it is fundamentally productive as much as it is necessarily destructive. Customarily we are taught to think of iconoclasm as a violent practice, aimed simply at destroying images; an opposition to art as much as imagination, and to *poiesis* itself. We are told that it is tied up with the historical development of the great monotheisms and conflicts over the relation of images to God; that there were those who desired to please God through the creation of iconic images as much as there were those who saw in the production of such images a blasphemy against a God who forbade the making of an image of himself. God, in such terms, was said to present himself as image, but could not be reproduced as such by those to whom he made himself present as image.

The foundations of this idea go back to the Hebrew Bible and, indeed, the Ten Commandments, which stated that 'You shall not make for yourself a graven image, or any likeness of anything that is in heaven above, or that is in the earth beneath, or that is in the water under the earth; you shall not bow down to them or serve them' (MacCulloch 2009: 443). This Jewish prohibition on the creation of images of the divine was, however, much contested by an iconophilia that had its roots in the Greek culture from which Christianity otherwise developed. The pre-Christian Greeks had regarded it as natural to represent the divine in human form, and their art was much characterised by such representations. Christ himself was said not only to have corresponded with but to have given a portrait of himself to King Agbar V of Osrhoene (MacCulloch 2009: 180).

Why then did iconoclasm, understood in this way as emerging from the prohibition on the making of images of the divine, and the subsequent destruction of such images, become a significant aspect of the historical development of Christianity? MacCulloch identifies its origins in Christianity in the military encounters of the Byzantine world with that of the Islamic during the eighth century, and the interest of the Christians in understanding what it was in Islam that accounted for the military formidability of Muslim armies at the time. The rejection of pictorial representations of the divine was said to be a feature of 'Muslim austerity', and Leo III was said to have been so impressed by this element of the Islamic faith as to have instigated iconoclastic policies among his own peoples (MacCulloch 2009: 442–3). Beyond the quite ungrounded assumption that there must be a connection between the rejection of pictorial representations of divinity in Islam and the military prowess of Muslim armies, the reasons for the development of iconoclasm in Christianity have remained to this day quite obscure, and indeed are still much debated, not least in the theory of art itself (Freedberg 1989).

In modernity we have been taught to associate iconoclasm with the rationalities of ideological movements concerned with the destruction of images which represent 'antithetical meaning structures', and the will to establish new meaning structures over the old (Tsongas 2018: 25). This is one reason why the practice is easily associated, in political terms, with Islamist terrorism, and especially Islamic State (ISIS). Given the ways in which it has documented its own iconoclasm in videos and pictures, deliberately disseminated in multimedia archives, it is often seen as part of a wider, very rational strategy aimed at inciting fear and anxiety in viewing audiences, as well as at recruiting new followers (Rossipal 2016). The fact that ISIS has destroyed images stored in museums and on archaeological sites has also led some critics to denounce the group, simply, as barbarians (Rutelli 2016).

As the art historian Omur Harmansah has pointed out, the fact that such condemnations of the group tend to arise in response to media images distributed by ISIS itself of its iconoclastic acts indicates something of a paradox or even a contradiction. 'How is it', he asks, 'that we are convinced of ISIS militants' hatred of idols and representations, while we consume the very powerful images that constantly flow through the global media, and those videos that have since ironically become some of the most iconic representations of contemporary violence against humanity?' (Harmansah 2015: 173). In doing so we overlook 'the obvious', Harmansah argues, which is 'ISIS's relentless production of images' (2015: 173). How can this movement that 'relentlessly' circulates images of its own acts of destruction of images claim to be iconoclastic? Is this not a contradiction in terms? Other theorists of iconoclasm in the philosophy of art have made similar points about ISIS, and urged us to address its violence towards images as part of a performative strategy, one that is deeply rational and calculative (Calchi-Novati 2017: 114).

Is the 'iconoclasm' of ISIS itself therefore merely an illusion, an image of a historical practice, now outdated and rightly understood as barbaric, cynically and knowingly manipulated by its purveyors in order to attack the imaginations of a naive spectatorship, and incite fear and anxiety? Is it simply to enhance their own image in order to attract new followers, moved by the illusion of a fidelity to the orthodox roots of Islam, all the while deploying ultramodern image-making and disseminating technologies that undercut that image, once seen for what they are. Or is there something to their violence towards images that reveals something else about iconoclasm itself? Something that has been lost in the scholarship on iconoclasm as much as it has been lost in the scholarship on terror? Should we approach it as a cynical expression of strategy or try to make sense of it as an expression of a practice, tied up with deeply philosophical and theological questions over the status of images themselves, and therefore with that originary *poiesis* which is 'the gift of the original space of man' (Agamben 1999: 101)?

Of course, there is no contradiction in the making of images of the destruction of images. The iconoclastic practices of ISIS mirror, perfectly, the iconoclastic powers of the imagination; its dual functionality, in production and destruction of images. In recognising iconoclasm as a higher power of imagination, we must also recognise ISIS and its terror as a deeply imaginative movement, and not, simply, a barbaric or backward group deserving of the kinds of moral condemnation that so many critics of its methods are inclined to subject it to. Those who point to the apparent contradictions in the iconoclasm of ISIS repeat a basic critique that has been made of various forms of iconoclasm historically. In art and culture the iconoclasm of figures identified with the avant-garde has been described as similarly contradictory, since it needs art to strive for the production of anti-art, as Ross Birrell has well argued (Birrell 2000). Philosophically, Jacques Derrida long ago made the point that destructive discourses and practices necessarily tend to inhabit the very structures they aim to destroy (Derrida 1978: 194; Birrell 2000: 276). If we reflect on Deleuze's 'people to come', as he discovered and described it in the space of post-war cinema, its comprehension is impossible other than in the ruins of old Europe and a society that it itself sought still to destroy. This is a people that, on its emergence, is perceived, always and necessarily, from the perspective of the dominant social form, as a sick kind of people (Reid 2013: 231). It has to struggle to constitute itself.

That a religiously defined movement such as ISIS is shaped by forces that can be seen at work in avant-garde movements in art should not surprise us. Giorgio Agamben has argued recently that the avant-garde movements of the twentieth century were basically liturgical, and that in being so, they were following developments in Christianity itself (Agamben 2019: 11). Liturgy concerns performance (Agamben 2019: 10). Twentieth-century avant-garde art aimed and perhaps succeeded in becoming what Agamben calls a 'pure liturgy' or 'absolute performance' (Agamben 2019: 11). While Agamben's engagement with actual art is fleeting, it is not difficult to put flesh on his claim. In the field of dance, for example, this liturgical dimension of the avant-garde found literal expression in the performance works of Ted Shawn, who deliberately incorporated liturgical gestures derived from Christian Methodist traditions (Schwan 2017: 31). Indeed pretty much the whole of the avant-garde in twentieth-century dance might be said to have a religious and liturgical dimension (Schwan 2017: 28). Religion has shaped the avant-garde every bit as much as the avant-garde may be said to have shaped the development of religion.

Agamben's text in which he develops this argument is concerned centrally with the status of avant-garde art, and performance art especially, in relation to what he calls 'the religion of capitalism' (2019). The gist of his argument is not simply that art retains a relation with religion, in its being liturgical, but that the liturgy it performs is in praise of the glory of capital, such that capital is its religion. We might well ask the same kind of question of the performative strategies and iconoclasm of ISIS. It is a fact that ISIS developed out of a modern tradition of political Islam that is notorious for its apparent opposition to Western capitalism (Qutb 2001; Al-e Ahmad 1984). Many have pointed to the seeming paradoxes of political Islamic groups, such as al-Qaeda before ISIS, which depended fundamentally on the structures of global capital to operate (Reid 2006). Does the same critique apply to ISIS and its performative iconoclasm?

The Image of Capital

We know, from thinkers such as Guy Debord, that the power and development of capital is heavily tied up with its capacities to deploy and exploit images. Debord's concept of spectacle famously described 'the means by which our experiences are constantly mediated by images that produce their own forms of alienated social relations' (Murray 2011: 166). It is not merely 'a collection of images, but a social relation among people, mediated by images' (Debord 2010: 4). For Debord the spectacle is aimed at controlling, not the means of production, but the entire social and cultural infrastructure, through the deployment of images; a deployment of images that works to destroy a public's very abilities to see, for it 'concentrates all gazing and all consciousness' (Debord 2010: 3) while finding vision to be the sense through which human subjugation can best be obtained (Debord 2010: 18). It is both the affirmation of appearance and the affirmation of human life as mere appearance (Debord 2010: 10). 'It says nothing more than "that which appears is good, that which is good appears"' (Debord 2010: 12). If earlier phases of the domination of capital over human life degraded their being into having, the contemporary phase has led to a shift from having into appearing, 'from which all actual "having" must draw its immediate prestige and its ultimate function' (Debord 2010: 17). The spectacle is by definition immune to human activity, inaccessible to any political intervention. It is the opposite of dialogue (Debord 2010: 18). It seduces us into believing that we are communing with it and its images, yet works tirelessly to prevent us from accessing it and to maintain a non-dialogical relation between power and audience (Murray 2011: 166). Images function for the spectacle to maintain an illusion of dialogue, while our imaginations become the source of our subjection. As such, the task of critique, Debord maintained, is to expose the spectacle as the 'visible negation of life, as a negation of life which has become visible' (2010: 10). Which is to render capital itself into the form of the visible, for 'the spectacle is capital to such a degree of accumulation that it becomes an image' (Debord 2010: 34).

The violence of ISIS, and its depiction in moving and still images, is commonly discussed as, simply, an extension of the strategy of spectacle on which capital relies; 'part of the spell that capital itself produces' as Gandesha and Hartle put it (2017: 13). The violence of ISIS, whether against people or images, from the perspective of the vast majority of the commentary and critique, is not to be considered as part of the potential or even real and existing 'counter-spectacle' which other movements, for example Occupy, are routinely identified as sources of (Gandesha and Hartle 2017: 14–15). ISIS, in these contexts, is commonly situated as a contrast to those movements which are concerned with changing real social relations, rather than simply contributing, further, to the vast spectacle of images to which the human subject is said today to be suborned.

Yet ISIS, in its direct and deliberate violence towards images, which is to say in its iconoclasm, might well be seen to embody counter-spectacle in ways that far exceed the achievements of Occupy or other movements in the West since 1968. To substantiate this claim, it is not necessary to refer to the obvious ways in which ISIS has gone about launching direct attacks on various sites of spectacle, such as rock concerts in Paris or the stadiums where globally televised football matches are taking place, and by deliberately taking out the spectators of spectacle (Gandesha and Hartle 2017: 13), even though that could easily be considered a form of 'counter-spectacle'. What is more compelling in ISIS is that which its critics determine to be its weakness, which is to say this apparently paradoxical relation that it has with images. ISIS is not the first to display this paradox, concerning which we have already gone into some detail. In the history of art there exist many examples of attempts to represent the danger of images, which is to say, to deploy images in denunciation of images, in ways that prefigure this paradoxical relation to images in ISIS. Consider, for example, those paintings of *The Dance Round the Golden Calf* made by Lucas van Leyden around 1530, and by Nicolas Poussin around 1634. These are both images that play out this paradox, being images of the worship of images, and images of the dissolution of the subject that results from that worship (Freedberg 1989: 378–85). Lucas and Poussin deployed images to express their denunciation of images; these are images that display 'the negative consequences of looking, admiring, and adoring' an image (Freedberg 1989: 384).

Does this deployment of an image to negate the image, such as by both Lucas and Poussin, somehow debase their iconoclasm? Can one be an artist, a maker of images, and still lay claim to being an iconoclast, or is this simply a contradiction in terms and therefore a failing? Clearly, within art criticism, there is room for debate as to the function of the image, and specifically the image of the worship of images, in the work of artists such as Lucas and Poussin. The historian of art David Freedberg has demonstrated as much in his enlightening discussion of the issues at stake in these particular paintings (1989: 378–85). For they concern not simply the relation of the artist, the maker of images, to the negative powers of images, but the relation of the viewer. 'We admire –

adore would not be entirely incorrect – a picture which has as its subject the epitome of the negative consequences of looking, admiring, and adoring' (Freedberg 1989: 384). Can one, in other words, be instructed by an image as to the risks posed by images, or is one's participation in the viewing of such a spectacular image as Poussin's itself debasing of the self?

Are these not the very questions that recur, today, not so much in the contemporary reception of art and its critique (a discourse that would on the surface of things seem to have long left behind at least the theological concerns of historical iconoclasts), but in debates on the integrity of ISIS and its peculiarly image-saturated iconoclasm? The iconoclasts in question, ISIS, debase their own practice by mediating their destruction of images via images, which are then deposited in multimedia archives. Theirs is a cynical manipulation of the image of the iconoclast, revealed by their real dependence on images; a dependence that reveals their debasement, as false iconoclasts, as we are told by many venerable art critics and political scientists alike.

It is curious, though, to say the least, that this revelation of the function of paradox and assertion of contradiction in the iconoclasm of ISIS should have been taken at face-value by their critics, in art as much as in the field of politics. Paradox is virtually the *sine qua non* of contemporary art, as one art critic, Boris Groys, has argued (Groys 2008: 4). Art that does not reach paradox does not fulfil the requirements of contemporary art, as he says, for paradox is itself the fundamental normative requirement demanded of all contemporary art. 'A contemporary artwork is as good as it is paradoxical – as it is capable of embodying the most radical self-contradiction' (Groys 2008: 4). Thus elementary to the greatness of Duchamp's *Fountain* is that it is art and non-art at the same time, and of Richter's paintings that they are realistic and abstract simultaneously, or of Malevich's that they are both geometric figures and paintings (Groys 2008: 3). We might say of the work of ISIS in Palmyra or Mosul that it is art in so far as it operates as both the destruction of images as well as the making and circulation of images of that destruction. We might say that this feature of their work is far from being a weakness, something that gives us an insight into their hypocrisy and cynicism, but is instead their greatest strength.

Conclusion

On the surface of things a group such as ISIS, and the violence it is identified with, would seem to be far removed from the image of the 'people to come' that Deleuze sought to fabulate into appearance. Political scientists of a progressive kind line up to condemn it, and seek out other movements in which to identify the birth of new sociopolitical orders, beyond capitalism, beyond neoliberalism, Western modernity and its attendant regimes of repression. In my view it is repressive not to concede the innovative elements of ISIS; elements that by and large escape the limits of critique of their violence, especially, towards images, in the different literatures wherein their iconoclasm has been subject to scrutiny. The image of terror offered up to us from the depths of the Western imaginary does not conform with what might yet still be said of its reality, when we take the concept of iconoclasm more seriously, and recognise its deep importance and intrinsic complexity to radical and avant-garde movements in the West itself, in theory and philosophy, as much as in art, and indeed in theological debates that continue to take place as to the origins and meaning of this particular practice, the status of which remains obscure.

> You ask me whether I believe in nomads as an answer. Yes, I do. Genghis Khan is nothing to sneeze at. Will he come back from the dead? I don't know, but if he does it will be in some other form. Just as the despot internalizes, the nomadic war-machine, capitalist society never stops internalizing a revolutionary war-machine. (Deleuze 2002: 260–1)

References

Agamben, G. (1999), *The Man Without Content*, Stanford: Stanford University Press.

Agamben, G. (2019), *Creation and Anarchy: The Work of Art and the Religion of Capitalism*, Stanford: Stanford University Press.

Al-e Ahmad, J. (1984), *Occidentiosis: A Plague from the West*, Berkeley: Mizan Press.

Birrell, R. (2000), 'The Radical Negativity and Paradoxical Performativity of Postmodern Iconoclasm: Marcel Duchamp and Anton Artaud', *Theatre Research International*, 25 (3): 276–83.

Calchi-Novati, G. (2017), 'The Biopolitics of ISIS' Iconoclastic Propaganda', in V. Emeljanow (ed.), *War and Theatrical Innovation*, Basingstoke: Palgrave Macmillan, pp. 101–18.

Debord, G. (2010 [1967]), *Society of the Spectacle*, Detroit: Black and Red.

Deleuze, G. (1989), *Cinema 2: The Time-Image*, London: Athlone.

Deleuze, G. (2002), 'Nomadic Thought', in G. Deleuze, *Desert Islands and Other Texts, 1953–1974*, New York: Semiotext(e), pp. 252–61.

Deleuze, G. (2005), *Cinema 1: The Movement-Image*, London: Continuum.

Deleuze, G., and F. Guattari (1988), *A Thousand Plateaus*, London: Athlone.

Derrida, J. (1978), *Writing and Difference*, Chicago: University of Chicago Press.

Foucault, M. (1993), 'Dream, Imagination and Existence', in M. Foucault and L. Binswanger, *Dream and Existence*, Atlantic Highlands, NJ: Humanities Press.

Freedberg, D. (1989), *The Power of Images: Studies in the History and Theory of Response*, Chicago: University of Chicago Press.

Fromson, J., and S. Simon (2015), 'ISIS: The Dubious Paradise of Apocalypse Now', *Survival: Global Politics & Strategy*, 57 (3): 7–56.

Gandesha, S., and J. F. Hartle (2017), 'Reification and Spectacle: The Timeliness of Western Marxism', in S. Gandesha and J. F. Hartle (eds), *Reification and Spectacle*, Amsterdam: Amsterdam University Press, pp. 9–20.

Groys, B. (2008), *Art Power*, Cambridge, MA: MIT Press.

Harmansah, Ö. (2015), 'ISIS, Heritage, and the Spectacles of Destruction in the Global Media', *Near Eastern Archaeology*, 78 (3): 170–7.

Langer, S. K. (1953), *Feeling and Form*, New York: Charles Scribner's Sons.

Lenco, P. (2012), *Deleuze and World Politics: Alter-Globalizations and Nomad Science*, Abingdon: Routledge.

MacCulloch, D. (2009), *A History of Christianity*, London: Penguin.

Murray, A. (2011), 'Beyond Spectacle and the Image: The Poetics of Guy Debord and Agamben', in J. Clemens, N. Heron and A. Murray (eds), *The Work of Giorgio Agamben: Law, Literature and Life*, Edinburgh: Edinburgh University Press, pp. 164–80.

Nail, T. (2013), 'Deleuze, Occupy, and the Actuality of Revolution', *Theory & Event*, 16 (1).

O'Sullivan, S. (2006), *Art Encounters Deleuze and Guattari: Thought Beyond Representation*, Basingstoke: Palgrave Macmillan.

Protevi, J. (2001), 'The Organism as the Judgment of God: Aristotle, Kant and Deleuze on Nature (that is, on biology, theology and politics)', in M. Bryden (ed.), *Deleuze and Religion*, New York: Routledge, pp. 30–41.

Qutb, S. (2001), *Milestones*, New Delhi: Islamic Book Service.

Reid, J. (2006), *Biopolitics of the War on Terror: Logistical Life, Life Struggles and the Defence of Logistical Societies*, Manchester: Manchester University Press.

Reid, J. (2010), 'Of Nomadic Unities: Gilles Deleuze on the Nature of Sovereignty', *Journal of International Relations and Development*, 13: 405–28.

Reid, J. (2013), 'A People of Seers: The Political Aesthetics of Post-War Cinema Revisited', in B. Evans and J. Reid (eds), *Deleuze & Fascism: Security, War, Aesthetics*, Abingdon: Routledge, pp. 78–95.

Rossipal, C. (2016), 'ISIS and the Global Image War: An Archival Perspective on Iconoclastic Performance and Bio-Political Authority', *Inquiries Journal*, 8 (11), <http://www.inquiriesjournal.com/a?id=1489> (last accessed 6 June 2022).

Rutelli, F. (2016), 'The Return of Iconoclasm: Barbarian Ideology and Destruction by ISIS as a Challenge for Modern Culture, Not Only for Islam', in N. Charney (ed.), *Art Crime*, Basingstoke: Palgrave Macmillan, pp. 143–9.

Schwan, A., (2017), 'Ethos Formula: Liturgy and Rhetorics in the Work of Ted Shawn', *Performance Philosophy*, 3 (1): 23–9.

Spinoza, B. (1972 [1677]), *Ethics*, London: Heron Books.

Chapter 9

Deleuze, the Simulacrum and the Screening of Terror Online

Yasmin Ibrahim

Deleuze encounters the phenomenon of the simulacrum not as a copy of the original but as the enunciation of difference in intrinsic form and reality. For Deleuze, we enter a world in which 'Simulacra are those systems in which the different relates to the different by means of difference itself. What is essential is that we find in these systems no prior identity and internal resemblance: it is all a matter of difference' (Deleuze 1990: 299). The transcendence of violent images online and their dissemination as affective screen images remakes the spectatorship of terror, where consuming terror through the simulacra of immateriality online (re-)produces new modes of birthing the terror-bound subject and terror as subsumed through post-indexicality. Here terror imagery reterritorialises the virtual sphere, producing new subjecthood with and through the semiotic capitalism of the internet. Terror imagery and its dissemination online reveals the simulacrum as a spectre in which circuits of consumption and assemblages re-enact it as a commodity for the masses, revitalising digital terror through capitalism and its hidden algorithms. In the process, it unleashes violence and the imaginary of terror as part of the 'sharing' economy, celebrating the simulacrum as both the recombination of (im)material forms and its abstraction by capital online.

Through the catechism 'God made man in his image and resemblance', Deleuze invokes a provocation through the Old Testament, highlighting the distinction between the copy and the simulacrum wherein man through sin lost the resemblance while maintaining the image (Watson 2005: 257). Crafted neither in inferiority nor as a copy of the copy, the simulacrum to Deleuze was about internal difference despite its external resemblance. Both arts and sciences through time have been saturated with robust debates about the conception of representation as well as mechanical reproduction. Today these discourses are renewed through the embedding of our everyday lives in new media platforms where the notion of 'virtuality' holds centre stage, thwarting our sense of the real through simulated environments and through an architecture in which reproducibility is celebrated and seamless through convergent technologies. Though the notion of the simulacrum has been juxtaposed and associated with the original or authentic, our renewed anxieties about truth and authenticity in the age of the digital reiterate how simulacra and the simulated have often been embroiled in the demise of the real and the effacement of the authentic. Deleuze, in *Difference and Repetition* (1968), contends that a whole differential economy is produced with simulacra that produces signification in its own right, without foreclosing why difference becomes a lens to understand difference from the original.

For Deleuze, 'Simulacra are those systems in which the different relates to the different by means of difference itself' (1990: 299). In Deleuzian philosophy, difference from the original is not only materially significant, it can provide a mechanism to deconstruct new modes of signification that the original may not necessarily allude to in instrumental and aesthetic terms. In so employing this trail of thought, this chapter foregrounds this theoretical premise of difference as a hermeneutical approach to deconstruct the transcendence of terror and violent imagery online in the digital economy. The term 'simulacrum' has gone through a rethinking through time, but in signifying a concept that can both signal association with and a rupture from the original, it confronts a fracture in its waves of theorisation, whether it is Baudrillard's (1994) notion of simulacrum as the 'hyperreal' in contemporary society, or Debord's *The Society of the Spectacle* (1983), where the whole of the world is subsumed through it. Its disruptive and sustained configuration in philosophical thought through time affirms its resonance as a prominent concept, particularly in the era of the digital.

The convergence of technologies and imaging facilities in communication devices such as the smartphone bridge connections between the gaze of the corporeal body and its ability to transmit images online temporally and spatially. The internet as a repository of personal photos as well as an accumulation of photo archives that collect vast amounts of content on a daily basis points to a human civilisation burdened by images and imagery stripped of their context of origin, and swimming through the deep and infinite terrain of the virtual realm. Decentred and floating as digital content, these connect through key search terms, search engines and algorithms to form assemblages and associations through both machine and human interfaces. As such, the digital image is a matter made for relentless duplication, alteration (morphing, photoshopping, cropping and so on) and virulent circulation. Its material form online is unstable as, copies of a copy, it acquires a life form of its own remediated through the processes and machinations of the internet washing up against content made to travel through a whole range of hidden and invisible processes online, while premising an economy of user-generated content.

Digital images through their mutability and movement on digital platforms come to embody a visual economy in their own right, where it is not their likeness (that is, resemblance) or association with the original that matters, but their deviation and the acquisition of distinctiveness through their deviation from the original that lends renewed scrutiny to the simulacrum. This deviation and acquisition of difference as a distinct category symbolises them as simulacra melding through an economy of consumption and desire that remakes them as unsettled and unfolding objects. In the realm of violent or terror imagery, these unstable online archives feed the ideological and aesthetic, producing their own wave of violence differentiated through their inability to represent the real, but equally for the ways in which they can be reappropriated to be recoded or to solidify the violent 'Other' in our social imaginary as modes of repetition, without foreclosing these as objects of play that can be politicised while being dislocated from the political. It is within the turbulent architecture of the digital economy that I want to locate the Deleuzian concept of the simulacrum, invoking its distinctiveness from the original in recognising that its difference presents new ethical challenges for humanity.

Deleuze and Difference

Deleuze problematises the notion of the simulacrum through readings of Plato, or in specific terms his 'reading of Nietzsche's reading of Platonism' (Smith 2005: 90). Deleuze in *Difference and Repetition* (1968) and *The Logic of Sense* (1969) propounds his own notion of the simulacrum in which 'the different relates to the different by means of difference itself' (1990: 299). In *Difference and Repetition* Deleuze seized on immanence and internal difference as key characteristics of simulacra. Deleuze's deconstruction of the simulacrum veers beyond the Platonic seminal notion of the copy and of the model as one of resemblance and the effects of simulacra as negative (1994: 294). For Deleuze, 'the copy is an image endowed with resemblance, the simulacrum is an image without resemblance' (1994: 257). If imitation takes on a pejorative dimension in Plato's discussion in relation to the simulacrum, where it is imbued with trickery or subversion, in so presenting it, it then appears as a problem and a 'provocative' concept in modern human thought (Smith 2005). Deleuze overturns Plato's idea of simulacra, seizing upon difference as an internalised characteristic rather than enacting it as a contentious device through its resemblance. In centralising difference as the central facet in his theorisation, Deleuze draws on the Christian notion of an image losing its resemblance. In his proposition, he argues that if God created man in his own image and as such resembling God, man on his part through sin has lost the resemblance, despite retaining the image, where semblance replaces resemblance to become a simulacrum. The simulacrum deviates from the copy by possessing an internalised differential nature which is not derived from the original. The simulacrum has a quality that contests both the notion of the original and the copy, undermining the distinction between the two, and in the process it can overturn, subvert and challenge the privileged position of the model (Deleuze 1994: 69). Resemblance as an effect of the differential machinery of the simulacrum then suggests that it has the potential to unveil and deconstruct assumptions about an 'originary model behind the copy, a true world beyond the apparent world' (Deleuze 1994: 106).

For Deleuze, the simulacrum does not operate on the premise of falseness in contrast to the original. As such the 'power of the false' (*pseudos*) becomes an instrumental and positive notion in its own right, and as such has its own immanent economy. Stripped away from the paradigm and form of truth, this truth is no longer juxtaposed to the sense of the false world that the simulacrum signifies. The simulacrum occupies its own truth through this disruption and fragmentation from the model. In so claiming, Deleuze argues that the simulacrum is based on a model of difference and from this 'internalised difference' it acquires its own power and autonomy (Smith 2005). Hence the Deleuzian assertion that 'Simulacra are those systems in which the different relates to the different by means of difference itself. What is essential is that we find in these systems no prior identity, no internal resemblance: it is all a matter of difference' (Deleuze 1990: 299). Deleuze, in emphasising resemblance as an external effect divorced from its internal characteristic, unleashes simulacra as imbued with possibilities to comprehend the disruptions they present through their immanent attributes different to the original.

In Deleuze's conception the simulacrum acquires a purity and a rebirthing into a positive light, which deviates from its negative depictions that as such warrant caution and expiation. The simulacrum requires a new formulation of ideas that are intrinsic to the simulacrum itself and premised on the notion of pure difference. The immanence of internalised difference is a central spine of the Deleuzian conceptualisation of simulacra. While Plato crafted difference as the dialectic between the copy and the model through the idea of sameness, Deleuze inverts this problematic. In so doing, he externalises resemblance and internalises difference. The copy is often imbued with an identity suggesting that this is the limit of its difference from the original, when in effect this difference alludes to more intrinsic processes than surface resemblance or identity. In addition, through repetition the simulacrum acquires an autonomous quality that ungrounds it from context, enabling it to transcend and be formless. Deleuze presents an invitation to think through difference and disparity rather than similarity or a priori identity. Deleuze's deconstruction of the simulacrum through its internalised difference is also about illuminating fundamental problems with contemporary thought, in which the modern world constructed through the simulated and the forces of simulacra points to the failure of representation (Smith 2005: 25). In Deleuze's later work, the concept of the simulacrum disappears and in its place the 'assemblage' appears, and for Deleuze 'things no longer "simulate" anything, but rather "actualise" immanent Ideas that are themselves real, though virtual' (Smith 2012: 26).

The dissipation of the simulacrum and its replacement with the concept of the assemblage (*agencement*), or rather the process of actualisation of the complex process of differentiation, reframes simulacra as non-linear and amenable to multiple iterations. Difference as a lens of inquiry then prevents the simulacrum from being a mere imitation that negates the model in gaining a hierarchy or primacy, scrambling any preconceived order in terms of its participation. The simulacrum as a differential machinery to the original despite its sameness or resemblance to the model is about unmasking processes and ontology which would otherwise be subsumed through the primacy of the original. In unmasking and ousting this differential machinery, new ideas immanent to simulacra become necessary, based on the notion of pure difference rather than resemblance.

For Deleuze, contemporary art bears a responsibility in providing a critical lens on the pervasiveness of mass production and replication, even before the onset of platform capitalism as we witness it today. With accelerated reproduction, which appears in our everyday life whether through consumerism or the standardisation of objects of desire, art can provide modes of inquisition into these modes of replication, where these coalesce into frenetic consumption on the one hand and/or our demise or death as a form of ultimate journey, teasing out the 'difference which plays simultaneously between other levels of repetition' (Murphy 2007: 165).

Deleuze and the Assemblage of Simulacra

In drawing on difference in the conceptualisation of the simulacrum, Deleuze in *Difference and Repetition* presents systems of simulacra as preceding and extending beyond the logic of resemblance, and the simulacrum's reduction of individuation relates it to a wider economy where it relates to difference acquiring intensity through its intrinsic qualities and quantities. As such, to understand the simulacrum we need a different set of ideas and notions to enact its immanent utility and characteristics. Systems of simulacra can relate to other mechanisms and forge linkages, and in so doing thwart their particularity by these linkages and movements. Such a theorisation of simulacra as a system not only eschews resemblance and its umbilical relations with the model, it emphasises its decentring and divergence as a mode of convergence. The simulacrum as a differential machinery means it can make elements foreign to itself. Modern life, particularly technological-mediated modernity with its incestuous relationship with intense replication and duplication, whether it be consumerism or celluloid cultures, has spawned a vast amount of criticism about modernity as a form of simulacrum (Giddings 2007: 419).

Similarly, Baudrillard (1994), through his seminal concept of the hyperreal, puts forth the contention that simulation is castrated from territory, referentiality or substance, generated through a notion of the real without origin or reality. For Baudrillard (1985), simulacra as signs become exchanged and interlocked with other elements instead of the real. The contemporary world is then experienced through this loss of the real, submerging it through a hyperreality. This hyperreality that supersedes the real illuminates the ascendancy of simulacra over representation and its significance for human civilisation. If Baudrillard stresses simulacra through the notion of hyperreality, Fredric Jameson (1991) traces this genealogy through Marxist paradigms to assert that the technologically mediated world through media and consumer capitalism permeates all spheres of culture and everyday life. This resonates with Debord's society of the spectacle where the world is transformed into images and consumed through spectacle. Reification of the commodity and spectacle determine how the simulacra predominate in modern life.

Similarly, Sean Cubitt (2001), in articulating a theory of simulation, posits that technology such as communications and media stand in for reality, effacing it while supplanting it with an unsteady world of materiality. This simulated world is not only subversive and disruptive but in essence introduces intense uncertainty in defining the boundaries of reality *vis-à-vis* interactive technologies and their relation to the real (Haladyn and Jordan 2010). The digital sphere and its embedding into our everyday life, art and science, and its transcendence into technological platforms means that the simulacrum as a differential machinery bearing external resemblance becomes an arena of renewed scrutiny (Rheingold 1991; Turkle 1996).

In not burying the simulacrum, Deleuze seeks to raise this phantasm from the shackles of being mere inauthentic copy or representation (Deleuze and Krauss 1983). Such premising of the simulacrum through modernity calls into question new modes of processes and relationships without foreclosing the connection ultimately with consumerism and capitalism, and their eking out of human vulnerabilities and affectivities. Creative thinking and aesthetic production become aspects that can remake simulacra, as developed in *A Thousand Plateaus*. The face of Christ, so joyfully harnessed by painters, does more than inspire creative aesthetic production, according to *A Thousand Plateaus*. It also sets in motion a new politics, one in which pictorial art plays a crucial role (Watson 2005: 257).

In *A Thousand Plateaus*, Deleuze and Guattari rearticulate the crisis of representation with the notion of faciality, pregnant with the ideological modes in which the world can be re-represented, and equally in the production of subjectivity. Their proposed 'schizoanalysis' of the psychoanalytic and social domains reveals that particular instances of literary discourse constitute 'desiring-machines' which break through the constraints of capitalist appropriation and thereby function as revolutionary investments of desire capable of exploding the fundamental structures of capitalist society (Stivale 1980: 46).

The breaking away from the compliance of the model or origin is important to Deleuze, when he invites his readers to think through divergence and difference wherein chains of surface resemblance are broken to affirm 'its phantasmatic or repressed power' (Deleuze 1990: 261). The simulacrum, unlike representation, is a rebellious breaking away from representation's zeal to conform and exclude eccentricity and difference. The notion of representation leads everything back to the model, including the human. The simulacrum as phantasm then scrambles hierarchies, unleashing them through nomadic and autonomous tendencies which create both chaos and modes of decentring (Watson 2005).

Deleuze and Semiotic Capitalism

Deleuze's own writings and his collaborations with Guattari reflect on capitalism as 'parasitic, inventive and without limits, of the virtual type' (Deleuze and Guattari 1980: 580). Modernity and schizophrenia hold together through the dislocating power of capitalism to cover the world with financial networks, while being able to elude control by states so as to establish its dominance by transforming all goods into commodities and recoding value where it deterritorialises the flows and operates in the smooth space of world capitalism (Vandenberghe 2008: 882). Through a 'general axiomatic of decoded flows' (Deleuze and Guattari 1980: 567) capitalism is conjured as premising the world through its own logic and forming an empire that no longer has an outside where there is nothing that is not enframed by capitalism, nothing that escapes the global flows of capital (Vandenberghe 2008: 882).

Capitalism seeps into the everyday, exploiting immaterial labour through a 'linguistic turn' where it is able to colonise lifeworlds. Here capitalism extends beyond the distinct spheres of production, and as such the domination of the subject is interiorised. Machinic enslavement entails a mutation from 'enslavement by the machine' into 'subjection to the machine', producing subjectivity through the production and consumption of goods and services (Vandenberghe 2008: 891). The opposition between enslavement and subjection, domination and submission, or alienation and subjectification, according to Deleuze and Guattari, is then overcome, advancing a human–machine symbiosis under the ambit of advanced liberal capitalism, which operates in global terms, without a centre or periphery, inside or outside. This machinery integrates the living subject as a constituent part of its own assemblage operating through the will and affectivity of these desiring subjects (Deleuze and Guattari 1980: 572). The collapsing of boundaries between culture and economy means that culture itself is commodified as part of the rationale of capital, in which it loses its autonomy.

The interpenetration of the economy with culture produces a shift from the production of goods to the production of signs, and as such in the postmodern world we are increasingly invested in the transaction and consumption not of material objects, but of semiotic objects or signs. In such an economy, with intense anaesthetisation of commodities, objects float devoid of their material content to be recalibrated as simulacra without referentiality to the original. Baudrillard's notion of hyperreality and Debord's society of the spectacle point to the global landscape of signs which dematerialise reality while illuminating the intense spectacularisation of commodity culture and consumerism. Deleuze and Guattari's schizoanalysis, drawn from a 'materialist psychiatry', examines human energy invested in all domains ranging from the production of political will to the economic production of labour. The linking of desire to the production of energy and endeavour then fuse the social and libidinal economies (Holland 1987: 20). In *A Thousand Plateaus* (Deleuze and Guattari 1987: 428) the mega-machine is recoded through human subjectivity in cybernetic paradigms in which heterogeneous components coalesce: human and non-human, organic and inorganic, semiotic and material, archaic and modern, signifying and asignifying; producing an ambivalent economy filled with opportunities and risk (Genosko 2015: 8). According to Guattari, this state of asignifying semiotics induces the virtual environment generated by machinic interactions such as acceleration and mathematical prediction whose existence is verifiable theoretically (Watson 2002: 35). Signifying a profound shift, the capitalist machine initiates an axiomatic system that is an asignifying syntax rather than a signifying semiotic. As such, it 'displays an indifference to meaning, qualitative measures, and distinctively non-capitalistic forms of production and distinct classes of goods. It employs decoded flows rather than extrinsic coded differences' (Genosko 2015: 11).

According to Maurizio Lazzarato, capitalism unfolds through an asignifying semiotics, one in which machinic enslavement produces a subjectivity through our bind with it. 'Unlike signifying semiotics, asignifying semiotics recognize neither persons, roles nor subjects' (Lazzarato 2006: 10). Where the power of semiotics resides in its ability to permeate the systems of representation and signification, machinic enslavement functions by setting things in motion by connecting us with the rationality of the machine and in activating affective and transitivist relations. Defined through cybernetic relations, mega-machines are not only about overt bondage but also their subjugative element.

Asignifying semiotics can be understood as any system of signification that dissociates itself in some manner from a meaning component (Genosko 2014: 13). For Guattari, asignifying semiotics recognises neither subjects, nor persons, nor roles, and not even delimited objects passing through signifying systems within which individuated subjects find themselves lost and alienated (Genosko 2014: 20). In transposing this to the digital economy, this libidinal economy and its relationship with immaterial labour online illuminates an economy where desires coalesce with social and economic production through the accumulation of data and value, which capital abstracts. Raw data as an immanent fabric of digital capitalism and its machinations can recode content online. The creation of smart environments online that work with algorithmic rationality means that humans as subjects and their desires can be anticipated, while their consumption patterns are reconfigured as profiles that can be sold back to the market, where desires can be further elicited and manipulated. Our conjugal assimilation with the machine and production of subjectivities through human–machine symbiosis means that capitalism increasingly depends on non-signifying machines.

Simulacra and Terror Online

The transcendence of violent images online and their dissemination as affective screen images remakes the spectatorship of terror, where consuming terror through the simulacra of immateriality online (re-) produces new modes of birthing the terror-bound subject equally in the consumption economy of terror. The visuality of terror imagery has always been problematic in terms of representation. Terror imaged from the vantage point of mass broadcasting or outed online through leaks enters new realms of remaking in the digital age with the design architecture of the internet and its colonisation by capital. The spectacular images of 9/11 and the burning Twin Towers as resonant and repetitive screen imagery provided a backdrop for reimagining and justifying new waves of imperialism and colonial subjugation under the banner of the 'war on terror'. In Deleuzian philosophy these can be interpreted through their external resemblance, yet as simulacra online they reiterate the affirmative qualities of repletion and are distinctive for the ways in which they remediate terror as a screen(ed) image. The terror event as an image on media and digital platforms appropriates a life force beyond representation, invoking resemblance as an external element to the event, while being abstracted into a biopolitical arrangement of power relations in which the Muslim body becomes rebirthed as the terror-bound subject, reterritorialising the internet through this 'social imagination' of the Muslim body as rife with violence. It conjoins its resemblance to other terror images, whether these show ISIS beheadings or men incarcerated through the symbolic imagery of their orange boiler suits. If the discourse of the 'war on terror' seeks to impose a similarity or linearity to the progression of these cumulativee terror images that imagine the 'Muslim' body, the internet architecture thwarts space and scrambles time, placing Muslim subjectivity within these machinations, yet creating new modes of gaining proximity and ownership of the Muslim body through play in simulated environments such as video games.

The cinematic violence of killing in video games invokes an intertextuality between the screen and contemporary politics, creating the possibility for the production of racialised bare lives through the aesthetic of the screen and the temporality of instant gratification. Simulated environments, which became a point of intense examination for Baudrillard and Debord, provide an inextricable tryst between gaming and terror in which violence provides a backdrop for pleasure seeking. Digital games such as *Splinter Cell* deal directly with terror-related issues, co-opting the 'war on terror' and premised on the events of 9/11, while *Counter-Strike* allows teams from opposing sides to take the role of terrorists as well as counter-terrorists. Equally, digital gaming has been used by al-Qaeda and Lebanese Hezbollah to present their own modalities of violence, 'to present their grievances and display their fighting prowess in ways that advance the organisations' strategic goals' (Al-Rawi 2018: 741–2). Digital games such as *Kuma War* and *Medal of Honour* as a reflection of popular culture reveal the kind of men that have to be targeted – Arabs with beards, wearing turbans – and show fights taking place in front of mosques (Schiffer 2011). A study that examined players of anti-terrorist games found that video game stereotypes can prime negative and aggressive perceptions and attitudes towards the stereotyped group (Saleem and Anderson 2013). As such, reality and the screen conjoin in the foreplay of 'pornotroping'.

'Pornotroping', for Hortense Spillers (2003), is the enactment of Black suffering for a shocked and titillated audience. Thus the production of the human as 'flesh' (Spillers 2003) or 'bare life' (Agamben 1998) is bound with the physicality of torture, where the target is lacking in bodily and human existence. Instances of pornotroping feature prominently in literary and visual conjurings of slavery, the Holocaust, colonialism and images from Abu Ghraib prison, as well as from the aftermath of Hurricane Katrina (Weheliye 2008: 71). In a similar vein, Pugliese, in examining the practices of torture perpetrated at Abu Ghraib, argues that the images of torture must be seen through their 'ritualised and codified repetition, as reproducing historical regimes of visuality predicated on White supremacist violence-as-spectacle' (Pugliese 2007: 256).

The construction of the Muslim body through the simulacra of associated imagery means it straddles a duality where it is imagined as a limit figure that can unleash terror on the world, while, on the other hand, there is no limit to the torture it can endure due to its aberrance. Guantanamo Bay as a site beyond jurisdiction, yet amenable to the purview of courts, builds terror within an economy that is both inside and outside juridical overview, presenting terror through visual and invisible economies in which visual archives of Muslim terrorism against the West justify terror and Islam being conjoined and bound through a visual archive of terror imagery in media and online platforms (Ibrahim 2007). Television and social media reportage on terror thrives through intense repetition of the image, as a visual archive that can justify military action and equally give coherence to inchoate strategies for contacting the Other or dispelling it; it produces affirmation through repetition but also autonomy of imagery through its movement and reappropriation online. The production of the Muslim terrorist as a terror-bound subject and his counterpart, the jihadi bride, feed a Western social imaginary through a virulent image archive that presses a seamless narrative on to disparate geographies and identities, marking them out as myths emerging as threats to the civility of the West (Ibrahim 2019; Ibrahim and Howarth 2019). The 'terror-bound subject' emerging through a visual archive of terror since 9/11 and its imposition of a subjectivity on the global Muslim community or Ummah (Ibrahim 2009) has meant the foreshadowing of Muslims through a visual archive in which the resemblance of these imageries in Western ideological discourses produce subjectivity through processes beyond the terror event.

Terror images that supposedly represent massacres or terrorist acts, when released online, acquire differential qualities in the virtual realm, forming associations despite being abstracted and decontextualised through the image archives of the internet. I want to draw on Allan Sekula's notion of shadow archives. In the *The Body and the Archive* (1986) Sekula contemplates image archives within a historical trajectory in which the coalescing of power and knowledge may impose a cultural intelligibility on images. For Sekula, the historic reservoir of images produces a 'shadow archive' where readings of images and their effacement could be coded through power. The photograph as an artefact performs to an imaginary economy where it contributes to the production of social memory in terms of its preservation, circulation and modes in which it might be curtailed.

This economy is then mediated by circuits of cultural and financial production and consumption, without foreclosing its relationship to ideology or hegemonic discourses. This enmeshing through discursive relations of knowledge/power locates the image archive as a disruptive platform continually articulated and effaced through the 'logic' immanent to this archive, where content and subjectivity are negotiated by positioning individuals within its body politic. Through the digital economy online, images as simulacra are characterised by disruptions in form and function in which they can be appropriated through machine logic and architecture, which means their difference is further accelerated through their immaterial modes in which they can acquire an ability to travel through the voluminous virtual sphere and be re-abstracted and remade through the governmentality of platform capitalism. Here data extraction, algorithms, search engines, hashtags and virality can accelerate the differential quality of the simulacra. Terror imagery online performs to the spectacular attention economy and yet can be abstracted through unrelated consumption, production and attention economies which thwart, disrupt and subvert in equal measure.

The birthing of visual archives built through semantic searches, tagging and disparate audiences and platforms illuminates the fact that new archives of terror imagery could emerge through a platform logic in which the simulacra would absorb the complex architecture of the internet and the ways in which search engines can organise and code content. Both the terror-bound subject and terror as a form of commodity are remade through virulent circulation and consumption online, where terror resides alongside trivia and the avalanche of content that fills the Web, forming relationships with hitherto unrelated objects and subjects. Subjectivity is imposed through our consumption patterns online in which profile cultures and data extraction reconstruct our profile through the enterprise of capital and its extreme appetite for transacting data. The commodification of terror and its consumption as entertainment, or its rearticulation through image archives which conjoin unrelated temporal events, remake terror from the vantage of platform economics. As such, these 'asignifying systems' in which objects and subjects are not enmeshed by signs or signifiers will build new connections through the assemblage patterns of the Web. If assemblages are seen as releasing structures from the order of hierarchy, image archives become bound through assemblages where these can be consumed and reposted or valorised through networked economies where they can accrue value or be diminished in significance through image and the corporate governance of platforms (Ibrahim 2017).

The idea of virulence pegged to an attention economy and value creation in platform capitalism means that the dissemination of images online responds to other mechanisms such as repetition, recombination of form (morphing, memes, filters, and so on) as well as modes in which images can swim without context and be reappropriated and curated through individual aesthetics. This reconfigures terror imagery through the spectacular economy in which referentiality is recoded through the internal signification of machines, whether these be programming languages or algorithms which interface with commands with a hidden logic. The governmentality of algorithms and the domination of social media empires means that content can be refiltered and enmeshed through their image governance, whether this be via outsourced censors going through content or user-agreements in which offence and gratuitous violence can be reinterpreted. Terrorist beheading videos, for example, can be livestreamed and watched by an audience, where media ethics can be subordinated to a screen culture where viewing through an immediacy of events is seen as social capital. If philosophy entails the art of experimentation or *tekhne*, it then comes to 'constitute time' (Stiegler 1998: 27). To seize an image, for Benjamin (1969), is to abstract it from the flow of time. And similarly, Baudrillard and Deleuze perceive the simulacrum as scrambling time as a linear format or sequence. The simulacrum constitutes a form of liberation for Deleuze where it can have its own temporalities and fluid movements.

One case in point is the livestreaming of terror as in the case of the New Zealand massacre in 2019, when fifty-one Muslim worshippers at a mosque were killed by an alleged right-wing terrorist. The massacre was livestreamed on a GoPro camera attached to the gunman's head (Regan and Gunter 2019), and was viewed 4,000 times before it was removed. Nevertheless people copied and reposted versions of the video across the internet, including on Reddit, Twitter and YouTube, with news organisations airing some of the footage as they reported on the slaughter (BBC News 2019; Lapowsky 2019). As the massacre metastasised across digital platforms, even the most technologically advanced companies were impotent to quell the online dissemination of the killings for mass consumption (Timberg et al. 2019). This massacre was made for sharing and was promoted through a social media trail on Twitter and Facebook, and was broadcast live on Facebook. A 74-page anti-Muslim manifesto was posted prior to the attack on Twitter and the extremist forum 8chan, decrying 'White genocide'.

Users on the site following the attack in real time, cheering or expressing horror, were immersed in a transaction economy of trading links to the shooter's hate-filled postings and to copies of his videos on various sites, while encouraging each other to download the clips before they were taken offline. Over the two days before the shooting about sixty of the same links had been posted across different platforms, nearly half of which were to YouTube videos that were still active after the massacre

(Timberg et al. 2019). Soon after the massacre, short clips of the footage were edited to include footage of YouTube personalities superimposed as if they were livestreaming a video game (Roose 2019). On Reddit, the videos were reposted for users to narrate and comment on in real time on forums named 'gore' and 'watchpeopledie', which Reddit subsequently banned. A moderator on the 'watchpeopledie' forum defended keeping the video online because it offered 'unfiltered reality', and the seven-year-old forum had more than 300,000 subscribers at the time of the massacre. While Reddit subsequently announced that any content containing links to the video stream would be removed in accordance with its policy, erasure of the video online proved challenging as users posted links to the videos, re-uploading them as they were deleted, and signposting new links to alternative 'mirror' sites, ensuring it as an artefact for sharing despite condemnation and criticism in sharing these posts on different platforms. Repostings, images on a loop and the virulent circulation of content marks the repetitive tendencies of the internet, where images multiply at alarming rates to leave copies of copies with an implicit ability to travel, attach to other content and morph in form without relinquishing their inner qualities of differentiation as a copy of a copy.

Deleuze, in *Difference and Repetition* (1994), argues that repetition is precisely the source from which affirmation draws its potency. In repetition, affirmation overcomes its weakness, becomes immune to reactive forces. For Deleuze, the difference between truth and appearance, between what is actually there and what has come to be through forgery, is not surrendered. On the other hand, it is undermined insofar as this difference does not exist between independent correlates, but only emerges in the self-reference of difference (Ellrich and Picker 1996: 478). Deleuze believes that truth can be derived from the very system that produces appearance, or illusion of semblance. In the process of repetition, the negative is not only filtered out, but an illusion, an image of identity, is simultaneously generated in the course of these revolutions (Deleuze 1994: 298–300). As such, repetition not only filters out the actually negative, but also simultaneously generates the simulated negative. In effect, affirmation is capable of doubling itself only by virtue of negativity and/or identity obtained from self-referential negativity. Repetition hence works to decentre identity, distort similarity and lead consequences astray.

Terror enmeshed in the sharing economy is not just a space of decontextualisation from the event or its temporality, but can invoke new modes of voyeurism. Sharing as part of value creation online and the possibility for content to go viral means these re-enact new terms of engagement while working in conjunction with platform capitalism. Consuming terror online involves the production of new data subjectivities in which our digital footprints become an important security resource. The traces of data we leave through everyday consumption can be subjected to analytics and risk scoring, and have come to occupy an important position in combating crime and terrorist activity. Border targeting systems such as the UK's e-borders programme and the US Automated Targeting System gather and analyse a range of passenger data as a means of combating security threats (Hall and Mendel 2012: 9). Borders are increasingly securitised through these data analytics through which passenger data can be subjected to algorithmic logic, amalgamating data from disparate datasets. Hall and Mendel (2012: 9) posit that the digital footprint used to combat terrorism can be associated with traditional forensic criminal investigation. Here biometric and digital footprints invoke associations with deposits or residues of the body. The data economy enables the anticipation of threatening behaviour before its full materialisation (Hall and Mendel 2012: 10). Hall and Mendel point out that bodily prints and metrics have historically been used to diagnose a subject's proclivities ahead of time. For example, fingerprints, beyond their instrumental provision as evidence from a crime scene, were in a larger iteration used for criminal coding of subjects and as a means of archiving knowledge about criminal subjects by linking bureaucratic records to abstracted biometrics, and, more importantly, in terms of identifying risky populations of recidivists and habitual criminals (Sekula 1986b). The print was an index of the subject's particularity, but also a way of diagnosing an individual's disposition; the means to visualise a person's future capacities before their manifestation (Hall and Mendel 2012: 10).

Paul Virilio, drawing on Deleuze, sees technology, whether in the guise of the machine gun or the camera, as imposing a world of trickery and illusion where we are no longer able to discern where reality begins or leaves off (Virilio 1995: 54). The conditions under which we produce reality in the virtual environment are not divorced from the sense of Deleuzian 'delirium' produced through the overwhelming proliferation of images in the postmodern condition, where these pose questions for humanity's sense of reality. In his seminal discussions on aura, Walter Benjamin explored our perceptions and relationship to art as remediated through reproduction processes and photography. The hermeneutics of treating the past as an image means that history itself is acquired and perceived through technological means and particular modes of reproduction (Benjamin 1968: 255). As such, technical image reproduction contains an immanent power to efface or reiterate the very power that may construct or valorise an image. The analysis of Deleuze's image as simulacrum lays bare how image reproduction can have revolutionary potential where the interrelationship between art, image, reality construction and technology may induce new anxieties, and perhaps, as Heidegger articulates, a 'way of revealing' or 'into being what is not' (cf. Stiegler 1998: 9). Terror is not only rebirthed on digital platforms, it acquires its own life force through difference and its human–machine symbiosis, which Deleuze and Guattari explore in *A Thousand Plateaus*. In the overarching discourses of the 'war on terror', the migration of terror imagery and its simulacra feed both the resemblance induced by copies and equally the intrinsic logic of semiotic capital, unleashing new ethical challenges for humanity and society.

Conclusion

Through the notion of the simulacrum, Deleuze opens up immense possibilities for liberating the image from being a mere copy by discerning it through its intrinsic difference. Employing Christian theology and schizoanalysis, he recodes the simulacrum as a complex phenomenon that can disrupt and reorder time and reality through its resemblance to the original, as a counterpoint to Plato's negative articulations. In seeking to examine the digital economy through the Deleuzian notion of image ethics and the simulacrum, the symbiosis between machine and human is further disaggregated through the dissemination of copies online and with particular reference to terror imagery stripped of time and context as well as its materiality, and becoming contiguous in terms of resonance and significance through machine–human interfaces in which visual archives, while producing a semblance of continuity about the terror-bound subject, cater to an expansive economy of spectacularisation and asignification. Terror commodified and unleashed through immaterial modes online combines with asignifying capitalism in complex ways. Abstracting, reiterating and thwarting terror imagery in terms of referentiality to the event, the phenomenon nevertheless seizes on repetition as a mode to affirm mainstream ideological discourses while remaking terror as an expansive enterprise, one in which relentless sharing, instant gratification, simulated environments and voyeurism reignite the crisis of representation, giving credence to Deleuze's aphorism of the simulacrum being distinctive by means of difference itself.

References

Agamben, G. (1998), *Homo Sacer: Sovereign Power and Bare Life*, trans. D. Heller-Roazen, Stanford: Stanford University Press.

Al-Rawi, A. (2018), 'Video Games, Terrorism, and ISIS's Jihad 3.0', *Terrorism and Political Violence*, 30 (4): 740–60, <https://doi.org/10.1080/09546553.2016.120 7633>.

Baudrillard, J. (1985), 'The Ecstasy of Communication', in H. Foster (ed.), *Postmodern Culture*, London: Pluto Press, pp. 126–34.

Baudrillard, J. (1994), 'Clone Story', in *Simulacra and Simulation*, trans. Sheila Faria Glaser, Ann Arbor: University of Michigan Press, pp. 95–104.

BBC News (2019), 'Facebook to Consider Live Video Restrictions after NZ Attacks', <https://www.bbc.co.uk/news/technology-47758455/> (last accessed 3 May 2022).

Benjamin, W. (1968), 'The Work of Art in the Age of Mechanical Reproduction', in *Illuminations*, ed. H. Arendt, trans. H. Zohn, New York: Schocken Books, pp. 217–51.

Benjamin, W. (1969), 'Paris: Capital of the Nineteenth Century', *Perspecta*, 12: 165–72.

Benjamin, W. (2003), 'The Work of Art in the Age of its Technological Reproducibility', in *Walter Benjamin: Selected Writings*, ed. H. Eiland and M. W. Jennings, trans. E. Jephcott, Cambridge, MA: Belknap Press of Harvard University Press, pp. 19–55.

Cubitt, S. (2001), *Simulation and Social Theory*, London: Sage.

Debord, G. (1983), *Society of the Spectacle*, Detroit: Black and Red.

Deleuze, G. (1990 [1969]), *The Logic of Sense*, trans. M. Lester and C. Stivale, ed. C. V. Boundas, London: Continuum.

Deleuze, G. (1994 [1968]), *Difference and Repetition*, trans. P. Patton, New York: Columbia University Press.

Deleuze, G., and F. Guattari (1980), *Mille Plateaux: Capitalisme et Schizophrenie, II*, Paris: Minuit.

Deleuze, G., and F. Guattari (1987), *A Thousand Plateaus: Capitalism and Schizophrenia*, trans. B. Massumi, Minneapolis: University of Minnesota Press.

Deleuze, G., and R. Krauss (1983), 'Plato and the Simulacrum', *October*, 27: 45–56.

Ellrich, L., and M. Picker (1996), 'Negativity and Difference: On Gilles Deleuze's Criticism of Dialectics', *MLN*, 111 (3): 463–87.

Genosko, G. (2014), 'Information and Asignification', *Footprint*, 8 (1): 13–28.

Genosko, G. (2015), 'Megamachines: From Mumford to Guattari', *Explorations in Media Ecology*, 14 (1–2): 7–20.

Giddings, S. (2007), 'Dionysiac Machines: Videogames and the Triumph of the Simulacra', *Convergence*, 13 (4): 417–31.

Haladyn, J., and M. Jordan (2010), 'Simulation, Simulacra and Solaris', *Film-Philosophy*, 14 (1): 253–73.

Hall, A., and J. Mendel (2012), 'Threatprints, Threads, and Triggers', *Journal of Cultural Economy*, 5 (1): 9–27, <https://doi.org/10.1080/17530350.2012.64 0551>.

Holland, E. W. (1987), 'Introduction to the Non-Fascist Life: Deleuze and Guattari's "Revolutionary" Semiotics', *L'Esprit Créateur*, 27 (2): 19–29.

Ibrahim, Y. (2007), '9/11 as a New Temporal Phase for Islam', *Contemporary Islam*, 1 (1): 37–51.

Ibrahim, Y. (2009), 'The Mediated "Ummah" in Europe: The Islamic Audience in the Digital Age', in A. Charles (ed.), *Media in the Enlarged Europe: Politics, Policy and Industry*, Chicago: University of Chichago Press, pp. 113–21.

Ibrahim, Y. (2017), 'Facebook and the Napalm Girl: Reframing the Iconic as Pornographic', *Social Media + Society*, 3 (4), <https://doi.org/10.1177/2056305 117743140>.

Ibrahim, Y. (2019), 'Visuality and the "Jihadi-bride": The Re-fashioning of Desire in the Digital Age', *Social Identities*, 25 (2): 186–206.

Ibrahim, Y., and A. Howarth (2019), 'Hunger Strike and the Force-feeding Chair: Guantanamo Bay and Corporeal Surrender', *Environment and Planning D: Society and Space*, 37 (2): 294–312.

Jameson, F. (1991), *Postmodernism, or the Cultural Logic of Late Capitalism*, London: Verso.

Lapowsky, I. (2019), 'Why Tech Didn't Stop the New Zealand Attack from Going Viral', *Wired.com*, <https://www.wired.com/story/new-zealand-shooting-video -social-media/> (last accessed 3 May 2022).

Lazzarato, M. (2006), 'Semiotic Pluralism and the New Government Signs', *Semiotic Review of Books*, 18 (1): 9–12.

Murphy, T. F. (2007), 'Artistic Simulacra in the Age of Recombinant Bodies', *Literature and Medicine*, 26 (1): 159–79.

Pugliese, J. (2007), 'Abu Ghraib and its Shadow Archives', *Law & Literature*, 19 (2): 247–76.

Regan, A., and J. Gunter (2019), 'Reaction to NZ Mosque Attacks', *BBC News*, <https://www.bbc.co.uk/news/live/world-asia-47578860> (last accessed 3 May 2022).

Rheingold, H. (1991), *Virtual Reality: Exploring the Brave New Technologies*, London: Simon and Schuster.

Roose, K. (2019), 'A Mass Murder of, and for, the Internet', *New York Times*, <https://www.nytimes.com/2019/03/15/technology/facebook-youtube-christchur ch-shooting.html> (last accessed 3 May 2022).

Saleem, M., and C. A. Anderson (2013), 'Arabs as Terrorists: Effects of Stereotypes within Violent Contexts on Attitudes, Perceptions, and Affect', *Psychology of Violence*, 3 (1): 84–99, <https://doi.org/10.1037/a0030038>.

Schiffer, S. (2011), 'Demonizing Islam before and after 9/11: Anti-Islamic Spin – an Important Factor in Pro-war PR?', *Global Media and Communication*, 7 (3): 211–14.

Sekula, A. (1986a), 'The Body and the Archive', *October*, 39: 3–64.

Sekula, A. (1986b), 'Reading the Archive: Photography Between Labor and Capital', in J. Evans and S. Hall (eds), *Visual Culture*, London: Sage in association with The Open University.

Smith, D. W. (2005), 'The Concept of the Simulacrum: Deleuze and the Overturning of Platonism', *Continental Philosophy Review*, 38 (1–2): 89–123.

Smith, D. (2012), *Essays on Deleuze*, Edinburgh: Edinburgh University Press.

Spillers, H. J. (2003), 'Mama's Baby, Papa's Maybe: An American Grammar Book', in *Black, White, and in Color: Essays on American Literature and Culture*, Chicago: University of Chicago Press, pp. 203–29.

Stiegler, B. (1998), *Technics and Time: The Fault of Epimetheus*, Stanford: Stanford University Press.

Stivale, C. J. (1980), 'Gilles Deleuze and Félix Guattari: Schizoanalysis and Literary Discourse', *SubStance*, 9 (4): 46–57.

Timberg, C., D. Harwell and H. Shaban (2019), 'The New Zealand Shooting Shows how YouTube and Facebook Spread Hate and Violent Images – Yet Again', *Washington Post*, <https://www.washingtonpost.com/technology/2019/03/15/fa cebook-youtube-twitter-amplified-video-christchurch-mosque-shooting/?utm_ter m=.bad7ef449d6f> (last accessed 3 May 2022).

Turkle, S. (1996), 'Virtuality and its Discontents: Searching for Community in Cyberspace', *The American Prospect*, 24: 50–7.

Vandenberghe, F. (2008), 'Deleuzian Capitalism', *Philosophy & Social Criticism*, 34 (8): 877–903.

Virilio, P. (1995 [1993]), *The Art of the Motor*, trans. J. Rose, Minneapolis: University of Minnesota Press.

Watson, J. (2002), 'Guattari's Black Holes and the Post-Media Era', *Polygraph*, 14: 23–46.

Watson, J. (2005), 'The Face of Christ', *The Bible and Critical Theory*, 1 (2), <https://doi.org/10.2104/bc050004>.

Weheliye, A. G. (2008), 'Pornotropes', *Journal of Visual Culture*, 7 (1): 65–81, <https://doi.org/10.1177/1470412907087202>.

Chapter 10

Islands of Sorrow, Ships of Despair: Nativism Resurgent and Spectacles of Terror

Arthur Kroker

What follows are four meditations in honour of the thought of Gilles Deleuze. Less a description from afar of the intellectual and political rupture in the order of everything that was the sure and certain mark of Deleuze's lasting contribution, but something else, a form of writing that is at once faithful to thinking power in terms of the language of descent promulgated by Deleuze and, at the same time, reflecting on the question of contemporary terror as the limit experience in this time after Deleuze. Here, the bodies of abuse that are the subject of Islands of Sorrow, Ships of Despair; the bodies tortured with all the signs of vengeful cruelty that inhabit the dreams of Caliphate; the bodies of broken dreams struggling on the streets of all the Maidans of the contemporary world; and the psychically possessed bodies of Trump's American 'Id slipping its chain' – all these are applications, in fact as well as in theory, of Deleuze's primary political insight, namely that the spirit of the fascist within has now broken out of the cage of individual solitude, becoming the emblematic geist of the twenty-first century. More than most, to honour the thought of Gilles Deleuze, to really assent to Foucault's understanding of Deleuze as the primary thinker of the current century, is to write the world anew in the spirit of Deleuze, to tell the stories attendant upon a time in which capitalism with its tangible hint of a resurgent death drive, governments gone pitiless in the their cold yet hostile indifference to asylum seekers and refugees, medieval dreams of religious fundamentalism with all their bodily terror, and the madhouse of nihilism are the centres of power. Deleuze would understand this. Telling the story of the fascist within as the essence of the language of terror, power and bodily dispossession by a form of writing that crystallises the world of terror through the optics of event-scenes, those psychically burned moments in the movement of political time, here the memory that is Gilles Deleuze precedes us, as it always has, by taking up residence deep down in the logic of all things in this unfolding century of Deleuze and terror. These are meditations, then, of a Deleuze who is in our future, not in the past. Not so much, though, the Deleuze of Difference and Repetition, *but something much more austere and, in that auterity, deliriously perverse, a future of no difference, no repetiion, with the blood language of terror streaming a globalised world shifting seamlessly and fluidly between the differential intensities of capitalism, religion, sexuality, ethnicity, race and the reinscription, again and again, of novel patterns of power that have not and will not be broken. So then, four meditations on this time after Deleuze.*

Seemingly everywhere now there is a global surge of increasingly reactionary populism taking the form of Brexit in the UK, authoritarian conservatism in Hungary, anti-immigration politics in Australia and the EU and the coming into imperial power in the United States of a president whose political stock in trade involves opening up the wounds, again and again, of an always threatened, angry, offended and defensive American version of global whiteness. But still, for all that, the real world of politics will not be denied, with all its complexity, contradictions and stubborn reiteration of deeply familiar histories of racialised violence, sexual discrimination, class warfare and growing economic inequality.

So then, four event-scenes focused on the contemporary political scene: 'Islands of Sorrow, Ships of Despair' with its story of white backlash against seekers of asylum and nomadic refugees; 'Dreams of Caliphate in the Theatre of Cruelty' with its reflection on the real-life politics involved in the 'management of savagery'; 'Maidan in Red Square: Cold War Supernova' – a story about the resurgence of Eurasian ideology; and, finally, 'The American Id Slips its Chain' as what happens when Hannah Arendt's concept of 'negative being' becomes the driving force of contemporary American culture. Here, resurgent nativism and the spectacle of terror are dominant signs in a political future that is as grisly in its details as it is grim in its prospects.

Event-Scene 1: Islands of Sorrow, Ships of Despair

On 19 July 2013 a joint press conference with PNG prime minister Peter O'Neill and Australian prime minister Kevin Rudd detailed the Regional Resettlement Arrangement (RRA) between Australia and Papua New Guinea:

From now on, any asylum seeker who arrives in Australia by boat will have no chance of being settled in Australia as refugees. Asylum seekers taken to Christmas Island will be sent to Manus and elsewhere in Papua New Guinea for assessment of their refugee status. If they are found to be genuine refugees they will be resettled in Papua New Guinea . . . If they are found not to be genuine refugees they may be repatriated to their country of origin or be sent to a safe third country other than Australia. These arrangements are contained within the Regional Resettlement Arrangement signed by myself and the Prime Minister of Papua New Guinea just now. (Parliament of Australia 2013)

What explains the epidemic of visceral political rage directed against contemporary seekers of asylum and refugees in panic flight from murderous violence, sexual violence and violent exterminatory cleansing campaigns based on religious, ethnic and political difference? Everywhere the same pattern of cruelty and indifference. For example, in Australia, an ongoing experiment in the political, and hence ethical, disappearance of refugees, with policies intended to prevent asylum seekers from actually entering the territorial space of Australia – policies of outsourcing refugees to mandatory detention centres in Manus and Papua New Guinea; or policies of imprisoning refugees on prison ships permanently floating offshore like a twenty-first-century incarnation of medieval practices of exclusion. In Canada, morally sanctioned policies of indefinite detention in specially designed centres of imprisonment for those in flight often from abusive violence, death and mutilation in the Global South. In country after country, always variations on the same pattern of public morality – the effective criminalisation of asylum seekers; the literal disappearance of refugees; the outsourcing to the new penal system of those who, in flight from fear or hope for compassion, place seemingly unacceptable demands for an ethics of care on a system wagered on an absolutist politics of pitilessness. Beyond questions of securing borders and faltering sovereignty, perhaps we are confronted here with something at once more basic to the human condition in the current century and definitely a tendency that will only proliferate in its ethical magnitude as future years unfold, namely what happens when refugees and asylum seekers from the real majoritarian population of the world – the apparently unassimilable remainder – come into physical contact with the space of the ruling codes of economic intelligibility, political self-interest and morally prescribed righteousness. Perhaps what we are witnessing in these episodic incidents of mandatory detention of refugee claimants and physical disappearance of asylum seekers are the first notes of a new executioner's song, a song that is as morally indifferent as it is politically indignant.

While it is tempting to describe such official violence against refugee bodies – the bodies of the unexpected, the unwanted, the uninvited – in terms of a resurgence of bunker archaeology, that is, the highly defensive walling-off of zones of economic privilege from the violent perturbations of the Global South, that is not really the case. In a way that is both more politically complicated and ethically perverse, refugees and seekers of asylum are not so much simply excluded as compelled to occupy the highly equivocal space of two bodies of signification – a physical body with an earthly history of flight from fear, poverty and violence, but also an increasingly phantasmatic body of the morally designated scapegoat (potential carriers of terrorism and embodiments of economic anxiety). While the biological bodies of refugees, whether individually or with spouses and young children, are the constant object of physical exclusion and indefinite detention, the phantasmatic body of the scapegoat is just the reverse – it is not only permitted to enter deeply into the symbolic language of domestic power but actually comprises a viral invader circulating in the deepest psychological recesses of the domestic citizenry. Like all those phantasmatic 'outsiders' before it – the alien, the savage, the stranger – the refugee occupies a symbolic position that is both interior and exterior to power – an object of exclusion and an enabling condition for the moral cohesion of domestic populations, both driving the rise of increasingly authoritarian forms of politics but also psychologically enabling the rebirth of the authoritarian personality as the normative basis of contemporary political intelligibility.

In his insightful book *Fanon's Dialectics of Experience*, the postcolonial theorist Ato Sekyi-Otu argues that this is our situation:

> An omnivorous transnational capital that requires repressive local agencies to discipline their populace into acquiescing to its draconian measures; a free market of material and cultural commodities whose necessary condition of existence is the authoritarian state; the incoherent nationalism of dominant elites who are in reality transmitters and enforcers of capital's transnational aims. (Sekyi-Otu 1996)

In other words, an active alliance of 'transnational capital dictatorship and local privilege'. However, my account of all those islands of sorrow and ships of despair indicates that the contemporary situation with respect to power and resistance may be more complicated than this. Perhaps the persistence of racism, growing class inequalities and continuing discrimination on the basis of gender and sexuality has produced a new global situation. Certainly a continuing alliance of transnational capitalism and local privilege, but also the piling up seemingly everywhere of surplus bodies originating in a new alliance of power and resentment, even anger, on the part of the world's most privileged populations against the poor, the weak, the powerless. And something else as well, namely the increasing projection of phantasmatic identities on the bodies of those who resist – the spectre of the foreign terrorist, the unwelcome immigrant, environmental activists perceived as threats to 'national security', indigenous resistance officially redefined as terrorism. In addition, there is also a resurgent suspicion that the security of the 'homeland' has been undermined from within by 'home-grown terrorists' – undetectable, messianic, the new direct action assassins. Literally, everything begins to intersect under the sign of power and resistance.

Power intersects with a much older story of racial exclusion. It is never 'transnational capitalism' alone but transnational capitalism that works to support certain forms of racial intelligibility. It is never resistance in its own terms, but political resistance that sometimes intersects regressively with the politics of anger of white privilege; and sometimes resistance that intersects progressively with challenges to racial domination, class inequalities, gender discrimination and anti-democratic forms of governance. But always, of course, the predominant moral fact of contemporary times, the literal disappearance of the globally dispossessed from the ethical intelligibility of the times in which we live. When the shadow of nihilism falls on contemporary consciousness, it most often takes the form of reducing into very real public invisibility the all-too-human existence of the new 'wretched of the earth', with their contingencies of despair and trajectories of hope.

Event-Scene 2: Dreams of Caliphate in the Theatre of Cruelty

We are no longer in the Cold War with its logic of cool deterrence, but a random series of hot wars with all the intensity of heated provocations. For example, consider those desolate, truly barbaric scenes of Islamic State fighters (ISIS) methodically carrying out media-staged executions of bound, helpless captives, usually by beheading, often by knives, but also by the burning cruelty of flames. In this new theatre of symbolic exchange, no carefully orchestrated design detail has been left to chance. Executioners are dressed in fierce black, their kneeling victims in orange jumpsuits.

With fast-circulating media imagery as the skin of the planet, the symbolic parallel is as clear as it is absolute. In this society of the (ISIS) spectacle, we are intended to understand intimately and immediately that this is Guantanamo Bay in reverse. Except this time not those densely media-streamed images everywhere in the recent past of similarly helpless Muslim prisoners, certainly some defeated warriors, perhaps even actual terrorists, but others simply randomly purchased bargaining chips provided by a supply chain of feeder states and clever clients to the global security apparatus; now it's just the opposite – bodies from the many nations of the ruling, Western empire – journalists, travellers, aid workers, Christians – fed by a hitherto invisible supply chain of Islamic fighters to the newly formed apparatus of extremist Islamic terror. And this time too, it is no longer those cold media images of Muslims glimpsed by waiting cameras isolated behind the chain-link fences of Guantanamo strapped to gurneys or walking unsteadily assisted by muscled guards on their way to the rituals of hard interrogation and torture, but specially chosen Western bodies – hostage bodies – from the empire of ruling powers as symbolic substitutes, perhaps for all of us, on the way to public execution. Like a grisly replay of the logic of sacrificial violence, heretofore usually exercised by the global security state against vulnerable outsiders, those selected to be publicly murdered are chosen from morally recognisable citizens of the global security state, all the better to position ISIS as the key challenger to the sovereignty of imperial power. Following the ineluctable logic of politics, attracting the predictable wrath of all players in the global security state is aimed at achieving the overall political objective of defining in advance the framework of this new theatre of war. In this case, ISIS as the representative spearhead of what, just as predictably, will follow the unleashed violence of the global security state – a highly motivated, persistently disenfranchised, moral community of interest among the domestic (Sunni) population, first in Iraq and Syria and potentially in many countries.

Consequently, in this scenario of twenty-first-century cruelty and humiliation, is what is being drawn into visibility simply a new form of parallel nihilism – an equivalence, in this case, between what Camus once described as murderous instincts and demands for absolute justice: one in the name of heightened security, and the other, more transparently, in the language of Islamic revenge-seeking? Or is what is being rehearsed by these highly visible and deliberately twinned scenarios of individual injustice to the point of death a new and more banal twist in the contemporary rituals of cynical power?

In this case, following de Tocqueville's lucid observation that the prison system in the United States has always functioned as a silent but powerful form of communication – communicating, that is, to society as a whole the acceptable framework of normative intelligibility and, at the same time, the harsh, disciplinary penalties awaiting those who violated juridical boundaries – Guantanamo Bay has always been deliberately positioned as a cold beacon of hard truth to an always feared and, at root, perhaps ungovernable world of remaindered populations. That this hard truth works only to confirm de Tocqueville's insight that disciplinary prisons such as Guantanamo are the material expression of how symbolic exchange in the name of heightened security functions in the contemporary world does not in the least minimise its cynicism. While the moral language of all the hidden, shadowy Guantanamos of the global security world may continue to display a moral equivalence between absolute murder and absolute justice, that's not really the essence of the cynicism on contemporary display. Perhaps at this point in the spreading wasteland of the twenty-first century it is no longer possible to speak meaningfully of a necessary conjuncture between absolute murder and absolute justice. When murder is put on public display for global media circulation, and when the question of justice itself is reduced to a carefully staged communication, Camus's reflections on violence and justice are finally blasted away by the powers of the phantasmagoria. Here, murder and justice have no meaning in themselves, but become sign-slides in the vertiginous flow of the media spectacle.

What really counts in this game of endlessly reversible signs is certainly not a more primary ethical equivalence between otherwise warring absolutes than the question of affect. All those tortured prisoners, those kneeling victims of beheadings and burnings, those helpless individuals divested of their lives, of their indispensable singularity, by guns, by knives, by flames are, in the end, disposable, transient props in the greater games surrounding the simulation of affect. Sometimes a prolonged simulation of the affect of globalised fear that seems to be the desired effect of those Guantanamo torture runs; and, at other times, intense simulations of something even more complex, namely a doubled affect of fear and pleasure – panic anxiety and cathartic joy – that seems to be the precise splitting of the information blast of affect that is so carefully contrived by ISIS in all its spectacular public executions. Panic anxiety, that is, for the bunkered-down populations of the empire and their nervous governments, which can only respond to this game of affect warfare by releasing conventional technologies of aerial combat – in effect, an increasingly surreal landscape of war in Iraq, Syria and

Lebanon that features sophisticated, supersonic fighter jets trying to bomb an affect, attempting, that is, to wipe out the spreading intensity of desires for revenge and dreams of the return of the Caliphate with terror from the air. In this scenario, there can only be a hyper-inflation of aerial weaponry on the part of the empire and its client states, because we are probably witness to one of the first incidences in the contemporary century of a more metaphysical struggle between space and time, beyond the strategies of territorial control of space premised on the total spectrum dominance of space by technologies of empire, precisely because the privileged horizon of ISIS is purely temporal – a time-biased strategy of warfare that links religious passion, political calculations and technological weaponry. Here, the space-bound hegemony of techno-corporatism, with all its desire for absolute mastery of territory, finally confronts something new, namely the temporal power of cosmology. Absolutist in its religious beliefs, nihilistic in its will to exterminate its opponents, conversionary in its politics and mobilised by a form of resistance affect that takes deep root in individual subjectivity, ISIS can be so menacing precisely because it is the first, and certainly the most fierce, of all the cosmological rebellions to come against the techno-corporatist idea of the West. Which is probably why all the client states of the ruling idea of the (techno-corporatist) West have suddenly found common cause in a very public execution of their own, specifically destroying by all military means necessary the possible realisation of an Islamic Caliphate.

This is our probable future, then, wagered on a contest between the panic warfare of technologised weaponry and the slow, contagious affect of Islamic dreams, sometimes expressed in public phantasms of revenge killings, at other times in the silent conversion for reasons both religious and political in the heartlands of empire itself, and, at other times, in political theologies of the Caliphate. In this hot war with all its heated provocations, what stands in the balance is a fatal sign-slide between two fundamentally irreconcilable phantasms of power: one spatial, the other temporal; one techno-corporate, the other religious; one a warfare of spatial extension, the other a politics of religious intensity.

Or something else? Perhaps like a real-life version of *Game of Thrones*, what's at stake here may be simply a persistent struggle for market share in the cold-eyed business of global security. From the perspective of empire, effortlessly overcoming territorial boundaries, preparing sacrificial (Muslim) bodies for public display as subservient signs of the futility of resistance to the symbolic exchange of empire politics, and putting the mark of power on those remaindered bodies at its disposal.

Not just abuse value for its own pleasure, but now abuse value for the collateral benefit of a greater circulation of power. Recircuiting this logic in the name of a greater market share of the pleasures of abuse value, ISIS may also be imitating empire politics in its technology of advanced cynicism. That its executions are so transparently cruel, so humiliating in their bodily degradations, may also be motivated by a doubled strategy of cynicism. Certainly, a repetition in extremist Islamic form of the moral equivalence of the moral absolutes of death and justice, but also something equally banal, namely a deadly contest with al-Qaeda for the larger global loyalty on the part of remaindered Muslim populations everywhere in resistance to the imperial empire. In this instance, the spectacle of executions as also about a multinational branding strategy in the games of Islamic terror, undermining lingering loyalties to al-Qaeda and positioning ISIS as symbolic heir to dreams of Caliphate.

Ironically, this is confirmed by urgent requests to the US Congress by presidents of different political parties for an effectively open-ended authorisation to wage continuous war against ISIS, against, that is, the global spectre of terrorism. Here, the demand for a global security state is energised by palpable insecurities generated by the media spectacles of ISIS, just as much as the global franchising of the ISIS brand of murderous cruelty is invigorated by the equally palpable injustices of the search for perfect security. In this theatre of symbolic exchange, what is actually the medium of exchange is perhaps only an *apparent* difference working to confirm the persistence of its opposite number. On the one hand, the new security state mobilised by the very real threat of terror; and, on the other hand, the reality of terror as a way of provoking global insecurity and all that follows – the politics of revenge in a world driven by the greater anxiety of phantasmagorical absolutes threatened or betrayed.

Whatever the ruling motivation in those brutal and highly mediated scenes of ISIS's public executions of hostages and prisoners, one trajectory is clear. Here, we are first witnesses to all the intensity and violence of a fundamentalist version of suicidal nihilism quickly, and deliberately, going viral on social media, the new nervous system of planetary communication. This has complex strings of meaning as its first results: *anguished grief* on the part of families and friends of the victims; *political confusion* on the part of the new security state; *psychically driven acts* of violent solidarity by lone 'terrorists' on the domestic scene, whether in France, Canada, Denmark or the United States; the first palpable *political sign* that what is really being revealed in this challenge to the death by ISIS is something larger, more haunting and complex, namely the inception of a third Iraq war which, while it may be politically expressed as a Sunni rebellion across Syria and Iraq, involves issues that are a matter of political theology – the sudden surfacing of the long-repressed idea of the Caliphate and, with that, the inception of a new Sunni crusade against the hegemony of the modern, putatively secular state. Even in military defeat, the idea of the Caliphate with its long-repressed dream of Muslim insurgency will likely remain to haunt the global security ambitions of the secular West.

Event-Scene 3: Maidan in Red Square: Cold War Supernova. Understanding Maidan as Precursor to the War in Ukraine

MOSCOW (AP) – For the thousands of Russians gathered near Red Square on Saturday, Maidan – the square in Kiev synonymous with pro-European protests last year – is nothing to celebrate.

'Maidan is a festival of death . . . Maidan is the smile of the American ambassador who, sitting in his penthouse, is happy to see how brother is killing brother . . . Maidan is the concentration of everything anti-Russian . . . Maidan is the embryo of Goebbels,' the organizers of Russia's new Anti-Maidan movement shouted from the stage.

Demonstrators vowed that last year's protests in Kiev – centered in the Maidan square which ultimately forced Ukaine's pro-Russian president to flee on Feb. 21 – would never be repeated in Russia. (Mills 2015)

If the Italian theorist Antonio Gramsci was correct that the real struggle over ideology is always a matter of soft power, that is, a struggle for ruling ideas, then Ukraine is already the victor in its conflict with Russia. Certainly not the visible Ukraine with its conventional symbols of political sovereignty complete with crony capitalism, corrupt judiciary and armed far-right Azov battalions, but the idea of a New Ukraine that is symbolised in all its democratic yearning and political potency by those tumultuous and globally inspiring events in Maidan Square. Like a classic rebellion from below, the social movement that was Maidan literally blew apart the governing structure of post-Soviet regimes, first in Ukraine and soon perhaps in Russia itself. Here, a social movement with all its contradictions, as anarchistic as it was libertarian, as democratic socialist as it was national socialist, as youthful as it was old, took to the streets and decisively won not simply a country, but the release of a new idea into contemporary political history. That's the reason for the current political protest against Ukraine and the West in Red

Square. That's also the reason for the crude caricaturing of Maidan in Russian mass media, why, in fact, that which was most dangerous about Maidan from the perspective of absolutist power, namely its courageous persistence through the cold of winter, through violence, through generalised indifference, through hopelessness itself, is what may ultimately release the much-repressed spirit of democratic populism in the Russian homeland. Ironically, Trotsky knew this best. In his *History of the Russian Revolution*, he identified the Russian *mass* as the truly volatile agent of insurrectionary political history – a Russian mass which may now and then slumber, but once mobilised by the passion of a new ruling idea, may well rise to realise the idea of Maidan in Red Square. Just as Stalin ordered the assassination of Trotsky for fear that his analysis of the revolutionary capacities of the Russian mass would be realised in the face of totalitarian socialism, so too Putin is now confronted with the long-feared spectre of a Russian mass that finally breaks its vow of silence – a second 1917, except this time the storming of that combination of command-state capitalism and Stalinist-era rule that is the Kremlin today. Utopian? Perhaps. But if that is so it would be well to remember that utopia is also another name for 'nowhere', and that which is not only nowhere now, but violently constrained by the psychic pressure of propaganda as much as by the politics of misdirected anger, often has a way of bubbling to the surface of life as the ruling idea linking past and future. Paradoxically, of course, the idea of Maidan is a born traitor to the world-vision of Trotsky, since it stakes its claim to the future not on the always manipulated idea of the mass, but on the enigmatic, and solitary, singularity of the individual.

In any event, like life itself, political history often follows a logic of reversal with its fantastic constellations of power expanding outwards until, like the explosion of a galactic supernova, its brilliant luminosity in the darkness of space indicates that it is already in the process of a fatal contraction, instantaneously compressing into the infinite density of one of those otherwise invisible black holes populating the galactic spaces of recorded and unrecorded time. Considered astronomically, that's the story of the contemporary conflict in Ukraine. With the heavily publicised fall of the Berlin Wall in 1989 and the sudden collapse of Soviet political hegemony in Central and Eastern Europe, the until then seemingly invincible Soviet empire simply disappeared from political history. Breaking with the slow and predictable chronological, almost normative, rhythms accompanying the rise and fall of other empires, the end of which could be anticipated due to political exhaustion, civil war and economic stagnation, the sudden, unexpected and massive eclipse of the Soviet empire was more in the nature of an astronomical event. Here, like the brilliant blast of a star going supernova at the end of its life cycle, the Soviet empire literally imploded into the dark density of still new, still unformulated national political formation that was Russia. Historical debris was everywhere with seventy-year-old socialist institutions – governing structures, centralised planning organs, the idea of Communism itself – as what Marshall McLuhan once described as 'cosmic dust', accelerating shards of the dissolving remainder of society, economy and politics, the traces of which gets in your eyes, disturbing human vision.

With a cry of joyous delight, the Western press instantly declared the end of the Cold War and the beginning of what was widely promoted as an irresistible movement to a capitalist-informed democracy in the newly market-based heartland of imperial Russia. While the British security establishment has spoken of this as a 'catastrophic strategic mistake' in misreading Russian intentions, the real error probably lies less in acceptable discussions of the varying strength of absolutism and democracy in Russian political subjectivity and its governing institutions, than in forgetting the implacable natural laws of astronomy. In this case, overlooked in the massive implosion of the Soviet empire was a curious scientific fact regarding the violent death of mature stars. In the story of galactic astronomy as in the history of contemporary politics, mature stars that suddenly terminate in the explosion of a supernova blast never totally disappear, but simply compress into dense concentrations of matter, densities so incalculable in their congealed energy that while never releasing any visually detectable sign of light, their presence can sometimes be detected in the form of violent event-horizons populating deep galactic space – always ready to consume the energy mass of any unsuspecting passing star. When what is known about the astronomical properties of deep space is applied to earthly politics, perhaps it would be more appropriate to theorise the Russian/Ukraine conflict in terms of the politics of the event-horizon, that point in space and time in which the passing Ukrainian mass threatens to be consumed by the raw, unpredictable energies of Putin's Russia. Once drawn into the congealed density of Putin's Russia, a different narrative applies. Definitely not the dominant Western narrative promoting the virtues of the technologically driven new universal state of capitalist democracy, but something strikingly different – the rise from the ruins of Soviet empire of a new Eurasian ideology, fully complicated in its strange alliance of nostalgia for Russian imperialism, mass psychological *ressentiment* over the loss of Soviet empire, hand-to-mouth direct action fascism in the streets, reincarnated tsarism as its absolutist style of governance, and an increasingly phantasmatic state media feeding on populist energies to create ever more spurious borderlines based on the changing fiction of friend and enemy. In an insightful essay, 'Fascism, Russia and Ukraine', Timothy Snyder has noted:

> The Eurasian ideology draws an entirely different lesson from the twentieth century. Founded around 2001 by the Russian political scientist, Aleksandr Dugin, it proposes the realization of National Bolshevism. Rather than rejecting totalitarian ideologies, Eurasianism calls upon politicians of the twenty-first century to draw what is useful from both fascism and Stalinism. Drugin's major work, *The Foundations of Geopolitics*, published in 1997, follows closely the ideas of Carl Schmitt, the leading Nazi political theorist. Eurasianism is not only the ideological source of the Eurasian Union, it is also the creed of a number of people in the Putin administration, and the moving force of a rather far-right Russian youth movement. For years Dugin has openly supported the division and colonization of Ukraine. (Snyder 2015)

It has been reported that one of the strange scientific properties of the event-horizon, that liquid, gaseous borderline between black holes and the surrounding space, is an *abrupt time-differential* – with time beneath the surface of the event-horizon, within, that is, the darkness of the black hole, radically different from measurements of time in neighbouring space. Consequently, the politics of event-horizons is always implicated by the question of abrupt shifts in the liquid flow of time between their interior kernel and exterior surface. A perfect way to visualise the conflict in Ukraine, with the European time of the exterior surface – the centrifugal pull of the market economy of the EU, the powerful spatial weaponry of NATO – contrasting sharply with the centripetal affective memory-time of *Novorussia*, with its viscous clustering of equally powerful memory fragments – tangible memories of fallen tsars, collapsed empires, lost lands of the Don Cossacks, brutal territorial battles of the Second World War in the Donbas region, a series of nineteenth-century Russian wars in Crimea and, most of all, that resurgent contemporary memory cluster that is represented in all its powerful psychological force by the twin *ressentiment* of Russian nationalism and Putin's frustrated will to political absolutism. Blocked from *without* by the twin threat of an always aggressive NATO taking up threatening positions in the former satellites of Soviet empire, from Poland and Lithuania to Georgia, and an expansionary American empire functioning skilfully behind the scenes to orchestrate seemingly spontaneous political events; and characterised from *within* by a Russian nationalist subjectivity constructed on the basis of the politics of anger and lost (empire) hopes, the time spectrum just beneath the surface of the Ukraine/Russia conflict is a doubled flow of wounded sensibilities and revenge-taking. Definitely not only a heavily media-promoted sense of wounded Russian nostalgia for its lost imperial past, but something more strikingly contemporary – something more definite, lucid and strategic.

In this eruption of the theatre of Russian politics, what is on full display in its unfolding logic is nothing less than a systematic attempt to historically materialise a new political narrative between Eurasian ideology and the 'New World Order' of neoliberal capitalism. Beginning with specific territorial objectives – reclaiming a larger territorial border zone with NATO, refusing the sea ports of Crimea to NATO warships and possibly linking the industrial centre of Donbas and its wealth of fossil fuels with Crimea, the new political narrative is driven by a powerful alliance between a superbly executed strategy of hybrid warfare and patriotic fury in the Russian homeland. From this perspective, there are always two Maidan insurgencies in political play. From the Western perspective, the democratic social movement that marked the street rebellion in Kiev's Maidan Square was a spontaneous populist rebellion, as formless in its organisation as it was utopian in its possibilities. From the perspective of the new Eurasian ideology, Maidan was precisely the opposite – a cleverly staged coup by the United States and Europe using the proxy of a democratic social movement to install an incipiently (Ukrainian) fascist power aimed directly at historically blocking the master narrative of Eurasian ideology. Ironically, with the former political administration in the United States having declared that 'NATO is obsolete' and redefined Putin as friend, not enemy, the future is as uncertain as it is liquid in its reversals.

Confronted by the truly unexpected, that is, by time-bound dreams of recovered territories and reasserted Russian power from the dying ashes of Soviet empire, the political confusion of Europe and the United States is dramatic. In a post-1989 world that was supposed to be frozen in the framework of the global projection of power that was the unipolar (American) new security state, this upsurge on the distant frontiers of empire – far from the contemporary Pacific realignment of American military forces and at odds with the flows of hegemonic German domination of market rationality in the EU – was a model of political opacity. Was the West suddenly in the presence of a replay of the Cold War with the sudden appearance of Russian nuclear-armed bombers straying across the English Channel and the Arctic regions of Canada?

Was this the last, desperate gasp of a collapsed empire, as politically exhausted in its absolutisms as it was reckless in its military adventures? The world may be moving towards planetary digital connectivity, the talk, until recently, may be all about the wonders of the quantified self of social media, the goal of science may be the final machine/human interface that is synthetic biology, but the time horizon that is the Ukraine/Russia conflict today is Cold War time – the reanimation of long-standing, smouldering resentment against the decisive disappearance of Soviet empire and, with it, the historical realisation of the trajectory of Russian imperialism; and the resuscitation once again of the pure binaries of Cold War history.

With a deadly mixture of confusion and uncertainty in the presence of the politically opaque, Europe and North America immediately combined to do what they do best – fight perceived military aggression with the weaponry of expanding (Ukrainian) armies and the ideological ferocity of known right-wing resistance battalions. In other words, a pure battle of space based on Western intentions to block resurgent Russian nationalism with force of arms while deploying purely economic weapons – the dramatic write-down of the energy market with its reduction of Russian investments to junk status – as a way of shaping events in the long term. That this will probably be the first of many failed strategies in the Ukrainian conflict is predictable since it has little relevance to what is actually occurring, namely a new form of politics in which what really counts is a battle over the meaning and direction of time itself.

What is the future? *Euro-time* with its bureaucratic normalisation of traditionally bitterly contested nationalist sensibilities and positivist celebrations of advanced market capitalism, or what might be called the *reanimation of supernova time* with its powerful mixture of the politics of (nationalist) anger and hybrid warfare? How, in the end, is warfare really waged at the liquid event-horizon that is the borderland between Russia and Ukraine? What happens when supposedly collapsed (political) supernovas such as the Soviet empire congeal in the form of the wounded subjectivity, economic corruption, disciplinary power and absolutist government that is contemporary Russia suddenly having predatory designs on a Ukrainian regime that is trying desperately to accelerate in the direction of Euro-time? Perhaps in the midst of resurgent Russian nationalism and profound Western confusion what remains most opaque is not possible military solutions, but something more complex and enigmatic, namely which vision of the flow of time will, in the end, take root in the subjectivity of contested domestic populations. In this case of the doubled sign with its two only *apparently* opposite political narratives, what really counts may be the ability of the ultimately winning power to play the game of the sliding signifier, to be both victim and executioner in a political scenario wagered on pure phantasmagoria.

And what of the rebellious events in Maidan Square that so inflamed Putin's Russia? Could it be that what is really contested in this game of the doubled sign is not so much the newly reheated logic of the Cold War, but something very different. Namely that what is actually the real objective of Russian intervention in Ukrainian sovereignty is the palpable fear of a future Maidan in Red Square. Not so much a contest over the doubled sign of the New World Order versus Eurasian ideology, but the upsurge at the walls of the Kremlin itself of a fundamentally new idea in Russian history – a democratically inspired social movement based on an ethical vision of global citizenship. We can know for sure that the introduction of this missing third term to the game of the doubled sign, neither the New World Order or Eurasian ideology, but an upsurge of the missing element of humanity itself, would quickly bring down on its (vulnerable) head the wrath of the New World Order as well as the angry backlash of Eurasian ideology. In this scenario, what really threatens is that which is fully indeterminate, so emblematic of courage, so full of promise, so deeply feared, namely Maidan as the once and probable future of Red Square. And all this ironically mobilised by the resurgence of a Cold War supernova.

Event-Scene 4: The American Id Slips its Chain

> But here you have the myth of the essential white America. All the other stuff, the love, the democracy, the floundering into lust, is a sort of by-play. The essential American soul is hard, isolate, stoic, and a killer. It has never yet melted. (Lawrence 2018: 108)

The American id wants to slip its chain and go on the prowl again. Restless, aggrieved, furious but most of all viscerally outraged by eight years of forced moral restraint under Obama's leadership and visibly repulsed by Clinton's appeal to the greater morality of identity politics, it wants to go hunting for the human remainder, to rebel against the hectoring counsel of comfortable elites, to smash things up, to make its mark on an indifferent world that is quickly escaping its control. The better angels of American subjectivity may well be best expressed by the hopeful lamentation that is *Amazing Grace*, but, in its blood track, American identity is also, and has always been, a relentless war-spirit.

Carefully playing the long game of liberal internationalism with its alliance of imperial US hegemony and global supply chain capitalism, Obama refused to bend in the direction of the cultural narrative of sacrificial violence. His political skills clearly lay in an unusual blending of the art of calculation and the artifice necessary to quiet, off-grid diplomatic persuasion mixed with a continuing commitment to drone strikes and special forces to keep dissenters against American hegemony at bay. It was all so rational, strategic, carefully designed for the long wave of US statecraft that it just as quickly led to its own immediate reversal. In the end, the phenomenon of Trumpism is America's id to Obama's controlling superego, Certainly a Freudian cliché, but for all that, an accurate one. When the long-repressed American id explodes on to the public scene, when it gets ready to express itself, sometimes by a way of speaking that just calls out from long-forgotten memories all the screaming and hollering of other frenzied crowd scenes in the past, when it finally is free to say publicly what it actually feels rather than what by all the governing expectations it is expected to say, then we can recognise that we are in the presence of the war-spirit, dusted off, brimming with energy, out for revenge, delighted by the sheer libidinal pleasure of breaking the rules, demolishing conventions, mocking, humiliating and taunting.

Most of all though, the war-spirit needs a goal, a direction, a war. The actual object of that war doesn't much matter. *Projected outwards*, that war will probably wear many masks in the future: trade wars with China, immigration wars with Mexico, tariff wars on the world, manufacturing war on the global supply chain, financial wars on NATO and, of course, the always dependable, always fully spectacularised 'war on terror'. That war, the war projected externally, will surely come, with the inevitability of a violent storm on the horizon and with the carefully manufactured predictability of a terrorist 'incident' intended to suddenly unify an otherwise discordant American political community around the common military pursuit of moral revenge on a designated scapegoat. That script of the future is probably already running. *Projected inwards*, the war-spirit will intensify what already exists by way of the enhanced security state, namely the control of the domestic American population by tracking, surveillance and databasing, but it will also engage in close-to-the-ground assaults on the statutory protections of human rights, whether racial, ethnic, gender or in matters of sexuality. In this case, the war-spirit that is the American id cannot help itself. That part of the 'American soul [that] is hard, isolate, stoic, and a killer' has been pent up too long, restrained, tied down, repressed, forced to keep its deepest feelings of anger to itself, compelled by the language of liberal 'political correctness' that it so despises to spike its rage.

Here, Obama's success through two presidential terms in restraining the most destructive energies of the American id may well turn out to be his most spectacular failure. In the absence of a full-scale war of sacrificial violence against a clearly defined external enemy, the American war-spirit long ago turned inward. Its psychic secretions have been everywhere in recent years: all that denigrating discourse of the birther movement, the Freedom Party, those viral flows in social media about shadowy 'globalist' conspiracies against the American heartland have long been the steady drumbeat of the war-spirit as it takes possession of the felt subjectivity of sixty-three million American voters. It is viral in its circulation, seductive in its affective appeal, the language of the lonely crowd in a suddenly connected world, a veneer of moral outrage over the reality of the very real pleasures to be had in finding common cause in abuse value – the American id unleashed. Reactive in the deepest sense, it wants to bait convention, to hear the howls of broken expectations, to say outrageous things, to provoke shocked counter-reaction from the objects of its abuse. Nothing in itself but a powerful discharge of what Hannah Arendt once called the 'negative will', it leads a hand-to-mouth existence. It provokes, lashes out, parodies, taunts and humiliates – anything to provoke a reaction and thus re-energise itself. That's the real logic of Trump's strategy of double down and double up: winning at all costs as, at first, a business formula but now the ruling intelligibility of American governance. The perfect media amalgam: it is a sign-slide between sadism and masochisism. Sadistic in just the way that Heidegger predicted: a future marked by the 'spirit of malice' finally free to openly speak the language of abuse value. But masochistic as well, this time in a way that Nietzsche prophesied. Here, the lonely crowd that is the anonymous essence of social media needs direction, needs to know the designated targets for the pleasure of scapegoating, needs really an 'ascetic priest' in the unlikely form of Donald Trump. Liberated from conventional political parties, highly skilled at summoning up the war-spirits of the American id, dexterous in his ability, whether by television or Twitter, to sign-shift between sadism and masochism, victim and executioner, possessing both a form of magnetism that gives earthly form to the war-spirit and a self-pity that betrays an inner fatigue, Trump *is* the symbolic exchange of the unleashed id.

Until now the 'negative will' – the will to nothingness – has always been provisional, biding its time, waiting in the wings of history for its full expression. But now, driven by the winds of racial hatred, animated by palpable fears of the menacing power of globalism, charged up to a high pitch of psychic intensity by the restless energies of the bored, the melancholic, the anxious, the distressed, the will to nothingness bursts right through the skin of American society to become its dominant cultural narrative. Feared by some as a time of chaos, interpreted by others as the product of working-class destitution, challenged by yet others as fascist demagoguery and criticised by establishment authorities for its palpable signs of corruption, the will to nothingness remains undisturbed as it takes possession of the future of the American cultural narrative. Energetic, emboldened, boundary-breaking, a matter of fused solidarities, its presence can be felt in the powerfully implosive trajectory of the silenced outsiders, the new invisible majority. A swirling mass of psychic energy, thrilled at the prospect of speaking in the language of power, exuberant in its meticulous preparation of lists of those to be summoned to the coming feast of sacrificial violence, the will to nothingness intends to make of US politics something risibly medieval in character – an orgy of violence with victims and executioners gathered together for this newest expression of the dance of death.

And how could it be otherwise? The future of the will to nothingness that is now has long been in the books, prophesied by Nietzsche, analysed by Bataille, with its animating spirits lured to the surface of popular consciousness by Baudrillard. The only question that remains, the only detail yet unresolved by the particulars of a dark history that is still unfolding, still emergent, just beginning to suck everything downwards into an indefinite spiral of negation is which history is about to be experienced. Nietzsche's 'nihilism', Bataille's 'sacrificial expenditure', Baudrillard's 'death of the social' or perhaps all of these in strange combination as the will to nothingness American-style reveals the full meaning of the death-instinct as the real trajectory of the future? Who hasn't really known in their heart of hearts that the present order of the neoliberal technological imaginary is as fragile in its hold on enduring human loyalties as it is precarious as a convincing ideology? Through the early years of the twenty-first century we have been saturated by an increasingly melancholic tech hype, namely that we are fast approaching the new eschatological time of the 'technological singularity' in which machines will finally outstrip the limits of the human in the perfection of their AI intelligence, the robotic labour, and their collapse of the circuit of production and distribution through the imposition of the remorseless logic of raw capitalism's global supply chain. Confronted with the visible nihilism of the technological singularity, with its enthusiastic disappearance of the labour of human effort and intelligence in the face a much-hyped technological world of AI, deep-learning robots and synthetic bodies, the humans destined to be left behind have lit some bonfires of their own, challenging the technological singularity that is the political singularity of right-wing movements everywhere. Like a fantastic moment of destruction with some of the circling crowd attracted by long-pent opportunities for revenge, while others just want to feel signs of life again, even of macabre scenarios of the death of life, and with still others deeply moved by the night-time warnings of all the info-wars of social media, the singularity movement has just been achieved. Definitely not technological, in open rebellion against all the AIs of the virtual world, a highly energetic, psychically charged revolt of the invisible majority against the fate that awaits it at the hands of the neoliberal technological imaginary, the singularity moment of right-wing movement places its bets on the instinctual gratifications of the spectre of death. And why not? It knows death at first hand: the melancholic death of the working class, the coming death of the middle class, the very real death of the social in the wasteland of the society of consumption, and most certainly the death of politics in the highly machine-processed world of pollsters, consultants and the conventional political apparatus.

And it is all so quintessentially American, a story that has been told time after time in all the blood campaigns of American identity, ironically a replay of General Sherman's bloodlust on his march during the American Civil War to the southern sea when he advised his military superiors that the object of his campaign was to 'make Georgia howl', to make civilians in the southern slave states feel directly, intimately and intensely the indifferent pain, the real hurt of war and the capricious fate of war, to know the hard truth of his response to complaining white citizens from Atlanta that 'war is cruelty and you cannot refine it'. Well, at this point that language of bloodlust, that spirit of revenge-taking, the war-spirit may have finally slipped the chains of the history books and re-entered the American imaginary. Politics in another campaign, electoral this time, that has as its purpose that very same Sherman-like spirit, except this time it's not the armed conquest of the slave states of the American South but the conquest of something more intangible. Consequently, if there's a little looting of the public treasury along the way and maybe a lot of mean-spirited legislation aimed at all the helping agencies of the societal community, well it is all in the end a way of making the American liberal imaginary 'howl again', making it feel the repressed rage of a predominantly white American (male-stream) ego structure that just wants to break its bondage to the perceived fetters of the liberal spirit of forbearance, compassion and restraint. That, in fact, just might be the real art of the deal that it about to be enacted in the coming years.

When what the French philosopher Gilles Deleuze described as the 'little fascist' hidden until now within the subjectivity of so many citizens finds common ground with capitalism unleashed, the trajectory of the future is clear: the politics of scapegoating, the violence of unrestrained policing, racial profiling, denigrating the poor, demeaning women, promoting conversion therapy for the LGBT community, purifying society under the putatively 'universal' sign of whiteness, under the banner of nativism, under the therapeutic of nostalgia for an America that never really existed. Perhaps what we are now experiencing is a long pent-up adventure in the final stage of nihilism, that point where nihilism no longer allies itself with the will to power but functions more as a will to nothingness, the negative will: the will, that is, to turn from complicated questions of difference to public declarations of indifference. Visible signs of indifference are everywhere: indifference to truth, indifference to racial discrimination, indifference to gender equality, indifference, in fact, to the possibility of difference itself. But more than that, the mood of indifference may be the premonitory sign of the movement of American society that now turns back into its own negations – a society that lives in the wasteland, transforming negation into raw political energy, the psychic residues of generalised indifference into a powerful will to disaccumulate, to tear down, to block, to animate itself by spectacles of loss, detritus and the ruins within. Not just a death-instinct, but something different: a death-instinct that fuses multiple motivations – the white nationalist, the racial supremacist, the disenchanted, the bored, the angry – into the uncontrolled, and perhaps uncontrollable, energies of the negative will – the will to nothingness as the capstone of Trump's America.

References

Lawrence, D. H. (2018 [1923]), 'Fenimore Cooper's Leatherstocking Novels', in *Studies in Classic American Literature*, New York: Rosetta Books, ebook, pp. 98–108.

Mills, L. (2015), <http://news.yahoo.com/thousands-gather-moscow-protest-fascist-coup-kiev-125253591.html> (last accessed 22 February 2015).

Parliament of Australia (2013), 'Transcript of Joint Press Conference with PNG Prime Minister Peter O'Neill: Brisbane: 19 July 2013: Regional Resettlement Arrangement', <https://parlinfo.aph.gov.au/parlInfo/search/display/display.w3p;q uery=Id:%22media/pressrel/2611766%22> (last accessed 3 May 2022).

Sekyi-Otu, A. (1996), *Fanon's Dialectic of Experience*, Cambridge, MA: Harvard University Press.

Snyder, T. (2014), 'Fascism, Russia, and Ukraine', *New York Review of Books*, 20 March, <https://www.nybooks.com/articles/2014/03/20/fascism-russia-and-ukraine/> (last accessed 3 May 2022).

Chapter 11

The Spectacle of Terror[1]

Samir Gandesha

In a celebrated passage of *City of God*, St Augustine asks: 'What is time then? If nobody asks me, I know: but if I were desirous to explain it to one that should ask me, plainly I know not' (Augustine 2016: 239). So what if one asks: What is terrorism then? If no one asks us, we know: but if we are desirous to explain it to one that should ask us, plainly we do not know. Images of terror are ubiquitous, yet no term is more contested and more opaque than 'terrorism'. We both *know* and *do not know* what it is. Terrorism's effect – which, of course, principally lies in its *affect* – is transmitted and felt not via the event-like eruption violence of itself, but via the *threat* of its purely arbitrary, contingent, random manifestation. Terrorists don't trade in fear as such, insofar as fear takes a specific, finite object, but rather in an infinite atmospheric anxiety. While *fear* results from a direct confrontation with the object that presents itself before us, *anxiety* is produced by a sense that the potential violence that surrounds us could be dynamised from what Deleuze calls the 'virtual' into the actual with lightning speed at the flip of a switch or, more likely, the click of a mouse, the swipe of a smartphone or tablet.

The seemingly sheer randomness of terrorism is, furthermore, compounded by the very nature of a society that keeps the truth about itself from itself. A society that both knows yet at the same time doesn't know the truth about terrorism; a society that is unable to face the way in which its own deterritorialisations contribute to terroristic forms of reterritorialisation. In this deterritorialising logic, according to the media, terrorism is the violence that mostly happens *over there* but whose effects are mostly felt *over here*, although, of course, this binary logic is becoming harder and harder to maintain. The way the logic of terror plays itself out in the West is through the anxiety that the *over there* will eventually bleed into the *over here*. Terror crystallises the transversal logics of the global capitalist order, either in the form of ISIS or in the form of fascist accelerationism inspired by Nick Land and Mencius Moldbug (Curtis Yarvin). In the former, the very vacuum of political authority resulting from the neo-conservative logic of regime change created the conditions for this molar political assemblage to, at least for a period, establish the semblance of sovereign power skirting the established borders of the nation-state in the region. In the latter, it is an attempt to destroy the formally egalitarian order and establish a neo-feudal ethno-state by unleashing the deterritorialising logic of a race war – a war, one might add, that feeds off the fascism that inheres in all of us, as Foucault remarked in his illuminating preface to *Anti-Oedipus*. This is, as he puts it, 'the fascism that causes us to love power, to desire the very thing that dominates and exploits us' (Deleuze and Guatarri 1983: xiii).

Such fascism is, itself, a function of a militarism that has become, *qua* spectacle, an end in itself. Walter Benjamin famously defined this as the 'aestheticisation of the political'. Ian Buchanan argues that with the Vietnam War, there was a noticeable shift in the logic of militarism in the US state. The very loss of the war was, in a strict sense, the triumph of a new logic of militarism in so far as such militarism now transcended the teleological categories of victory and defeat. As Buchanan puts it,

> The B52 pilot unloading bombs on an unseen enemy below knows just as well as the suicide bomber in Iraq that his actions will not lead directly to a decisive change, that in a sense the gesture is futile; but, he also knows, as does the suicide bomber, that his actions will help create an atmosphere of fear that, it is hoped, will one day lead to change. Deprived of teleology, war thrives in an eternal present. Terror is not merely the weapon of the weak, it is the new condition of war, and no power can claim exception status. (Buchanan 2006: 30)

The rise of authoritarian populism from the US and Canada to Europe, Turkey and India can be understood, in part, as an attempt to address such deterritorialisation by policing borders and building walls. Indeed, the spectacle of terror is the site of convergence of the twin global strategies of the so-called leader of the 'free world' in supposedly 'liberating' both markets and states. The liberation of markets is justified by a doctrine that would germinate during the war years and several decades into post-war reconstruction via the Mont Pelerin Society and seize the moment in the crisis of 1973. This is a doctrine that would come to be known as neoliberalism. The liberation of states is justified by a post-Cold War doctrine that crystallised the experiences of the proxy war fought via the mujahedin in Afghanistan against the Soviet satellite regime of Najibullah, and that under George W. Bush sought to effect regime change throughout the region, after the attacks of 9/11. It sought to define the 'New American Century' in the absence of the Soviet enemy. The effects of both of these doctrines: deepening socio-economic insecurity and precarity combined with political and military blowback for its interventionist policies created the groundwork for the ascendancy of the Tea Party and, finally, Donald Trump. Globally, it has spurred on the rise of the far right.

In order to prevent terror's natural history of destruction from crushing them, citizens of Western states are seemingly prepared to assent to an ever-widening assault on their liberties –one sees this in the US with the passage of the Patriot Act, in Canada with the Anti-Terrorism Act of 2015 formerly known as Bill C-51 – legislation that is not just about preserving state power but also the existing regime of property relations. The power of the spectacle is, in other words, nowhere more all-consuming than in the image of terror itself. Think of the endless loop of the image of the two planes crashing into the Twin Towers – a spectacular version of the compulsion to repeat that originates in the *fort/da* game of the child who uses it to cope with the traumatic absence of his mother (Freud 1990). To come to terms with the spectacle of fascism today, it is imperative to confront the problem of terrorism.

It is against this background that it is worth revisiting Guy Debord's account of the society of the spectacle which is, I shall argue, uniquely able to help us understand terrorism not as somehow, as Jurgen Habermas, Jacques Derrida (Borradori 2003) and Jasbir Puar (2007) seem to want to suggest to varying degrees, *exterior* to the West, even if instigated by it in complex ways, but rather as somehow internal to its very sovereign power. It is possible to say here that terror complicates the logic of universal history in *Capitalism and Schizophrenia*: it suggests a certain logic of combined and uneven development which is itself part of the global intensification of capitalist social relations. This is akin to Louis Althusser's suggestion that one could find differential modes of production within one and the same social formation. In this case, the aspiration towards the instantiation of the sovereign body of power (ISIS) is, itself, inextricable from the very axiomatics of the law of value and the abstractions to which it gives rise that supposedly replaces it with the destruction of the feudal order. There is, in other words, a hidden link between the nihilism of theology, on the one hand, and that of the abstract logic of instrumental reason and the value form, on the other. In each we see, as Nietzsche first pointed out in the *Genealogy of Morals*, a politics of debt at work.

The view of terrorism as somehow external can feed into the idea (infamously introduced by Syrian entrepreneur Raja Sidawi) of the West as a 'culture of life' and the Arab world as a 'culture of death' (Ignatius 2015). If we look closely enough, however, it is also possible to discern at the heart of the West a culture of death, or as Nietzsche had already shown, a nihilistic will to 'nothingness'. Against such a will to nothingness, Nietzsche proposes 'Wille zur Macht', appropriated, of course, by Deleuze and Guatarri as an affirmative desiring production. 'The Unconscious is not a theatre but a factory' (Deleuze and Guatarri 1983). In this, despite disagreements over the status of dialectical logic, they were in full agreement with Debord.

As is well known, in his epochal *Society of the Spectacle* Debord differentiates the spectacle into its *concentrated* and *diffuse* forms. The first is that of fascism, in which the spectacle revolves around the cult of personality of leaders such as Hitler, Stalin and Mao, to which we might add figures such as the 'Eternal General Secretary' of the Workers' Party of Korea, Kim Jong-il, his son Kim Jong-un, and the 45th president of the United States of America. The diffuse spectacle manifests itself in post-war consumer society, dominated by advertising images in which the worker participates not simply in the shadowy realm of production but also in the glittery realm of consumption, which is how capitalism manages to solve, within the framework of the nation-state, its accumulation crises.

In his 1988 *Comments on the Society of the Spectacle*, Debord identifies a third form which is the cancelling and preserving (*Aufhebung*) of these two forms: 'This is the *integrated spectacle*, which has tended to impose itself globally' (Debord 1990: 8). Debord claims that while Stalinist Russia and Nazi Germany had elaborated the concentrated spectacle, and the US the diffuse spectacle, it was Italy and France, with their combination of capitalism, weak democratic traditions and relatively rigid bureaucratic structures in Stalinist parties and trade unions, that had elaborated the third form of spectacular society. Each society is measured by the degree of negativity it allows: 'When the spectacle was concentrated, the greater part of the surrounding society escaped it; when diffuse, a small part; today, *no part*' (Debord 1990: 9, emphasis added).

The integrated spectacle, according to Debord, is characterised by five main characteristics: incessant technological innovation, integration of state and economy, generalised secrecy, unanswerable lies, an eternal present. Uncannily anticipating the advent of a truly planetary form of capitalism, Debord argues that the dialectical *Aufhebung* of the diffuse and the concentrated spectacle in the integrated spectacle entails 'the globalization of the false and the falsification of the globe' (1990: 10). If the third form of the spectacle entails a hybrid of the concentrated and the diffuse, we might recognise it today in the form of neoliberalism mediated by ever more rigid and bureaucratic forms of international law and international organisations – a 'democratic deficit' that goes well beyond its original referent, the European Union.

And this is precisely where Debord's conception of the 'integrated spectacle' fails to convince. It can scarcely be maintained, today – as indeed it could have in the late 1980s – that Italy and France were the vanguard of the integrated spectacle. Rather, the 'globalization of the false and the falsification of the globe' that the integrated spectacle heralds ought to be understood in terms of the rise of China. But also, of course, at least in part, in terms of the shifting role of the American state specifically. Debord's argument about France and Italy, however, has to do with the way in which the revolutionary energies in these countries in the 1960s and 1970s (and here he might have also included the Federal Republic of Germany) were increasingly absorbed via the French Socialist and Green parties (think of Daniel Cohn-Bendit and Joschka Fischer, for example) or Italian Eurocommunism by either incorporating them or pushing them beyond the pale of democratic life by marking them as 'terroristic'.[2]

The place of terror, then, becomes key to understanding the nature of the integrated spectacle: terror, here, remains simultaneously exterior yet also interior to the integrated spectacle. It is in the phenomenon of terror and its construction by the state that we see the various elements of the integrated spectacle. As Debord argues:

> Such a perfect democracy constructs its own inconceivable foe, terrorism. Its wish is *to be judged by its enemies rather than by its results* (emphasis in original). The story of terrorism is written by the state and it is therefore highly instructive. The spectators must certainly never know everything about terrorism, but they must always know enough to convince them that, compared with terrorism, everything else must be acceptable, or in any case more rational and democratic. (1990: 24)

It is not difficult to see the way in which the five elements of the integrated spectacle crystallise in the contemporary ongoing 'war on terror'. 1) *Incessant technological renewal*: the production of new knowledge/power about terrorism and concomitant discourses of securitisation, specifically in the following areas: i) systems integration; ii) biometrics; iii) non-lethal weapons; iv) data mining and link analysis technologies; v) nano-technology. 2) The development of such technologies is one important axis of the *integration of state and economy*, often referred to as 'military Keynesianism', and, as we have recently seen, the staggering 10 per cent increase to the US military budget bears this out. 3) As the terrorist threat looms, there is an *increase in general secrecy*. According to the ACLU, the fifth worst abuse of state power since the attacks of 11 September 2001 is the increasing reliance on secrecy to block legislation from judicial review.[3] 4) The *spread of unanswerable lies* has, of course, become endemic in the form of 'fake news' in recent years, since the inauguration of Trump, and the state has always relied on the dissemination of the false. However, the use of the 9/11 attacks to justify the Bush regime's restructuring of US power in the 'New American Century',[4] and, in particular, the invasion of Iraq, required, it could be argued, an especially deliberate policy of lies. 5) Finally, the integrated spectacle was, as suggested above with the other forms of spectacle, the unfolding of the logic of reification and therefore *the present made eternal*. Another way of stating this, in the wake of the dominance within the integrated spectacle of the power of the purest logic of commodification, namely money-capital or finance, is the literal colonisation of the *not yet* via derivatives and futures markets.

On one reading, the notion of the 'society of the spectacle' is simply to be understood as a society dominated by *images*. For cultural and media studies, the spectacle denotes the predominance of what one-time Situationist fellow-traveller Baudrillard calls the simulacrum, or the copy untethered to an original (Baudrillard 1994) – that is, those objects that are constructed to outstrip, in their quality, the original. From such a perspective it might be possible to make sense of terrorism in terms of the tactics and strategy whereby media-savvy organisations such as ISIS are able to produce martyrdom videos invoking the idea of an uncanny 'unkillability' as effective recruiting devices for would-be suicide bombers; and a whole host of electronic platforms to coordinate, execute, document and disseminate images of their attacks, such as, for example, the infamous image of the assembly-line execution of twenty-one Coptic Egyptians on a Libyan beach.

The circulation of these images through Western societies is the principal means by which fear and hatred are spread. The former because it suggests an image of an invasion culminating in the forcible imposition of sharia law – the idea promoted by neo-conservatives in the US of 'Eurabia'; hatred insofar as it feeds on extant racism in formerly metropolitan centres of European colonialism such as London, Paris, Brussels. In both cases, the sheer fact of circulation of images of terror helps to secure ISIS's trifecta of objectives which, along with establishing a caliphate in North Africa and the Middle East, and drawing the West into the morass of Syria and Iraq, entails a radicalisation of moderate Muslims living in the so-called 'grey zone' between nominally secular and pluralistic civil society, on the one hand, and radical Islam, on the other. In other words, by these means, ISIS confronts neoliberal globalisation with the prospect of what Giorgio Agamben (2015) has called a 'planetary civil war'.

While it may be tempting to understand Debord as offering an account of social domination via the image, this would be an error. And he seems to anticipate the tendency to read his work in this way. The spectacle is not the domination of the image per se, but rather is a form of social mediation or relation characterised by 'separation': 'The spectacle is not a collection of images, but a social relation among people, mediated by images' (Debord 2005: §4). Debord thus provides a genealogy of the spectacle that places it in line with the concepts of the fetishism of commodities and reification developed by Karl Marx and Georg Lukács respectively. In his introduction to 'Critique of Hegel's *Philosophy of Law*', Marx states that the 'criticism of religion is the premise of all criticism' (Marx 1975: 175). Later in his supposedly 'scientific writings', he provides an account of the alienated forms of the categories of political economy. In Lukács's account of reification, the logic of fetishism is shown to penetrate both philosophical concepts and human intuitions, revealing them to be both empty and blind.

If the origin of Marx's critical theory is the detachment or separation of the sacred from everyday life, and its projection into the heavens, then the spectacle is the technologically mediated culmination of this logic. In fact, as Johan Hartle and I argue in *The Spell of Capital: Reification and Spectacle*, commodity fetishism can be said to roughly correspond with the phase of the entrenchment of liberal capitalism, the concept of reification with the crisis of the liberal order with the onset of Fordism and the Great War, and the concept of spectacle articulated on the eve of the crisis of Fordism itself. The spectacle, then, as 'the concrete inversion of life, is the autonomous movement of the non-living' (Debord 2005: §2). The spectacle is not simply a veil that obscures social relations from outside but rather a socially necessary illusion; not an ideal abstraction that conceals the true nature of the world but, rather, the 'real abstraction' (Sohn-Rethel 2020: 50–6) of the commodity – a form necessarily extricated from production relations. Debord states that

'Objective reality is present on both sides. Every notion fixed in this way has no other basis than its passage into its opposite: reality rises up in the spectacle, and the spectacle is real' (2005: §88). While both Marx and Lukács had called for philosophy not just to be criticised, but also to be *aufgehoben*, simultaneously negated and realised, as not just the idea of freedom but also its practice, the spectacle perpetuates conditions under which it 'philosophizes reality. The concrete life of everyone has been degraded into a speculative universe' (Debord 2005: §19). Yet philosophy, particularly in Hegelian guise, which is to say, in *speculative* form, was unable to supersede theology. Therefore, according to Debord,

> The spectacle is the material reconstruction of the religious illusion. Spectacular technology has not dispelled the religious clouds where men had placed their own powers detached from themselves; it has only tied them to an earthly base. The most earthly life thus becomes opaque and unbreathable. It no longer projects into the sky but shelters within itself its absolute denial, its fallacious paradise. The spectacle is the technical realization of the exile of human powers into a beyond; it is separation perfected within the interior of man. (2005: §20)

This passage is key to understanding Debord's many references to Feuerbach and the early Marx throughout this text: the spectacle is, ultimately, theological. It is, in other words, the culmination of the logic of the commodity form. By this, Marx held that the commodity was a strange object insofar as it embodied both sensuous use value and supersensuous value as such. The commodity was the product of the concrete labour of men and women whose labour power is purchased to produce an object that would, ultimately, go its own way independently of their will and, as capital or dead labour, would subsequently return to bear down upon them with force and, indeed, violence.

Just as believers bow down to the products of their own theological labours, namely the idea of God, workers are subordinated to the products of their own sensuous labour, namely the commodity form which is, at its most abstract, money-capital. In contradistinction to Matthew 6:24, therefore, God and mammon cannot, ultimately, be distinguished. That most abstract commodity, money-capital, was the ground for the constitution of concrete, embodied labour power – *both its productive and reproductive power* – to be rendered commensurate or equivalent. In other words, the uncanny nature of the commodity, its theological-cum-material attributes, has to do with the fact that it embodies both concrete and abstract labour, use value and exchange value or simply *value*.

What, then, does Debord have to teach us about terror? Debord's lesson is exemplified by a play entitled *The Invisible Hand* by Pakistani-American writer Ayad Akhtar, in which a cunning US investment banker is kidnapped by a Pakistani political group led by an imam. The imam, who has been progressively radicalised by deepening corruption in Pakistani society, puts the banker to work to manipulate the markets to raise funds for the organisation's social welfare wing. Ultimately, he 'shorts' or bets against the Pakistani dollar, and then proceeds to have an influential and powerful Pakistani politician, who controls numerous valuable assets, liquidated. His murder triggers a collapse in the currency that the organisation profits from. The work suggests that global terror must be seen as inextricable from what Christian Marazzi (2009) calls the 'violence of financial capitalism' – that their effects are parallel.

Today, of course, terroristic violence is dependent upon deterritorialised flows of money-capital, for example, from Western client state Saudi Arabia to ISIS in Syria and Iraq, from Tehran to Hezbollah in Lebanon, from Washington through its intermediaries in the Pakistani Intelligence Services to the mujahedin. At the same time, the material effect of finance was clearly exemplified in the immediate aftermath of the 2015 bailout referendum in Greece, as increasing numbers of old age pensioners were pushed out into the streets and as infant mortality rose in exact proportion to the extent to which basic medical supplies dwindled as a direct result of the decisions taken by the Troika. This was not unlike a terror attack. Both terror and finance are *invisible*, each in its own way. Kant argued in *Critique of Pure Reason*: 'Thoughts without content are empty, intuitions without concepts are blind' (Kant 1998: 193–4). 'Terror' is an empty concept while 'finance' is a blind intuition. In its utter concreteness, its historical and social embeddedness, its politically overdetermined nature, it is not possible to provide a conceptual, which is to say *universal* and *impartial*, definition of 'terrorism', hence the platitude 'One man's terrorist is another man's freedom fighter.' Conversely, we know what we are speaking about when we use the word 'finance', namely 'money-capital'; yet because of its very algorithmic abstractness, it is impossible to intuit, apprehend or represent finance directly. Western authoritarian populists and ISIS propagandists alike maintain that while the West is a culture of life, radical Islam is a culture of death, though this is, of course, not an opposition that can be maintained. Terrorism takes on the appearance of the theological negation of the worldly, while in fact it is the manifestation of the cold rationality of means and ends; finance takes on the appearance of the cold rationality of means and ends, while in fact embodying what

Marx called the 'theological subtleties and metaphysical niceties' of the commodity form which, as Walter Benjamin suggests, culminates not in the 'reform of existence but its complete destruction' (Benjamin 1996: 289).

Notes

1. I would like to thank Am Johal for comments on a previous version of this essay. Many of the ideas were generated in a panel discussion with Adel Iskandar and moderator Minelle Mahtani devoted to the topic of 'Auditing Terrorism' on 31 March 2016, with specific reference to Ayad Akhtar's play *The Invisible Hand* mounted by Pi Theatre and directed by Richard Wolfe.
2. And here it is worth pointing out parenthetically that Toni Negri was denied a visa to participate in academic events in Canada, including at the Institute for the Humanities, because of the Anti-Terrorism law.
3. <https://www.aclu.org/other/top-ten-abuses-power-911> (last accessed 9 May 2022).
4. <https://web.archive.org/web/20050205041635/http://www.newamericancentury.org/statementofprinciples.htm> (last accessed 9 May 2022).

References

Agamben, G. (2015), *Stasis: Civil War as Political Paradigm*, trans. N. Heron, Palo Alto, CA: Stanford University Press.

St Augustine (2016), *Confessions Vol. II*, trans. and ed. C. J. B. Hammond, Cambridge, MA: Harvard University Press.

Baudrillard, J. (1994), *Simulacra and Simulation*, trans. S. F. Glaser, Ann Arbor: University of Michigan Press.

Benjamin, W. (1996), 'Capitalism as Religion', in *Selected Writings Vol. 1: 1913–1926*, ed. M. Bullock and M. W. Jennings, Cambridge, MA: Belknap Press of Harvard University Press, pp. 288–91.

Borradori, G. (2003), *Philosophy in a Time of Terror: Dialogues with Jürgen Habermas and Jacques Derrida*, Chicago: University of Chicago Press.

Buchanan, I. (2006), 'Treatise on Militarism', in I. Buchanan and A. Parr (eds), *Deleuze and the Contemporary World*, Edinburgh: Edinburgh University Press, pp. 21–41.

Carafano, J. (2005), 'The Future of Anti-Terrorism Technologies', The Heritage Foundation, 6 June, <http://www.heritage.org/homeland-security/report/the-future-anti-terrorism-technologies> (last accessed 9 May 2022).

Debord, G. (1990), *Comments on Society of the Spectacle*, trans. Malcolm Imrie, London: Verso.

Debord, G. (2005 [1967]), *Society of the Spectacle*, Detroit: Black and Red.

Deleuze, G., and F. Guattari (1983), *Anti-Oedipus*, trans. R. Hurley, Minneapolis: University of Minnesota Press.

Freud, S. (1990 [1920]), *Beyond the Pleasure Principle*, New York: W. W. Norton.

Ignatius, D. (2015), 'How ISIS Spread in the Middle East, and How to Stop It', *The Atlantic*, 29 October, <https://www.theatlantic.com/international/archive/2015/10/how-isis-started-syria-iraq/412042/> (last accessed 9 May 2022).

Kant, I. (1998 [1781]), *Critique of Pure Reason*, trans. P. Guyer and A. W. Wood, Cambridge: Cambridge University Press.

Marazzi, C. (2009), *The Violence of Financial Capitalism*, trans. K. Lebedeva, Cambridge, MA: MIT Press.

Marx, K. (1975), 'Critique of Hegel's *Philosophy of Law*: Introduction', in *Karl Marx and Frederick Engels: Collected Works, Vol. 3: 1843–1844*, New York: International Publishers, pp. 175–87.

Puar, J. (2007), *Terrorist Assemblages: Homo Nationalism in Queer Times*, Durham, NC: Duke University Press.

Sohn-Rethel, A. (2020), *Intellectual and Manual Labour: A Critique of Epistemology*, Leiden: Brill.

Notes on Contributors

Claire Colebrook is Edwin Erle Sparks Professor of English, Philosophy and Women's and Gender Studies at Penn State University. She has written books and articles on contemporary European philosophy, literary history, gender studies, queer theory, visual culture and feminist philosophy.

Clayton Crockett is Professor and Director of Religious Studies at the University of Central Arkansas. He is the author and editor of a number of books, including *Derrida After the End of Writing* (Fordham University Press, 2017) and *Energy and Change: A New Materialist Cosmo-theology* (Columbia University Press, 2022). He is also a Distinguished Research Fellow for the Global Center for Advanced Studies, and a co-editor of the book series 'Insurrections: Critical Studies in Religion, Politics, and Culture' for Columbia University Press.

Anup Dhar, formerly a Professor of Psychology (2011–17) and Professor of Philosophy (2018–21) at Dr B. R. Ambedkar University Delhi, is currently Senior Fellow at Livonics Institute of Integrated Learning and Research (https://www.liilr.livonics.com/). His co-authored books include *Dislocation and Resettlement in Development: From Third World to World of the Third* (Routledge, 2009), with Anjan Chakrabarti; *The Indian Economy in Transition: Globalization, Capitalism and Development* (Cambridge University Press, 2015), with Anjan Chakrabarti and Byasdeb Dasgupta; and *World of the Third and Global Capitalism: Between Marx and Freud* (Worldview, 2012), with Anjan Chakrabarti and Stephen Cullenberg. His co-edited books include *Breaking the Silo: Integrated Science Education in India* (Orient Blackswan, 2017), with Tejaswini Niranjana and K. Sridhar; *Psychoanalysis from the Indian Terroir: Emerging Themes in Culture,*

Family, and Childhood (Lexington Books, 2018), with Manasi Kumar and Anurag Mishna; and *Marx, Marxism and the Spiritual* (Routledge, 2020), with Anjan Chakrabarti and Serap A. Kayatekin.

Samir Gandesha is Professor of Modern European Thought and Culture in the Department of the Humanities and the Director of the Institute for the Humanities at Simon Fraser University, Vancouver, Canada. He is co-editor (with Lars Rensmann) of *Arendt and Adorno: Political and Philosophical Investigations* (Stanford, 2012). He is co-editor (with Johan Hartle) of *Spell of Capital: Reification and Spectacle* (University of Amsterdam Press, 2017) and *Aesthetic Marx* (Bloomsbury, 2017) also with Johan Hartle. He is editor of *Spectres of Fascism: Historical, Theoretical and Contemporary Perspectives* (Pluto, 2020) as well as co-editor (with Stefano Marino and Colin Campbell) of *Adorno and Popular Music* (Mimesis, 2021) and co-editor (with Stefano Marino and Johan Hartle) of *The Aging of Adorno's Aesthetic Theory* (Mimesis, 2021). He is also co-editor of the *Journal of Adorno Studies*.

Yasmin Ibrahim is Professor in Digital Economy and Culture at Queen Mary, University of London. Her research explores the sociocultural dimensions of digital technologies and their implications for humanity. She also writes extensively on race, migration, border controls, Islam and terrorism. Her forthcoming book is entitled *Technologies of Trauma: Cultural Formations Over Time* (Emerald). Her most recent books are *Posthuman Capitalism: Dancing with Data in the Digital Economy* (Routledge, 2021) and *Migrants and Refugees at UK Borders: Hostility and 'Unmaking' the Human* (Routledge, 2022).

Don Johnston is a veteran international humanitarian aid worker and an independent researcher whose multidisciplinary work examines health and vulnerability in the Global South. He is the author of *Diagnosing Postcolonial Literature: Deleuze and Health* (Lexington Books, 2021); he has had various essays published in edited collections, and is the lead or co-author of multiple, research-based policy papers outlining international humanitarian programs in response to natural disasters, pandemics and conflict. He is the senior director of Socorro: Global Humanitarian Consultants (www.socorroglobal.com).

Arthur Kroker is an internationally known writer and lecturer focusing on technology, politics and culture. His most recent publications include *Body Drift* (University of Minnesota Press, 2012), *Exits to the*

Posthuman Future (Polity, 2014) and *Technologies of the New Real: Viral Contagion and the Death of the Social* (University of Toronto Press, 2021). With Marilouise Kroker he founded and edited CTheory, the global review of politics, theory and society. He has just completed a new book co-authored with David Cook, *The Quantum Revolution: Art, Technology and Culture* for the University of Toronto Press.

S. Romi Mukherjee is Senior Lecturer in the Social Sciences at New York University in Paris and Visiting Lecturer in the Political Humanities at L'Institut d'études politiques de Paris (Sciences Po). He has published widely, mostly in political theory, philosophy and the history of religions. Selected monographs and edited volumes include *Durkheim and Violence* (Wiley, 2010), *Social Memory and Hypermodernity* (Blackwell, 2012, with Éric Brian and Marie Jaisson), *The Political Anthropology of the Global* (Wiley, 2013), *Nouveaux visages du religieux dans un monde sécularisé* (2014, with Lionel Obadia) and *Equality in an Age of Neo-Liberalism* (Wiley, 2018, with Beth Epstein, Janie Pellaby, and Réjane Senac).

Julian Reid has been Chair and Professor of International Relations at the University of Lapland in Finland since 2010. He taught previously at King's College London, SOAS and the University of Sussex. He has held visiting positions at Virginia Tech and the University of Bristol. He is the author and co-author of several works on the political philosophy of Deleuze and Guattari, including *Deleuze & Fascism* (Routledge, 2013), co-edited with Brad Evans. His most recent book is *Becoming Indigenous: Governing Imaginaries in the Anthropocene* (Rowman and Littlefield, 2019), co-authored with David Chandler).

Janae Sholtz is Associate Professor of Philosophy at Alvernia University, Coordinator of Women's and Gender Studies, Neag Professor and research collaborator for the project, *Gilles Deleuze and Cosmology*, funded by SSHRC Insight Grant in Canada. She is the author of *The Invention of a People: Heidegger and Deleuze on Art and the Political* (Edinburgh University Press, 2015), *Deleuze and the Schizoanalysis of Feminism* (Bloomsbury, 2019), and co-editor of *French and Italian Stoicisms: From Sartre to Agamben* (Bloomsbury, 2020), with Kurt Lampe, and editor of the special issue *Infinite Eros:Deleuze, Guattari, and Feminist Couplings* in *Deleuze and Guattari Studies* (2018). Her research is primarily in twentieth-century and contemporary Continental philosophy, feminist theory, philosophy of art, and social and political philosophy. She has a strong interest in aesthetic practices and how affects created through these practices contribute to new modes of thought which may impact social and political life.

Janell Watson is Professor of French at Virginia Tech. She is author of two books, *Literature and Material Culture from Balzac to Proust* (Cambridge University Press, 2009) and *Guattari's Diagrammatic Thought* (Bloomsbury, 2011), and editor of *the minnesota review: a journal of creative and critical writing* (Duke). She is currently completing a book-length study of Michel Serres.

Index

EU representative:
Easy Access System Europe
Mustamäe tee 50, 10621 Tallinn, Estonia
Gpsr.requests@easproject.com